HARRY'S WAR

From Chiltern Valley to France; the story of Harry Withers an Australian soldier of World War One

First Published in Great Britain 2021 by Mirador Publishing

Copyright © 2021 by Max Carmichael and Glen, Carolyn and Linda Reiss

All rights reserved. No part of this publication may be reproduced or transmitted, in any form or by any means, without permission of the publishers or author. Excepting brief quotes used in reviews.

First edition: 2021

References to places and people are made with due respect. Any offence caused by references in the narrative is completely unintentional.

A copy of this work is available through the British Library.

ISBN: 978-1-914965-21-0

Mirador Publishing
10 Greenbrook Terrace
Taunton
Somerset
UK
TA1 1UT

HARRY'S WAR

From Chiltern Valley to France; the story of Harry Withers an Australian soldier of World War One

MAX CARMICHAEL

Foreword

THIS BOOK IS THE STORY of Harry Francis Withers, my great uncle, a man I never knew, but with whom I feel a great affinity. My mother, Beverly Reiss (nee Fanchi) was the niece of Harry Withers. Her mother, Violet Fanchi (nee Withers) being a younger sister to Harry Withers. Upon the passing of my mother, stewardship of an eight-inch by three-inch brown tin box came to myself and my sisters, Linda and Carolyn. Within this tin box were what can only be described as "family treasures"; letters written by Harry, who was serving with the Australian Imperial Force in England and France, to his family back home in Australia, on Ullina Station in the Chiltern Valley. Simple, honest letters, talking about training, fighting and leave time in England, France and Scotland. In the collection, is Harry's field service notebook with recollections of events and happenings written when time permitted him.

Growing up, my sisters and I were aware that family members, including our Great Uncle Harry, had served in World War One. However, it was not until reading Harry's letters and content of his field notebook did I develop some type of understanding of the man and his experiences. Whilst we have no letters from Harry's family to him, we see Harry's responses to enquiries and some observations as to his experiences as well as information regarding relatives and family acquaintances he encounters.

Having these family treasures in our possession, we felt compelled to preserve and share these memoirs, making them available to the wider

Withers clan and also to ensure Harry Withers is more than another name on an Honour Roll.

My sisters and I are thankful to Max Carmichael, himself a veteran and now author of several historically based works, who accepted this project by first preserving and transcribing the documents before researching and developing this book and bringing Harry's words to life. Harry's letters and the words in his notebook are sometimes sparse with their detail, recollection sometimes differs to reflection in his Battalion's War Diary and dates of key events may differ to official records but the etching of the man that was Harry Withers develops.

Harry was a little older than some around him, he missed the land he grew up on, the family who nurtured him and his writings clearly reflect a rural worker's Christian worldly innocence. While there are parts of Harry's story that are unknown, Max has researched Harry's infantry battalion, the 24th Battalion, as well as the situation observed in Harry's letter and notes and intertwined these with historical facts. Where unknown aspects of Harry's experiences have arisen or hidden inferences in correspondence is evident, conjecting possibilities and perspectives, Max offers possibilities that realistically cultivate scenarios that allow us to contextualise the ultimate affect that wartime experiences have on Harry.

Max breathes life into Harry's story. Touching on early Withers family settlement in Victoria's Chiltern district and highlighting the relative simplicity of life at the turn of the century, Harry experiences a bewilderment as to the savage activities of war and a loss of his rural innocence. I close my eyes and I can feel there is also a fundamental deep sense of love and appreciation. A love and appreciation of a son for his parents, siblings and large family, his home, farming his land, the life he left behind in Australia and his fellow battalion mates. Perhaps also there was the possibility of a new love in Scotland.

6426 Private Harry Francis Withers fulfilled his oath of duty and I'm honoured to be able to introduce the panorama that is … Harry's War.

Glen Reiss

Major (Retired), qtc, MMngt (Proj)

Chapter 1

The Withers

IN 1840 JASON WITHERS AND his newly wed wife Hannah, boarded the good ship *Himalaya* to undertake the long and potentially hazardous journey from England to Australia. The newlyweds were young. Jason in his twenty-fifth year and Hannah her twenty-second, and they were ambitious… an ideal combination to undertake the rigors of the adventures that lay ahead of them. So, no doubt with dreams of wealth and a better life they sailed toward distant Port Phillip Bay.

It was a fruitful migration, although at first Jason's initial foray to the Euroa area was hindered by a war of resistance being waged by the local indigenous people against the European invaders. Concerned at the risk this war posed to his wife and at that stage, three young children, Jason relocated the family to the Black Dog Creek area, in what is now north-eastern Victoria. This new area was somewhat more peaceful and by 1845 Jason and Hannah had secured a grazing licence for 19000 acres of land at Black Dog Creek which they named 'Ullina Station'. The 1849 Squatters' Directory of the Port Phillip District noted the Withers were at that time grazing some 5000 head of sheep on the run. In that same year the couple's fifth child, a boy named William, was born on 7 April, the first of the Withers children to be born at Ullina Station, and as far as this story is concerned, a particularly important male addition to the Withers' line.

As the young William Withers matured, he became a willing worker, skilled in bushcraft and an expert and fearless horseman. As an illustration of his prowess as a horseman, a family story tells of a black stallion on a neighbouring station that no one could master. The station owner had offered ten pounds to anyone who could ride the stallion and break it in, but he was confident his 5money was safe. That is until young William arrived at his door to accept the challenge. A small crowd of station hands and other interested bystanders gathered for the fray, and the horse was duly taken to the stockyards where it was saddled, and William helped aboard. Once he was firmly seated William asked for the slip rails to be removed and he then urged the stallion outside into the open land. A mighty battle ensued as the stallion endeavoured to remove William from its back. However, William was never unseated, and returned to the stockyards victorious to collect his ten-pound reward.

Not all of William's dealings with horses had such a successful ending. A few years after his success with the black stallion, William was working with Ullina Station's purebred Clydesdale draught stallion when the animal kicked him in the leg. Willian never fully recovered from the injury, and he was left lame for the rest of his life. In spite of this handicap, he continued to work in the grazing industry.

On the 1st of July 1851, the colony of Victoria separated from the colony of New South Wales. The new colony had its own Legislative Council which could pass its own laws and regulations, and in 1869 the Victorian Legislative Council passed a new Land Act revising the conditions for land ownership and its use as covered by previous relevant Acts. The new Act made provision for lands to be made available to settlers who could select up to 320 acres of land. The new settler was required to fulfil certain requirements and to pay an annual rent to the government. Failure to meet any of these requirements rendered the settler liable to eviction. However, under this new Act there was a problem for those who had established large grazing runs, as areas of land they had claimed were now liable to redistribution to the new settlers. Under earlier Land Acts and included in this new Act, provision was made for the purchase of land by the lessee or licensee giving those persons a pre-emptive right to do so if certain conditions had been fulfilled[1]. The new Act immediately impacted on Jason Withers, who held Ullina Station under pre-emptive right granted by an earlier New South Wales Land Act. A clause under the new Victorian Government Act caused a significant problem for Jason. The new Act required that he fence his property[2], a requirement that involved significant cost and one he was unable to meet. His only solution was to sell the station; a heartbreaking decision for a man who had journeyed from the other side of the world to seek his fortune. However, the sale may have galvanized William and his younger brother Thomas into action for in that same year the two brothers formed a highly successful partnership. Thomas was a man with similar skills and drive to William and by 1880 the brothers had resumed the management of Ullina Station where they continued to run sheep and cattle. Of the six sons born to Jason and Hannah, William and Thomas were the only two who married. William married Margaret McDonald in 1877 and Thomas married Anne Munroe in 1879. Thomas's wife was the daughter of a nearby station owner, but the family of William's wife had come to Australia to search for gold.

The Australian gold rush was to have a profound impact on Ullina Station. Gold had first been discovered in the Black Dog Creek in 1858, but little importance was placed on this discovery and sheep and cattle remained as the mainstay of the local economy, the main gold rush being centred on Ballarat and Bendigo. However, by 1880 the Watch Box Swamp on the upper reaches of the Upper Black Dog Creek had become a focal point for many prospectors and miners. They brought with them a variety of livestock for their own requirements, however as far as the Withers brothers were concerned the miners' animals presented an immediate issue as the additional animals represented unwanted competition for the available grass and water in the area. The two brothers were viewed with some hostility by the miners and small land holders when they endeavoured to protect the boundaries of Ullina Station. The situation became worse when large alluvial

---

[1] https://researchdata.ands.org.au/registers-purchases-section-act-1869/156027
[2] https://trove.nla.gov.au/newspaper/article/28588259

mining companies began to operate in the area, the waste from their operations covering acres of land and polluting the creeks and water courses. It is likely that the impact of mining on the local area contributed to William and Thomas deciding in 1896 to dissolve their partnership. In addition, it is also likely that the two brothers were planning for their own sons' and daughters' futures, dividing by two was far less complicated than it might have been had they maintained the partnership further. In any event, Ullina Station was divided between the two of them, with William retaining the original homestead and Thomas another area which he named "Woodlands".

The end of the partnership did not mean the two families were estranged. The children of both brothers attended the Chiltern Valley School, even though for Thomas's children there was a closer school at the nearby village of Lilliput. They also maintained contact through attendance at church. Both families were devout Christians and keen supporters of the Chiltern Valley Methodist Church. The Withers were also a patriotic family staunchly maintaining their ties with the mother country and loyally supporting their king and the British Empire. It was into this environment on 14 March 1884 that William and Margaret's fourth child, Harry Francis Withers was born.

Having survived infancy, an achievement in itself at that time, school was the next formative step for young Harry. From 1872, education in the colony of Victoria was free and compulsory up to and including the age of fifteen[3]. Literacy and numeracy were considered essential for the common good, as an educated population was seen as crucial for any move toward effective self-government for the colony. A single syllabus was approved for each school grade, to be applied to all schools in Victoria. Discipline, reading, writing, arithmetic, spelling, geography and history were the major subjects to be covered, however military drill was also taught.

Initially children as young as three years of age could be enrolled, however in 1892 an Order in Council lifted the enrolment age to five years of age.[4] It is unclear whether Harry and his siblings commenced their education at the earlier age. However, what is certain is that their father had

---

[3] https://www.nma.gov.au/defining-moments/resources/free-education-introduced
[4] https://www.parliament.vic.gov.au/papers/govpub/VPARL1894-95No3.pdf, p7

a keen interest in education and no doubt insisted that his children received the best schooling available.

All of William and Margaret's children attended school at Chiltern Valley. Records show that a primary school was first established in the valley in 1887[5]. The 1894 Education Report tabled in the Victorian Parliament by the Minister for Public Instruction, The Honourable A.J. Peacock, reported to Parliament that the Chiltern Valley School consisted of two wooden buildings, a portable school room and teachers' quarters, "of the new style". The facility was reported to cater for 30 scholars[6], a number of whom were William and Margaret's children. However, other records show that enrolments at the school in the next few years rose considerably. At its busiest up to 122 students. The increase in enrolments prompted local interest in increasing the school building's capacity, and in 1896 William Withers led the way in trying to address the issue. He canvassed the Chiltern area for funds to enable the relocation of the old and disused Doma Mungi School which was situated about three kilometres west of Chiltern Valley, to the Chiltern Valley School facility. Harry would have been at school long enough to enjoy the fruits of his father's fundraising efforts.

Harry was probably an attentive student. However, his wartime letters suggest he was not a great achiever scholastically. His handwriting is poor, and he appears to struggle with the composition of his letters home. He probably left school in 1899 the year he turned fifteen and would have been faced with the challenging task of finding employment. This would not have been easy.

During the 1890's Australia was in the grip of a serious economic depression. Overseas investments evaporated, banks failed, the price of wool plummeted, and the colony's Gross National Product fell by 17%. Of all the major centres, Melbourne suffered the most and by 1893 a third of the workforce was unemployed. One in ten Melbourne houses were repossessed by the banks, and people in the poorer quarters were starving. In desperation,

---

[5] https://www.victorianplaces.com.au/chiltern-valley
[6] https://www.parliament.vic.gov.au/papers/govpub/VPARL1894-95No3.pdf, p37

large numbers of men left Melbourne in search of work in the bush[7]. Harry probably had high hopes of finding employment in the Chiltern Valley, but he would have faced fierce competition for every available position. In addition to the depression and its outcomes, the situation was exacerbated by severe drought that gripped much of Australia from around 1895 to 1903. Rural communities already impacted by the economic decline began to suffer additional privations. Stock feed dried up and blew away and rivers, creeks and waterholes evaporated leaving a dry and barren landscape. Those farmers and graziers, who could, sold their animals, those who could not, were forced to watch their animals wither and die. Not a few farmers simply walked off their properties in utter defeat. [8]

The depression and the drought had impacted on the Withers's enterprises, even so in 1905 William managed to take advantage of lower land prices and purchased additional property. However, from 1911 the bad times began to bite, and he began to sell off portions of Ullina Station in order to keep afloat.

The whole environment for those involved in rural based industry of any kind was toxic. However, one aspect of the Withers family life that must have helped steel their resolve to hold on was their unshakable Christian faith. The family were regular attendees at the Chiltern Valley Methodist Church. Some of the Withers girls taught at the Sunday School, and it was reported that at the 1905 Methodist Church anniversary service seven-year-old Walter, the family's youngest son, provided an entertaining rendition of the song "Please give me a penny, sir":

> *Please give me a penny, sir?*
> *My mother dear is dead,*
> *And, oh, I am so hungry, sir,*
> *A penny please, for bread?*
> *All day I have been asking.*
> *But no one heeds my cry,*

---

[7] https://australianfoodtimeline.com.au/1890s-depression/
[8] Op. cit.

Will you not give me something?
Or surely, I must die.

Chorus.
Please give me a penny, sir?
My mother dear is dead,
And, oh, I am so hungry, sir,
A penny please, for bread?

Please give me a penny, sir?
You won't say no, to me,
Because I'm poor and ragged, sir.
And, oh, so cold you see.
We were not always begging,
We once were rich like you,
But father died a drunkard,
And mother she died, too.

Chorus.
Please give me a penny, sir?
My mother dear is dead,
And, oh, I am so hungry, sir,
A penny please, for bread?

Please give me a penny, sir?
Is heard on every side,
Lisped by little trembling lips,
And singing on life's tide.
Oh, listen to their pleadings,
And pity these, the poor,
Then blessings brought from heaven,
Will shine on thee the more.

Chorus.
Please give me a penny, sir?
My mother dear is dead,
And, oh, I am so hungry, sir,
A penny please, for bread?[9]

During the performance in response to the lad's impassioned pleas, the audience threw pennies at his feet.

There were other events too that held the family's attention. In 1907 Margaret and William's eldest daughter, also named Margaret, married John Stewart, the son of a local mine manager and by 1908 the couple had produced their first child whom they named after his father. In 1909 there were further nuptials when William and Margaret's fifth child Grace married John Mitchell the son of another mining family. Then in 1914, there was another wedding, this time of the couple's youngest daughter Ellen, also known as Nell, who married John O'Neil. However, along with these happy occasions, there was also sadness. In 1899 Jason Withers, whose ambitions had brought the family to Ullina Station, died and was buried in the family cemetery at Ullina Station. Then in 1910 Jason's wife Hannah passed away and she was buried next to her husband. However, in 1905, one particular event occurred that was to have a dramatic impact for the Withers family as a whole, but most particularly for Harry.

---

[9] https://nla.gov.au/nla.obj-190803035/view?partId=nla.obj-211068211

Chapter 2

A Life Changing Event

AFTER LEAVING SCHOOL, HARRY WORKED as a farm labourer, although whether this employment was at Ullina Station or at some neighbouring property is unclear. However, remembering that his father was partially crippled by a kick from a horse, and his older brother Alexander was a sickly fellow often requiring time away from home for treatment, it is likely that the majority of his work was on the family farm. The work would have involved droving stock, shearing sheep, milking cows, fencing, horse work and so on.

Away from this work, Harry decided to serve the nation and he enlisted in the local militia unit, Number 3 Squadron of the 8th Australian Light Horse Regiment.

The militia was the equivalent of today's Army Reserve, its members serving as part-time soldiers. The 8th Australian Light Horse Regiment was raised in 1884 and continued to serve the nation through to 1912 when the unit was absorbed into other militia units[10]. In general, members of militia units were provided arms, equipment and uniforms; however, in the case of Light Horse units, members were required to provide their own horses. All members of the militia were paid an allowance, and Light Horsemen also received an extra allowance for their horses, which was in fact more than the amount paid to the riders. Training generally occurred on Saturday

---

[10] The 8th Light Horse was re-raised in September 1914 as an AIF unit and saw considerable active service at Gallipoli and during the Desert Campaigns that followed.

afternoons and over the course of a year, was the equivalent of twelve days' full-time training.[11] At this time militia training was not compulsory, but it did require a firm commitment if a militia man was to enjoy his training or complete his initial enlistment obligations. For a lad like Harry, used to the outdoor life, who enjoyed riding and shooting, service in the Light Horse was perhaps a logical extension of what was a pretty good life. However, all this was to change dramatically.

One Wednesday evening in June 1905, Harry and a friend were riding toward home, when Harry's horse put its foot in a hole, causing the animal to trip. Harry was thrown headfirst to the ground, sustaining a severe concussion. The local paper reporting this incident noted that while Harry's condition had improved, he was in a serious condition. Indeed, it may be safely assumed that he had suffered what is known today as a "Traumatic Brain Injury" or TBI. At that time the prognosis for such an injury was not good, as death or disability were common outcomes.

It is important to note that TBI is not the same as a head injury. The term "head injury" covers a multitude of possible afflictions including injury to the face, scalp and skull. All of these can occur without necessarily damaging the brain. TBI is as the title suggests an injury to the brain, acquired by severe impact to the head, causing the brain to be slammed against the inside of the skull, tearing, bruising, and twisting the brain tissue, causing bleeding and swelling. In Harry's case, when he was thrown headfirst from his horse, his brain would have suffered considerable damage from the impact. The results of these kind of injuries range from momentary loss of consciousness, to a long-term coma. There is also the strong possibility of long-term damage to the victim's physical and cognitive function.

Recovery from TBI is dependent on the extent and location of the brain damage, the age and general health of the person, the speed of first aid received and the quality of treatment. At the time of the accident, Harry was twenty-one years of age, so in this regard he had a good chance of recovery. However, for the rest of the recovery indicators, his recovery was less certain.

---

[11] http://alh-research.tripod.com/Light_Horse/index.blog/1846485/australian-militia-activity-location-list-1910/

The part of Harry's brain that was damaged is not known. However, the fact that his condition was reported as "serious", suggests the damage to his brain was not insignificant. As a result, from the moment his head hit the ground, his chance of a complete recovery had slipped into negative territory. This negativity increased due to the time taken for aid to reach him. At that time, the horse was still the most used form of transport, particularly in the bush. A dazed Harry may have been able to remount his horse and ride home, however if he was unconscious his rescue would most probably have been affected by a horse drawn vehicle. In either event, by the time Harry received first aid, he would have been at high risk of developing secondary brain injury. This complication develops when the injured brain swells to a dangerous level within the constricting space of the skull, causing further damage to the brain.[12]

By 1905 treatment for brain injury had greatly improved from the "vinegar and brown paper" treatment used to treat Jack's broken crown in the old nursery rhyme of Jack and Jill. However, out in the Australian bush, medical practitioners generally lacked the facilities to address injuries such as those Harry had suffered. The family physician, Doctor Harkin attended Harry after the accident, and he probably implemented a standard form of treatment in vogue at that time. This would have included bed rest, cold compresses applied to the head, and possibly the administration of bromide. Bromide was used as an anticonvulsant (convulsions or fits being a possible symptom of the brain injury) and as a sedative. Doses as high as six grams per day may have been recommended. Other than this, the family would have been recommended to pray for Harry's recovery. Somehow, Harry survived, but the kind of life he once enjoyed was now lost to him forever.

A minor aspect of this loss was that his injury necessitated his discharge from the militia. However, of far greater importance was that his injury seemed to have limited his ability to perform normal day to day tasks. Evidence of his overall condition and the impact that had on his family, is demonstrated in an incident that was to take place ten years after his accident.

---

[12] https://journals.lww.com/ajpmr/Fulltext/2010/08000/The_History_and_Evolution_of_Traumatic_Brain.13.aspx

On the 3rd of September 1913, Harry allegedly committed a serious assault against one of his cousins. The following day he was arrested and interrogated by the police in regard to this offence, and according to the arresting officers, when confronted with the crime, he confessed to being the offender.[13] At his trial, conducted at Benalla on the 14th of October 1913, the prosecution based his case against Harry, on this confession. The defence, however, presented compelling evidence, suggesting that Harry's confession was invalid, and medical evidence regarding Harry's mental state.

The defence barrister argued that the police should not have identified Harry as the perpetrator of the assault. One witness provided evidence that footprints left by the offender at the scene of the assault, were of a different size to Harry's feet. In addition, the victim believed the attacker was shorter and of a heavier build than Harry and was surprised when the police identified Harry as the offender. The evidence regarding the footprints and the victim statement, were either rejected, or overlooked during the police investigation[14]. Interestingly some members of Harry's family firmly maintain to this day that Harry was innocent of this crime, and that he was either pressured into the confession, or that he was sacrificing himself to cover for a friend.[15]

Defence also produced evidence of Harry's mental condition. Doctor Harkin, the Withers' family physician, gave evidence, that since the horse-riding accident in 1903, Harry had been subject to emotional and melancholic moods, often confused, and that he suffered from epileptic fits, conditions the doctor believed would only worsen in time. The doctor also stated, Harry had suffered an additional head injury in 1910, when he was thrown from a gig[16], and ten days prior to the crime being committed, Harry had been struck on the head during a game of football. The result of all these accidents in the doctor's opinion, was that Harry could hardly be considered to be sane, and that in his confused state of mind quite possibly accused himself of the crime. The doctor also advised the court that on the 5th of

---

[13] Benalla Standard 17 October 1913, p3
[14] Benalla Standard 17 October 1913, p3
[15] Glen Reiss 2020
[16] A light, horse drawn, vehicle

September, after the football incident, he had been summoned to treat Harry again, and found him in a highly agitated state. At that consultation he had prescribed for Harry, 16 doses of 20 grains of bromide to be taken every three hours. The doctor was unsure if Harry had taken the drug.

In support of Doctor Harkin's evidence, Harry's brother, Walter, also gave evidence. Walter stated that Harry's mental state had been a source of family concern for some years, and that at times he believed his brother was "out of his mind".[17] All of this, defence argued, meant that Harry was in a confused and agitated state when he was interviewed by police, and his "*confession*" should have been disregarded.

One piece of evidence was not presented to the court, and that concerned the side effects of the drug bromide. Taken at a level of just six grains per dose, bromide can cause a form of intoxication.[18] . If Harry had been compliant with the doctor's directions of 20 grains every three hours, it is likely he would have been in a highly drug affected state when interviewed by the police. Was bromide the reason for his confusion, and his apparent confession?

The evidence presented in Harry's defence did not sway the presiding judge Mister Justice Cussen. He rejected the evidence regarding the claim that Harry was not the assailant. However, he was apparently impressed with the claims regarding Harry's sanity. He recommended the jury consider the attack as the "work of a madman". After due consideration the jury returned a verdict of not guilty on the grounds of insanity. Mister Justice Cussen then sentenced Harry to an indefinite period of incarceration at the Governor's pleasure. [19]

Harry was first imprisoned at the Beechworth Gaol, possibly because it was the closest major prison. He remained in Beechworth until the 11th of December 1913, when he was transferred to the Melbourne Gaol. His family had not completely forsaken him, and in January 1915 they petitioned the Victorian State Governor, Sir Arthur Lyulph Stanley, for Harry's release. That petition failed. However, on the 17th of June 1916, Harry was suddenly released.

---

[17] Benalla Standard 17 October 1913, p3
[18] https://www.google.com/search?client=firefox-b-d&q=bromide
[19] ibid

Harry's release was made under a special condition of the *Crimes Act 1914* (the Act) which allowed the State Governor to exercise mercy. So, what had occurred in Harry's case, that led Sir Arthur Stanley to change his mind?

It is possible that Harry's mental health, in spite of Doctor Harkin's prediction of a poor prognosis, had instead improved. Harry had now been in prison for three years, during which time there was no record of any breach of prison regulations listed on his record. It seems his behaviour behind bars had been exemplary. Indeed, prison may well have been good for his condition. The routine of prison life removed many of the factors that prior to his incarceration had precipitated instances of mental illness, allowing his brain the opportunity to repair. In addition, it is now known that Traumatic Brain Injury may, over time, improve to a point where the sufferer can resume a "normal" life. So perhaps the prison authorities reported Harry's improvement and Sir Arthur was moved to order Harry's release as an act of mercy. There was provision for such an action under Section 21D of the Act.[20]

It may also be that on reviewing the evidence regarding Harry's trial and conviction, Sir Arthur decided Harry had been wrongly convicted. Section 85ZR of the Act allows the Governor General, or a State Governor to pardon those considered to have been wrongly convicted.[21] Interestingly Harry's prison record states he was released under "Special Authority – Section 563 of the Crimes Act".[22] Contemporary legal advice indicates that this section of the Act does not in fact exist, and it is therefore assumed the entry "563" is a clerical error. However, Sir Arthur certainly had the authority to order Harry's release under one or other of the sections of the Act.

There is a more sinister possibility regarding Harry's release. For while Harry was in gaol, world events had been shaping the destiny of his generation.

---

[20] http://www5.austlii.edu.au/au/legis/cth/consol_act/ca191482/s21d.html
[21] http://www5.austlii.edu.au/au/legis/cth/consol_act/ca191482/s85zr.html
[22] WithersHarryFrancisNo33421

Chapter 3

The Unthinkable War

ON THE 28TH OF JUNE 1914 the Archduke Franz Ferdinand and his wife were assassinated. That violent event is often held to be the spark that ignited World War One, but there were a myriad other factors that built the funeral pyre for the 40 million people who would die during that conflict.

In the decades before 1914 there had been a series of diplomatic clashes between the European Great Powers. From 1867 Italy, France, Great Britain, Germany, Austria-Hungary and Russia had been jockeying for position over European and colonial interests. Britain in particular was keen to secure the security of its Empire in relation to France in North Africa, and Russia in Persia and India. In this regard an alliance known as the Triple Entente was agreed between these three powers. However, either by accident or design, this entente had the effect of isolating Germany and of hampering that country's own imperial ambitions. In addition, the Entente promoted the friendship between Russia, France and Britain, but it demoted the importance, for Britain in particular, of maintaining good relations with Germany. These diplomatic activities pushed Germany toward a much closer alliance with Austria-Hungary and in 1879 the two powers signed the German-Austrian treaty or Dual Alliance. Germany also endeavoured unsuccessfully to drive a wedge between Britain and France and to oppose French attempts to unilaterally increase its influence in North Africa.

International tensions were hardly relieved when in 1910 Italy began to pursue its own colonial ambitions regarding Libyan provinces that were under the control of the Ottoman Empire. Tension was further escalated in 1912 when Russia encouraged the formation of a coalition of the states of Serbia, Bulgaria, Greece, and Montenegro that successfully attacked the Ottoman Empire in the Balkans, thus changing the balance of power in the region to the detriment of Austria-Hungarian interests. [23]

In the face of these tensions and diplomatic fallouts, the major powers began to prepare for war. Britain concentrated her efforts in this regard on increasing the size and improving the capabilities of the Royal Navy. The British naval expansion spurred Germany to similar action, whilst other powers introduced conscription systems and began to stockpile arms and munitions. War seemed inevitable but all believed that when it came it would be of a short duration and the plans they made reflected this belief. By 1914 plans and preparations were all but complete; all that was needed was a catalyst. In fact, it would have been almost too much effort not to have a war.

Half a world away the Australian Government had a different focus. Prior to Federation the individual colonies main defensive concerns focused first on the French and later the Russians. However, national defence was an unpopular topic in a population that felt itself sufficiently isolated from potential enemies not to have to worry unduly about creating its own military force.

British settlers in Australia had always supported their motherland. William Withers a staunch supporter of Britain, demonstrated his British patriotism in 1901 by donating a flag to the Chiltern Valley School and joining the students and teachers in the singing of 'God Save the King' and other patriotic songs perhaps like the popular song of the time 'Awake Australia':

> *Awake! Awake, Australia!*
> *Old Britain's bracing cheer*
> *Is borne across the waters far,*
> *And all her children hear.*
> *The echoes are replying*

---

[23] https://www.britannica.com/topic/Balkan-Wars

> *From chimes o'er all the world*
> *Australia fair must lead the van,*
> *With banner bright unfurled!*
> *Beneath thy bright blue skies,*
> *Australia Fair, arise!*

Indeed "old Britain's bracing cheer" had led to a small New South Wales contingent being deployed to the Sudan War of 1885, and a somewhat larger contingent of troops from all six Australian colonies deployed to the South African War of 1899-1902. These military commitments to Britain were a forerunner of what was to come.

The catalyst for war came with the assassination of Archduke Franz Ferdinand and his wife, resulting in a domino effect of European nations declaring war on one another, culminating in Britain's declaration of war on Germany on the 4th of August 1914.

Government reaction in Australia to the European situation might best be described as measured. Up to the day Britain declared war the Australian Government had been more concerned with the perceived threat posed by the Japanese in the Pacific region. Nevertheless, on the 4th of August 1914, Australia followed Britain's lead and declared war on Germany and her ally, the Ottoman Empire.

The pro-British, white Australian public was whipped into a patriotic fervour by rousing speeches and jingoistic songs such as 'Australia Will Be There':

> *There are lots and lots of arguments*
> *Going on today*
> *As to whether dear old England*
> *Should be brought into the fray*
> *But all right-thinking people*
> *Know well we had to fight*
> *For the Kaiser's funny business*
> *It wants some putting right.*
> *Rally 'round the banner of your country*
> *Take the field with brothers o'er the foam*

> *On land or sea*
> *Wherever you be*
> *Keep your eye on Germany*
> *But England, home and beauty*
> *Have no cause to fear*
> *Should auld acquaintance be forgot*
> *No, no, no, no, no!*
> *Australia will be there*
> *Australia will be there.*[24]

On the 15th of August 1914 the government announced the raising of an Australian expeditionary force for overseas service. The new force was titled the Australian Imperial Force, but better known simply as the AIF. The AIF's initial strength was limited to 20,000 men, and as these men donned uniform and commenced their training, the civilian population began to be indirectly impacted by the conflict. The Australian public were shielded from the worst of the economic conditions, but in Europe, there were food shortages, and the cost of everyday items dramatically increased. Late in 1915, the Withers obtained some idea of the situation faced by their relatives in Scotland in the following letter:

> *Oct -18-1915*
> *Ardveinnie*
> *Edderton*
> *Ross Shire*

My Dear Cousin

Your most kind & welcome letter give me great pleasure to hear from you. I was longing to hear from you although I was always hearing how you were from Sarah. Dear Cousin I was glad to see by your letter that you was well and that you are in good health it is a great blessing for word obscure might be you to be in good health. I was also glad to hear that Mr Maynard and your family was well. I see by your letter that your oldest son got married he is very young and so is the wife he got I hope she is all right by

---

[24] https://www.nfsa.gov.au/collection/curated/australia-will-be-there

this trouble the war is a terrible bad thing if it gets a good hold it is a common thing among the soldiers. Dear Cousin I am glad to say that we are all quite well just now my husband is keeping fairly well only he is complaining always of rheumatism he always goes about but it is not easy for him at times. I am keeping pretty well myself we have always so much to do here keeping the place right my family is all keeping quite well and they are none of them at the front yet but if things are not to get better soon I think all the men in the country will be called up it is just on the brink of that great war. Dear Cousin I see by your letter that some of your family is at the front also I see by the papers that there is a lot of boys from Australia and that they got it pretty hot at times from the Germans but they did good work

The papers here give a good account of the Australian boys at the front there is hardly a young man left around about here but what is away serving the King & country. Dear Cousin this is a terrible war and no sign of it getting finished it only looks worse than ever the Germans is a bad lot with all the dirty work they did hear. Cousin I am not hearing from August how Normans family is and Uncle Donalds family they are a long way from me but they are all quite well so far as I know and for Uncle Georges I never hear anything about him. Dear Cousin you was saying that the food is very dear in Australia we are paying very high for everything here we pay 4 ½ d for a 2 lb loaf butter 2d a lb meat is about the same as you have eggs is 2/6 a Doz all kind of meal & oats and clothing is almost double so it is pretty hard for poor people to make a living if this war is to last long I don't know how people will pull through. Dear Cousin you was asking if all my family was married I have two sons & a daughter married the other two sons is still with me and the married daughter. I was glad to hear that Mr & Mrs Withers & family was well, tell them I was asking for them Now Dear Cousin I must close with kind love to everybody not forgetting yourself and don't be so long in writing again I always hear from Sarah I remain your loving cousin Mrs West

Along with family news, the examples of the cost of food items, and an accurate prediction that the war would worsen, Mrs West's letter acknowledges the Australian forces contribution in the fighting. However, she appears confused as to who the Australians were fighting at that time, for the enemy the AIF confronted was not the German Army, but the Turkish Army of the Ottoman Empire.

Initially the majority of the 20,000 men who enlisted in the AIF, were deployed to Egypt. There they were to complete their training and assist in countering the Ottoman Empire's ambitions in the Middle East. In April, after just four months of training, the Australians, with troops from Britain, New Zealand, and France were deployed by sea to land on the Gallipoli Peninsula. The aim of this deployment was to seize control of the Dardanelles Strait, and to capture Constantinople, the Turkish capital.[25]

On the 25th of April the Australians landed on a narrow beach later named ANZAC Cove, gaining a precarious hold on ridge lines above the beach. From that position many attempts were made to break through the Turkish lines, all of which failed. On the other hand, repeated Turkish attempts to dislodge the Allies from their positions also failed. This stalemate lasted until late December 1915 when the Australians and New Zealanders were evacuated. [26]

The Gallipoli campaign cost Australia 26,111 casualties, 8,141 of whom were either killed in action or died of their wounds. While many legends were created during the campaign, it was in reality a costly military defeat. The casualty bill was also the genesis of a situation that would eventually affect Harry Withers.

---

[25] http://anzaccentenary.vic.gov.au/history/australias-contribution-wwi/index.html
[26] ibid

Chapter 4

The Call to Arms

HARRY'S RELEASE FROM THE MELBOURNE Gaol, must have been greeted with great joy by his family, but also with some concern. After all, the Harry they knew before he went to gaol, was mentally fragile and subject to epilepsy. So far as they knew, his condition had not altered. It may be imagined, on welcoming Harry home, that they showered him with love, and sought to protect and care for him in every way. However, from the date of his release through to October the 18th 1916, there is no surviving documentation regarding Harry's thoughts, his whereabouts, or what he was doing. The next hard evidence of his whereabouts is provided by his AIF enlistment documentation.

Harry's release from prison had coincided with a crisis for the AIF. As a force comprised entirely of volunteers, the AIF relied on a steady stream of additional voluntary recruits to replace its losses. The losses incurred at Gallipoli shocked the Australian public, and the number of men presenting at recruiting stations began to diminish.[27] In conjunction with this, following the evacuation, the AIF underwent a major restructure, an activity that emphasised the shortage of Australian reinforcements[28]. However, the situation was shortly to become far worse.

After the evacuation from Gallipoli, and a brief period of rest in Egypt, the majority of the Australian infantry units were redeployed to the European

---

[27] https://www.awm.gov.au/collection/event/ww1/1916/essay
[28] https://www.awm.gov.au/collection/E84708

theatre. The first major engagement in which they fought in Europe was at Fromelles. The village of Fromelles had an evil reputation. British troops had engaged the enemy around the village in 1915 and had suffered heavy casualties. The Australian 5th Division, and the British 61st Division, were sent to attack the Fromelles ridge on the evening of the 19th of July 1916. This attack was supposed to be a diversion, designed to draw German forces away from the Somme, where the Allies planned a major advance. However, the Fromelles attack was a complete disaster. The Australians suffered over 5,000 casualties, a figure that included over 2,000 fatalities, and no ground was taken. [29]

Less than a week later, on the 23rd of July, the 1st Australian Division made an assault on the village of Pozieres. This attack was a success, in that the Australians captured, and held Pozieres. However, in forty-two days of intense fighting they suffered a staggering figure of 23,000 casualties, 6,800 of which were fatalities.[30]

The casualties suffered during the Gallipoli campaign had shocked the Australian public, however, the casualties suffered at Fromelles and at Pozieres left the nation reeling. AIF recruitment plummeted and replacing the horrendous numbers of casualties became a major issue for war fighters and for government. In an effort to address this shortfall in voluntary enlistment, the notion of conscription was raised in Parliament. Then in October 1916, the Prime Minister William Hughes, took the issue of conscription to the nation in a referendum. The referendum was narrowly defeated, leaving the AIF at the mercy of a slow trickle of volunteers.[31]

To increase the flow of recruits, the AIF altered its strict physical requirements, and many men who had previously been rejected as medically unsuitable were enlisted. Initially the requirements had to be 19 to 38 years of age, a minimum of five foot six inches in height and a minimum chest measurement of 34 inches. They had to have good teeth, and good eyesight. During the first year of the war around 33 percent of all volunteers were rejected. In June 1915, following the high casualties at Gallipoli, the age

---

[29] https://www.awm.gov.au/collection/event/ww1/1916/essay
[30] https://www.awm.gov.au/collection/event/ww1/1916/essay
[31] https://www.nma.gov.au/defining-moments/resources/conscription-referendu

range was changed to 18 to 45 years of age, and the minimum height reduced to five feet. Dental and ophthalmic standards were also lowered. Recruits were also required to pass a medical examination, however as events in Harry's story will demonstrate, there must be some doubt as to the thoroughness of that particular process.

There is also anecdotal evidence of another initiative that may have been instigated to boost recruitment. Apparently, under this initiative, when some criminals were brought to court, just before final sentence was passed, they were offered a choice of "join the army, or go to gaol", or for those already in gaol... "promise to join the army, and you will be released". However, if this practise ever existed in Australia, no legislation providing the framework for such a practise is available.

As has been established, Harry enlisted in the AIF on the 18th of October 1916. Is it possible that his enlistment was the condition for his release from gaol? This question requires investigation.

Harry was released from the Melbourne Gaol on, or about, the 16th of June 1916, and it would seem logical that if enlistment was a condition of release, that immediately on walking out the gaol gate, his next stop would have been the nearest AIF recruiting office. However, this did not occur, and in fact it was four months before he joined up. If this scheme existed, it is unlikely the authorities would have agreed to a four-month delay between release from prison and enlistment. If Harry had instigated such a delay of his own volition, it is probable the authorities would have seen such a delay as non-compliance, resulting in his arrest and return to prison. Therefore, even supposing this scheme existed, it is unlikely he was released from gaol in order to join the army. Instead, Harry almost certainly owed his freedom to one or other of the options open to Sir Arthur Stanley as previously described.

What is beyond any doubt is that Harry enlisted in the AIF. However, whilst other families may have been proud their sons had enlisted to fight the foe, it is difficult to imagine Harry's parents being over pleased with their son's enlistment. The thought of Harry, a man who in the recent past would become agitated at the slightest provocation, being able to endure army training, let alone the stress and danger of war, must have filled them with despair. It is likely Harry was aware of his parents' likely reaction, and he possibly feared they would try to prevent his enlistment. It would have been a simple matter for his parents to advise the AIF recruiters of Harry's mental health issues and his epilepsy, and his enlistment would have been rejected. This may well be the reason why Harry in the company of another Chiltern Valley man, Tom Henderson, journeyed to the township of Castlemaine, a distance of some 290 kilometres to the west of Chiltern Valley, where both of them enlisted.

Prior to enlistment, Tom Henderson and Harry had both been labourers, although in his enlistment papers Harry made the distinction of labelling himself as a "farm labourer". The two men were well acquainted, it may even be that they were cousins, as Harry's great-uncle Jason, had married a Mary Henderson. Tom, it seems, was a free spirit, with a carefree attitude that may have darkened his reputation within the more conservative elements of the Chiltern Valley community. Later that free and easy attitude was to land Tom in trouble in the army. He was ten years younger than Harry, but the two were certainly on friendly terms, and it seems they had renewed contact after Harry's release from the Melbourne Gaol.

The question as to why Harry chose to join up is one of life's imponderables. He may have been moved by patriotic fervour, or he may have been seeking adventure. Perhaps it was Tom Henderson's idea, and he just went along with his mate. Or maybe service in the AIF was a means of escaping an overprotective family. In any event given his previous mental health history, submitting himself to the stresses associated with the enlistment procedures was an ambitious step. However, a perusal of Harry's enlistment papers show that not only was he able to cope with the process, he was quite capable of manipulating the process to his own advantage.

Harry's "Attestation Paper" has been completed in a clear bold hand, and while no doubt the recruits were coached through the questions on the paper, there are no errors in Harry's responses, no indication of any anxiety he may have felt. His father, William Withers, is listed as his Next Of Kin. His previous service in the militia was registered, as is the fact that he had been discharged due to head injuries suffered after a fall from a horse. The attesting officer recorded that Harry had understood all the questions asked of him. However, it is in the papers associated with his medical examination that the extent of Harry's new confidence and ability to deal with stress becomes apparent.

During the course of the examination, the medical officer tested Harry's eyesight, examined his teeth, noting Harry had a denture, and listened to his heart and lungs. Harry's physical appearance and statistics were listed as:

"Age 32 years and 6 months
Height 5 feet 10 ½ inches
Chest Measurement 36/38 inches
Complexion Fair
Eyes Blue
Hair Brown
Religion Methodist[32]"

Establishing a recruits religion appears to have been more important than other aspects of the medical exam. So far Harry was passing with flying colours. However, the medical officer then signed off on the appropriate section of the form which begins... *"I have examined the above person, and find that he does not present any of the following conditions..."* The form then goes on to list a variety of diseases but included are: *"defective intelligence"*, and *"he declares he is not subject to fits of any description"*.[33]

Clearly Harry has provided an edited account of his health, and he has omitted any reference to his mental health issues and epilepsy. But perhaps the fault may not entirely lie with him. The AIF recruiting team was probably working toward a quota, and even if Harry had appeared a little slow when they interviewed him, they didn't need masterminds in the front line, they just needed able bodied men able to hold, aim, and fire a rifle. In fairness, the available means of checking personal information in 1916, was

---

[32] https://recordsearch.naa.gov.au/SearchNRetrieve/Interface/ViewImage.aspx?B=8855783 page 1
[33] https://recordsearch.naa.gov.au/SearchNRetrieve/Interface/ViewImage.aspx?B=8855783 page 6

limited and slow, so there was little chance the medical officer would check Harry's story. So long as Harry kept his nerve and remained calm, all would be well.

Having passed all aspects of the enlistment procedure, Harry was duly sworn in as a private soldier in the AIF, to serve until the end of the war and a further period of four months, unless sooner lawfully discharged. Rightly, or wrongly, Harry was now a soldier.

Of course, even after Harry had joined up, had his parents been aware that he had misrepresented himself during his medical examination, they could have informed the authorities and had him discharged. However, they were either unaware, or so angry at his deception that they chose to let him suffer the consequences, and those consequences were about to begin. Harry's next stop would be a recruit training camp at Royal Park in Melbourne.

Chapter 5

Army Life

IT SHOULD ALSO BE NOTED that at this stage of the war, the AIF was not forming new units, rather it was reinforcing existing ones. On enlistment, Harry was allocated to the infantry and posted as a reinforcement to the 24th Battalion, while his mate Tom Henderson went to the 22nd Battalion. At the time Harry enlisted, the 24th Battalion was in France, and Harry would have to complete his training before he would be sent to join the unit as a replacement for someone who had been killed or wounded. The AIF reinforcement system for recruits destined for the European theatre involved a recruit completing initial training in Australia, another course on arrival in England, and another in France prior to a posting to the Battalion. So Harry was to undertake a considerable amount of training before he got anywhere near the enemy.

On enlistment recruits were allocated to a reinforcement draft, generally consisting of two officers and up to 150 other ranks. Initially these drafts were assigned to specific deployed units, the reinforcement even being recruited from the same area where the unit they were assigned to had been first raised, although the 24th Battalion was a generic Victorian unit. Harry was assigned directly to that unit, but for his initial training he became a member of K Company, 24th Battalion 18/Reinforcement unit, located at Royal Park Melbourne.

The camp at Royal Park had grown out of the enthusiasm for young Australian men to enlist in the AIF. At the outbreak of war, a camp had been established at Broadmeadows, but that camp's facilities were unable to cope with the huge numbers of recruits that had flooded recruiting offices in 1914 and 1915. In autumn 1915, a combination of wet weather, poor drainage, and very basic facilities resulted in a rapid increase in sickness among recruits. Fuelled by sensationalist press coverage, there was a public outcry, and as a result a series of additional camps were established at outlying places including the towns of Ballarat, Geelong, Seymour and the suburbs of Flemington, and Royal Park. Accommodation at these camps was tented, and while the general facilities remained basic, by the time Harry arrived at Royal Park there had been improvements in the standard of accommodation. The tents were provided with prefabricated "duck board" flooring, and each recruit slept on a straw filled palliasse. They had blankets, but no sheets were issued. Ablution blocks provided cleaning and toilet requirements, and bulk cooked meals were served in large mess tents. Recruits were expected to wash and mend their own clothing. In the winter this accommodation would have been pretty uncomfortable. However, Harry arrived at the camp in late spring, early summer, so even taking into account the notoriously fickle Melbourne climate, he and his fellow recruits would have been comfortable enough.

The Royal Park camp had been established in a particularly rough part of Melbourne. There were health concerns and accusations that an increase in prostitution and other vices had followed the establishment of the new military camp. Many of the recruits were wild and undisciplined fellows. There had also been a number of riots in city streets, mainly involving recruits from the Broadmeadows camp, but the soldiers at Royal Park were not exactly passive. With a few beers under the belt, they were capable of all kinds of mischief. Certainly, they received sufficient pay to be able to be able to enjoy themselves.

In fact, soldiers of the 1st AIF were among the highest paid of the war. A private soldier received five shillings a day, plus an additional one shilling per day to be held over until he was discharged, providing the soldier with an overall daily rate of six shillings a day, and leading to the nickname of "six bob a day tourists". Married men were required to allot two shillings a day for their dependents with an additional separation allowance paid to them after 1915. Given that the soldiers were fed, housed, clothed and had their health issues addressed at no cost, the rate of pay was at least equal to that of the average civilian worker.[34]

As a single man, Harry would have had spare cash, and at some stage he used some of his pay to purchase a pistol. Why was he moved to do such a thing? Had he been threatened and felt he needed to be able to protect himself? These questions are impossible to answer, however shortly before his embarking for England, he had second thoughts about the weapon and sent it home.

The training at Royal Park was of six to eight weeks in duration and included basic training in drill, bayonet fighting, and musketry. At the start of the war this training had not always been of a high standard, and those early recruit drafts received a very rudimentary training prior to being embarked for overseas service. Many of the officers had been appointed on the basis of their level of education and social position, rather than military knowledge, and once appointed, they received no special training to prepare them for command. Instructional staff were generally poorly trained too. Equipment was in short supply, and in some cases access to rifle range facilities for live firing of weapons was very limited. By 1916, the training regime was better-established, and conducted as a relatively smoothly running program. [35] The first few days of training may have been exciting and new for the recruits, but soon their initial enthusiasm for army life waned. The seemingly endless days of parade ground drill, the monotony of fatigue duty such as peeling potatoes and scrubbing out storerooms, guard duty, and lectures on various aspects of the training, was hardly the sort of thing they had signed up for. There may also have been the occasional route march to start to build up the recruits' fitness. Sunday would be their only day off, but only if they weren't on duty.[36]

There is no report of Harry's recruit training achievements, and perhaps more importantly, no report of a return of his anxiety attacks or epilepsy. So, it must be assumed he handled the training quite well too. Perhaps the army

---

[34] https://en.wikipedia.org/wiki/First_Australian_Imperial_Force
[35] https://anzacportal.dva.gov.au/wars-and-missions/ww1/military-organisation/training
[36] Op. cit.

life was similar in structure to life in prison…you got out of bed, you did what you were told, you got fed at regular times, you went to bed, you went to sleep. The fact that the army instructors shouted orders, and the nature of the training was sometimes trying, does not seem to have concerned him. Maybe his previous service with the 8th Light Horse Regiment, helped Harry too. Soon enough the Royal Park training drew to a close and Harry was assigned to a draft to embark for England.

Interestingly, only one letter from Harry's days at Royal Park has survived. That letter was written to his mother, dated 23rd of November 1916, on the day of his embarkation. Is the lack of any other letters an indication that his parents, and perhaps his mother in particular, were still displeased with their soldier son? Or had Harry refrained from writing home in case his parents made efforts to see him discharged from the army? Perhaps his mother only started saving his letters after his deployment. It is of course impossible to say, however, once Harry was overseas, he became a regular correspondent, and his mother began to save his letters. In that letter from Royal Park, Harry refers to the pistol he purchased, and he is clearly excited at the prospect of the imminent sea voyage:

"Royal Park
23/11/16

Dear Mum

Just a few brief lines to let you see I am ever thinking of you all. The revolver which I have sent home I bought for 10/6. I was going to take it with me. Then I thought it better to send it home so you can keep it for me. Tell Wal he can get cartridges at any of the iron mongers in Melbourne. I have been busy in distributing the sea kit to the men as we are to be up at 4 o'clock in the morning. The boat has been in since yesterday it is a lovely big boat. There are something like 300 troops to sail. I have very little news so I shall close with love to all. From Private H Withers K Company, 24th Battalion 18/Reinforcement"

There is nothing in this letter suggesting that all the excitement of preparing to embark had caused Harry to become anxious. Indeed, his words are rational, and articulate. He even indicates that he has been given some responsibility assisting in the distribution of sea kit to the other members of the draft. Whilst this might not indicate leadership potential, such details were usually reserved for well performing soldiers.

Chapter 6

The Long Sea Journey

THE "LOVELY BIG BOAT" HARRY referred to was His Majesty's Australian Troopship *Hororata*. The *Hororata* was a vessel of 9461 ton, launched in 1914. Originally designed to serve the New Zealand emigrant trade, she had five first class berths and 1066 in steerage class. She was originally owned by the New Zealand Shipping Company Ltd, London, and in 1915, on her maiden voyage from New Zealand to Brisbane, she was requisitioned, and leased, by the Australian Government for use as a troopship. [37] That same year, the *Hororata* took part in the first convoy taking Australian troops to Egypt. On that voyage she carried 67 officers, 2000 other ranks, and 124 horses[38]. She then continued to ferry Australian troops to England through to 1917, after which time she came under control of the British Admiralty. Troopships had a long and dangerous war, and during the course of the conflict many were sunk, or damaged by enemy action. However, luck was with the *Hororata*; she survived World War One, but sadly she was torpedoed and sunk in World War Two.

The *Hororata*, with Harry and Tom Henderson aboard, sailed from Melbourne on the 23rd of November 1916. Hundreds of well-wishers packed the pier at Port Melbourne to see the soldiers off. Paper streamers were thrown from the wharf to the ship, the ends to be held by families at the pier

---

[37] http://www.poheritage.com/Upload/Mimsy/Media/factsheet/93338HORORATA-1914pdf.pdf
[38] http://www.poheritage.com/Upload/Mimsy/Media/factsheet/93338HORORATA-1914pdf.pdf

end and the soldiers on board. As the ship began to move away, the streamers lengthened, then broke, ending the last contact many of those on board would have with their loved ones. However, Harry's family was not among the crowd on the pier. It is easy to forget at this distance in time, in 1916 a journey from Chiltern Valley to Melbourne was a major undertaking. Add to this, there would have been uncertainty as to the date of Harry's departure, coupled with the need to care for the farm and its animals making such a journey impractical. However, it is possible his parents were still angry at his joining up and chose to show their displeasure by staying at home. Yet in the letters Harry subsequently sent home, and in the diary he kept, there is no hint of bitterness regarding his parents' absence, suggesting that whatever the reason for their absence, he accepted it.

A long sea voyage now faced Harry and his fellow soldiers. They were to follow a similar passage to that taken by around 44 troopship "convoys" that left Australia with troops for the AIF during the four-year war. The term "convoy" is used loosely, for after the third convoy to leave Australia, the initial stages of the voyage was often made by unescorted individual troopships. When the troopships arrived in waters where enemy contact was more likely, formal convoys were formed, and escorting warships were sometimes provided. It was only in 1917, when Germany declared a policy of unrestricted submarine warfare, that all troopships were escorted[39].

Generally, troopships such as the *Hororata*, made the voyage from Melbourne to England in four stages. The first stage of her November 1916 voyage took her across the Great Australian Bight to the Western Australian port of Fremantle. There she took on more coal, the main fuel used to produce the steam that drove the ship's engines, in preparation for the next stage of the voyage, across the Indian Ocean to Africa. Her first African port of call was Durban, where again the ship took on more coal and supplies, and the soldiers were allowed limited shore leave. On leaving Durban, the *Hororata* sailed in the company of two other Australian troopships, the *Port Napier* and the *Kyarra.* This tiny convoy moved northward to Cape Town, arriving there on Boxing Day. Again, the ship refuelled and resupplied and

---

[39] https://anzacportal.dva.gov.au/wars-and-missions/ww1/military-organisation/transport#3

the soldiers were allowed limited shore leave. Cape Town was also the assembly point for a larger number of Australian steamers, and on the 27th of December the convoy of three had grown to seven, and included the troopships *Kyarra, Wanganui, Tahiti, Hororata, Suevic, Beltana,* and the *Borda*. In addition, an escorting warship was provided, *HMS Glasgow,* a light cruiser, guarding and guiding the convoy as it steamed ever closer to England. The next port of call was Freetown. Here the troops were not allowed ashore, but the ships were again resupplied with coal and other supplies. In addition, the escort changed, *HMS Glasgow* returned to Cape Town and her place was taken by another cruiser *HMS Almazora*. As the convoy entered the English Channel this escort was further increased by the presence of seven British destroyers, one for each troopship[40]. Finally, after ten weeks at sea, the *Hororata* completed her voyage and disembarked her precious cargo on the 23rd of January 1917.

Harry provided a very brief account of the voyage, in his diary:

"...Troop Ship Hororata left Port Melbourne Nov 23rd 1916 for England with seven hundred men. After five days of sailing we reached Albany and anchored for coal and left at 1 o'clock after coaling the boat went on to further her journey. The next port we passed was St Elenor which was reached after two weeks and five days, later we reached Serbone there was two men buried ashore which died of meningitis. Two days later there was another man buried at sea. After which we called at Durban. The boat pulled in to the warf and remained in port for nine days during which time we were allowed to go anywhere we liked after being dismissed from the ship and to return by eleven o'clock at night. When leaving the ship first there was five other lads joined us ancillary others. We spent our Xmas on the boat the days before reaching Scapa Flow there we marched through the town and then was dismissed in front of the town hall. Next day we left port at 3o'clock and joined a convoy guarded by one cruiser.

---

[40] http://www.diggerhistory.info/pages-asstd/schwinghammer.htm

> *Thence we called at Portsmouth England which was in all 10 weeks and three days. It was about 5 o'clock in the evening 20th January when we disembarked..."*

It is clear that Harry made this diary entry some considerable time after the voyage had ended and creates the impression it is all he could remember of the trip. Perhaps he made the entry in a free moment during his training in England, or more likely, when he was out of the line in France. As a result, it is likely his memory played tricks on him regarding dates and detail of the journey. For example, he recorded Scapa Flow as the convoy's final destination. He corrects this in a letter to his mother, written soon after his arrival at camp in England, where he more accurately provides details of the voyage route, and the ship's final destination as Devonport.

In addition, many of Harry's diary entries, including the one regarding his voyage, are light on detail. For the voyage must have been much more interesting than his diary suggests. In the same letter to his mother, he indicates he was having a "good time". He does not however, elaborate on his definition of a good time. Yet the troopship probably suited him quite well as the daily routine was even more similar to life in gaol, than normal army life.

Life on board a troopship was a considerably more structured existence than Harry had faced at Royal Park camp. The troops slept below deck, on hammocks. They took their meals on a mess deck. When the weather permitted, regular periods of drill, weapon training and military lectures were conducted. Concerts, boxing contests, and regular church parades, were also features of life on board[41]. The church parades in particular would have pleased Harry. However, there were negative aspects of the voyage. The deaths of soldiers from meningitis, debilitating seasickness, and the crowded uncomfortable conditions. Yet these factors don't seem to have impacted too much on Harry and there is no indication that he has suffered any kind of mental health, or epileptic episode.

Harry is almost noncommittal regarding the shore leave he took and there is no mention at all of the different cultures he must have seen. He doesn't

---

[41] https://anzacportal.dva.gov.au/wars-and-missions/ww1/military-organisation/transport#4

mention crossing the Equator and the good-humoured ceremony that was attached to that occasion. On another ship in Harry's convoy, another diarist, Private George Schwinghammer recorded the light hearted ceremony that took place on that vessel, with all those crossing the Equator for the first time being "dipped" in tank of water. [42]

Nor does Harry mention *HMS Glasgow* firing a warning shot at an unidentified ship, or of the ant-submarine guard duty the troops were required to mount once they neared England.[43] So when all these omissions are taken into account, the uneventful voyage Harry recorded in his diary, was in fact action-packed. However, as he and his mates made their way down the *Hororata* gangplank to land on English soil, an even greater adventure awaited them.

---

[42] http://www.diggerhistory.info/pages-asstd/schwinghammer.htm
[43] ibid

Chapter 7

Salisbury Plain January – February 1917

PRIOR TO AUGUST 1916 THE AIF had established its training facilities in Egypt to enable reinforcements to be more easily moved to the Gallipoli campaign. However, after the withdrawal from Gallipoli, AIF training groups were moved to England where dedicated camps were established across the Salisbury Plain. Each brigade had its own training battalion, and it was to the 6th Brigade's training battalion that Harry was destined.

Immediately after they disembarked Harry's draft boarded a train to Exeter, arriving at that destination in the early hours of the 31st of January 1917. Waiting on the Exeter platform was a civic reception party headed by the mayor of the town and numerous supporting citizens. Harry recalled the occasion in his diary:

> "...It was about 5 o'clock in the evening 20th January when we disembarked. We took train to Exeter and before leaving the station there was a bun and cup of coffee given to each man by the Mayoress of the town..."

In addition, each of the newly arrived Diggers was handed a small card wishing each man "good luck". That however was the last of the niceties for the day, as a rude awakening to the reality of life immediately followed this welcome. A five-mile march to Lark Hill, Salisbury camp followed, and they arrived at their destination at around 5pm.

At this distance in time, it is difficult to say what the conditions were during that march. It may be assumed the soldiers would have carried their rifles, and echelon bags, cylindrical shaped canvas bags commonly referred to as sausage bags in which spare clothing and other personal items were stored. Along with this load they would have worn their basic equipment, an assortment of pouches, straps and packs. The basic equipment Harry and his mates were issued in Australia may have been of a different pattern to that used in the European theatre, which was the British 1908 pattern. However, it is possible that by 1917 the 1908 equipment was being issued to recruits prior to their embarkation in Australia.

The 1908 pattern equipment was made of webbing and had been specially designed to enable the soldier to hold all of the articles he would require to maintain him in battle. There were pouches for ammunition, a holder for a water bottle, pouches and packs for personal items such as a shaving kit, eating utensils, toothbrush, pocketknife, housewife (sewing kit) and his pay book. In a larger backpack might have been a greatcoat, rubberised groundsheet-cape, food, a weapon cleaning roll and first-aid kit. The equipment was also designed to be easily put on, and just as easily taken off. When required, all the soldier had to do was to seize his rifle and basic equipment and he would be ready in moments to move where he was required. A full set of this equipment and its contents, plus a bayonet, around 150 rounds of ammunition, a gas mask, a steel helmet, rations and defence stores meant that an infantryman might carry into battle around 114 pounds or 52 kilograms. This weight excluded the weight of the soldier's personal weapon.

Harry and his mates would not have carried anything like this weight on that first march to Lark Hill, nevertheless for soldiers softened by ten weeks of sea travel that five mile, or 8.04672 kilometres march to the camp carrying their personal equipment and clothing would have been a testing experience.

On the 4th of February Harry penned off what was possibly his first letter home, providing a broad description of his adventures to date:

"D Company 18/24th Bat 6 Brigade
Salisbury Plains

Dear Mother and Dad
Just a few lines to let you know I am well, trusting this will find you all

well. Dear Mother I have been looking forward to a letter from home but have not yet received one. We had a great send off from Melb Pier the day of our embarkation one of the best send offs any of the men have had. We had a good voyage over we called at various places) on our way over at Albany, Durban, Capetown, St Helena, Sierra Leone so you see we have had a good time. It took 10 weeks and 3 days to get to Devon Port Plymouth. We got there about half past five in the evening on Monday and took a train to Salisbury There we had A five mile march to camp it was five in the morning when we got here. The boys all feel the cold very much. We are having a lot of falls of snow today it has been snowing nearly all day, the ground is covered an inch or two. We have been for a few route marches yesterday we went for a ten mile march and arrived to dinner at ½ past 1 then we had the afternoon free. I have met Bill Grail two or three times. He told me he had a letter from Violet. Dear Mother it seems a long while since I saw any of you how I would like to see you all. I pity you women with the washing if there is one thing we detest it is this all the men are the same we have just finished our dinner and taken a stroll to the YMCA hut to write our letters and some have a cup of tea and some buns. Our pay were taken from us a few days ago and sent to London as soon as we get back we will get four days leave. Some men left for France Thursday evening they were the 16/24 the 17/24 are to go next and then I suppose we will have to go. I think we shall be here for three months yet. We had very little sickness on our boat till we got to the tropics. This is a very large camp I am told that there are camps over the plains for a distance of seventy miles. There were about eight hundred. It was so hot for a few days that a lot of men got sick with the mumps, measles and other complaints. There were three deaths one was buried at sea the others were buried at Sierra Leone and the ministers asked if the Officers and Men if they would give anything toward getting tombstones which they did and got something like sixty-six pounds. Do not forget to answer at once and let me know Jack Mitchells address and Frank Smiths, I was told that George Murry has been here and has just gone back to the front. Dear Mother not much to write about, but will if I'm spared be able to tell a great deal more *than I can write. How did the boys get on with harvesting I was pleased Wal did not have to come over here, it is not the game it is cracked up to be, although we are having a good time. It is surprising the men that have been passed into the army. A lot of men should not be able to see their nose in front of them should they lose their glasses. One man took several sets on the boat. It is surprising how the men help one another. We had all kinds of sport on the boat and there was some good prize money given. I have little to tell now so I think I will close with love to all. Remember me to Mr Coopal and all the people in the valley, also to Willy, Alice, Nell, Frank and all the others. God bless and keep you all till we meet again. From your fond son No 6426 Private H.F. Withers, D Company, 18/24 Batt, 6 Infantry Brigade, Salisbury Plains, A.I.F."*

Harry was clearly impressed by the vastness of the Salisbury Plain military complex. It was indeed huge. Lark Hill alone consisted of a city of huts capable of housing around thirty-four infantry battalions…close to 28,000 men. However, in 1917, such a large number of men living in close proximity to one another, combined with one of the most severe winters for many years, provided a recipe for serious health issues. This was particularly so for the newly arrived Australians who had yet to acclimatise to the English conditions. In a worrying postcard sent to his parents in February 1917 Harry provides a brief description of the living conditions:

Dear Mother and Father

Just a few lines to let you know I am ever thinking of you. It is now three weeks since we arrived here. Dear Mother this is a dreadful cold wet place there have been an awful lot of deaths something like an average of ten a day. We have nice huts to sleep in there are thirty men to a hut. There is only twenty-one in our hut now as the others have gone to the front. There is something like two hundred men before the Doctor either with colds or mumps or else measles every day so you can see this a very hard place for us Australians. Dear Mother I am very anxious to hear from you all I have written several letters but don't know if you have received them or not. I do not feel like writing I would sooner be reading one from home. Dear Mother give my love to all at home. I expect to go to London next week with the other men who came over with us. I was picked out of the 4 ranks on parade the other day to go up for half a dozen fresh scones. There are a lot of German prisoners here. Love to all

Britain held a large number of German prisoners of war and other alien civilians in camps right across Britain. By 1918 there were almost 529 internment camps across the nation holding around 250,000 individuals.[44] Harry made no further mention of the German prisoners he saw at Lark Hill. Almost certainly any contact with those prisoners would have been forbidden, however if he had communicated with them, he would have discovered they were a disillusioned and bored lot. In 1916, in an effort to placate the trade union organizations, Britain avoided using prisoners of war on any kind of labouring tasks. This practise ended in 1917 and German prisoners were then engaged in a variety of work.[45]

Indeed, in some ways the German prisoners were better off than the young Australians who inhabited the training camps. The "nice" huts Harry wrote of, were in fact corrugated iron clad structures which offered minimal shelter from the elements. The cold temperatures proved to be major concern for the newly arrived Australians. For many of the young Australian soldiers, their arrival in England gave them their first sighting of snow and they reacted with boyish delight making snow men and throwing snowballs. However, the novelty of the snow soon wore off, to be replaced by discomfort and misery associated with being constantly cold. Soon the cold would prove to be only one of the factors that would test the newly arrived soldiers' resolve.

A visit to the Lark Hill dental surgery was a requirement for any of the new arrivals who had their own teeth. In 1917 the army's approach to dental health was "if in doubt take out". Toothache, were it to occur in the trenches, would greatly reduce a soldier's effectiveness and so bad teeth were simply extracted and false teeth provided. False teeth don't ache. It is interesting to note that on enlistment the medical officer had noted Harry wore a denture, however in a later letter he reports he has a new plate. Whether this was

---

[44] https://www.amazon.com/Captured-Germans-British-Camps-First/dp/1783463481
[45] https://www.bl.uk/world-war-one/articles/prisoners-of-war

because Harry had more teeth extracted, or because his original plate was in a poor state, is not recorded.

Another health risk at Lark Hill was the training regime. This was physically demanding and designed to toughen the troops prior to their deployment to France. However, it would seem those conducting the training were unaware of the dangers to health posed by very cold weather. These dangers were not lost to the trainee soldiers. F.V. Culverhouse, who arrived at Lark Hill around the same time as Harry, described the training as:

> *"Alternating periods of violent exercise followed by standing still as we gradually freeze. Alternately giving exercises that caused you to get overheated and then such drills as would let you freeze. That made sure that only the fittest could survive it."*[46]

Other soldiers made similar observations, some reporting that Australian reinforcements were forbidden to wear their great coats on parade or during route marches. Catching a chill under these conditions was almost impossible to avoid. Added to this the living conditions in the accommodation huts virtually guaranteed colds, measles, and mumps would pass freely from man to man. This situation was made worse by ill-advised medical care. Stories abound of men who on reporting sick, were seen as malingerers and returned to normal duty. By the end of February 1917 the level of sickness in AIF training units in the United Kingdom reached ten percent, a level that would not be exceeded even at the peak of the 1918 influenza pandemic. This was a serious situation, and not only for those undergoing training. Sick men could not be sent to reinforce the Australian battalions in France, where in the aftermath of the battles of Fromelles, Pozieres and Mouquet Farm they were desperately needed.

Harry of course was not aware of these statistics. However, his first two months at Lark Hill had been a life changing experience, one that he was not at all sure he enjoyed.

46

http://books.publishing.monash.edu/apps/bookworm/view/Australians+in+Britain%3A+The+Twentieth-Century+Experience/137/xhtml/chapter06.html John Oxley Library, State Library of Queensland, OM64-31/7.

Chapter 8

February/March 1917 Deployment Blues

THERE IS NO DOUBT HARRY and his mates suffered from the climatic conditions, sickness, and the toughness of the training. However, another malady would also have a severe impact on many of them. Sometimes flippantly referred to by today's soldiers serving overseas, as the "deployment blues", in reality this is now, and was in 1917, a serious affliction. If not addressed sympathetically, acute mental illnesses may develop. There is no cure as such for the deployment blues, however, communication with friends and loved ones has proven to be the key to successfully navigating through this ailment. In this regard the soldiers of today have a distinct advantage over their 1917 forebears. E-mail, social media, and international telephone calls, which were unheard of then, now greatly reduce the impact of separation and isolation that may accompany deployment. During World War One, homesickness, anxiety, stress, and culture shock were not so easily addressed.

In 1917 surface mail, or "snail mail" in the modern parlance, was the only means available to Harry and his mates to keep in contact with their loved ones at home. This means of communication under the best of circumstances was slow, but the war added a new perspective to the slowness. At times, enemy action slowed the mail to a trickle, sometimes stopping it altogether as ships carrying precious letters were sunk, or land vehicles carrying the mail were destroyed. All of this added to the anxiety experienced by the soldiers, and of course by their families too. Given

Harry's mental health record, he was at high risk of succumbing to this condition.

Indeed, over the first few weeks at Lark Hill, Harry's letters indicate that he was almost certainly suffering the classic symptoms of deployment blues. The first signs of this are evident in his concern at the lack of letters he had received from home and his concern for the well-being of those he had left at home.

His letters at this time are populated with anxiety and appeals for letters. In an early February letter to his sister Nell, he really unloads his problems in this regard:

> "D Company 18/24 6 Brigade
> A.I.F. Lark Hill Salisbury
>
> Dear Nell
>
> Just a line to let you know I am anxious about you all I have received no letters from home yet. This place does not agree with the Australians. I think we will be getting removed to Marsselies as a lot of the boys have gone to catch the Motor Car for Salisbury I should have gone only for having a cold. Tom Henderson told me he saw Jim Matherson. Dear Nell this is a very large camp it is like a town. The camp throughout the plain covers about seventy miles. There are about seventy thousand troops here. There were a lot of artillery left here for France last evening. I hear them saying that their artillery is better than any that has gone to the front. They have been training for five years and are waiting for the Spring. Dear Nell when you write let me know how you all are and how things are going. I will forward you some views another time. Dear Nell is Jack still at the farm, remember me to him and kiss the little ones for me. How is Reggie going with work he was going for. Let me know the address of the Smiths & Jack Mitchell and G Murray. How is the Murrays getting on. Dear Nell I will close as space is limited trusting to hear very shortly. Some of the boys have received letters from their people, but I have only got three from Melbourne. Love to yourself and all at home your ever fond brother Priv H.F. Withers"

Tom Henderson, the Chiltern Valley man who had enlisted on the same day as Harry, is mentioned in this letter, and it would seem at this stage the two are still in regular contact. Unfortunately, any details regarding the other man referenced in this letter, Jim Matherson, are unavailable, but it is assumed he too was a Chiltern Valley man.

This letter is littered with questions from Harry regarding the family at home and of his brother-in-law, Jack Mitchell. No doubt the raft of questions was made in the hope of fostering a return letter. However, interestingly he first complains that he received no mail, and that other men in the camp are getting mail, but then admits to receiving three letters from Melbourne. Who the correspondents in Melbourne were, is not revealed, but it would seem he was not quite as badly off as he believed.

At this point it should be noted that the letters Harry received from home have not survived. The many letters he received from his family and friends were not returned to Australia. This is not a criticism of the AIF administrative system, for it's unlikely Harry retained these. A World War One soldier on active duty generally travelled light, and items that could not be kept in his basic equipment, or kitbag, were rarely kept. His mother on the other hand, kept his letters, providing a one-sided view of the exchanges of correspondence that occurred during Harry's war.

By March he had received a letter from his parents, but the news had not been good:

"No 6426
Priv H F Withers
Lark Hill Camp
18/24 Battalion 6 Brigade
Salisbury Plains
A.I.F Salisbury Plains
9/3/17

My Dear Mother and Dad
Just a line to let you know I am well. I was very sorry to hear of Dad being so ill but was pleased to hear him getting better again and poor Alex also how he does suffer poor boy. I have just been for a walk about a couple of miles to a YMCA hut to get some post cards which I am sending also.

Dear Mother I am ever thinking of you all, just fancy us being nearly fourteen thousand miles apart. There some nice young chaps in our Company, two of the men out of our hut have parted for the Motor Transport. Today it has been very heavy snow falling until this afternoon. The men have been pelting one another with snow ball and making statues with the snow. It was snowing so heavily that we did not go out on parade today. We are to go for a twelve mile route march tomorrow if it is a fine day. I have had a letter from Mrs West, I wrote to her and told her I would very likely go and see them. I will not go yet as she said they were having a lot of trouble as her husband is very ill, but she would be pleased to see me later on. Dear Mother we have been bombing and bayonet fighting. We have to go through the gas yet and also our musketry. I wish this war was over and that I was home once more. I will close with fond love from your son Priv H.F. Withers. Love to all.

PS John 14 verse 1. God bless and keep you all is my prayer. "

The passage from the Bible that Harry refers to is one of comfort:

"Let not your heart be troubled: ye believe in God, believe also in me"

The message Harry is trying to impart to his parents is clear…they should not worry about him. Perhaps he is hinting at his improved mental health, without revealing to the authorities who may have read his letters that he had been unwell. This letter also provides an indication of Harry's growing commitment to his faith. In his previous letters he provides no blessing, nor does he quote a passage of scripture. From this letter and in almost every other letter and card he sent home at this time, he demonstrates his staunch Christian faith.

The Mrs West mentioned in this letter, was a cousin of Margaret Withers senior. She had married a Scot named West, and the couple had settled in Ross-shire in Scotland where they were involved in farming. Even if Mrs West had been able to receive Harry at that time, it is doubtful that he would have been granted leave to make a visit.

In addition to his anxiety and the lack of letters from home Harry, along with many of his comrades, was suffering culture shock. In spite of the predominantly British nature of 1917 Australia, life in Britain was decidedly different from the way of life Harry and the other Australians were used to. Aside from army discipline which many of the young Australians found difficult to come to terms with, they found the climate abominable, the landscape foreign, the customs and way of life of the English people difficult to understand, the food strange, and when they went on leave, the expense of basic items was exorbitant. Harry was to write several letters to family members making it abundantly clear he was not entirely enjoying the English experience, and at this stage of his deployment it seems he was sure there was no place like Australia, and no people like Australians.

In March 1917, Harry exhibited another alarming aspect of deployment blues…he had in the words of the soldiers of today: "gone feral". In Harry's case this does not seem to have manifested in any refusal to dress properly, or to disobey orders…although he may have come close. The one aspect of Harry's former life that had sustained him through this period of discomfort and dislocation was his faith, but at one stage it seems authority attempted to isolate him from that too. In a letter he wrote to his father in March 1917 he exposes a slightly rebellious side of his character that had previously been hidden:

> "No 6426
> Priv H.F. Withers
> Lark Hill
> 18 Reinforcements 24 Battalion 6 Brigade
> 18/3/17

A.I.F Salisbury Camp

Dear Dad just a line to let you know I am well trusting you and all are in the best of health. Dear Dad we had a very trying time the first two or three weeks with the cold and wet, but the weather is lovely now. I am going into Amesbury to Church after dinner. We are not allowed to go to Church as some of the men at the camp have the mumps so we are isolated till the 28th if you call it isolation it is only a farce like a great many other things. I have little news as I have not been away from the camp during the week I did not go on the route march yesterday as I hurt my ankle, the one that I hurt *footballing. Dear Dad I think we will go to France in about a month. Dear Dad I have not much news I have joined a fellowship class at the YMCA. I was at a concert at the YMCA to a send-off to some of the men going to France. I will close.*

Priv H.F. Withers your ever fond son. May God bless and keep you until we meet again."

Leaving camp, even to go to church, without leave and particularly when the camp was quarantined because of the mumps, could have landed Harry and his mates in trouble. However, there is no indication in his army record that he was charged with any offence. Therefore, it must be assumed he either decided against going to church that day, or he still went to church but wasn't caught. Nor does his injured ankle seem to have attracted any negative response from the authorities. Others who had presented with injury had been accused of malingering, but not Harry. It is probable that Harry's eager participation in sport saved him from this ignominy. Sport, so far as the army was concerned was good, particularly team sport, and Harry had sustained his injury playing football.

The deployment blues is now, and was then, an insidious condition. While it is apparent that Harry had overcome his first attack of the complaint, it was a condition that was to revisit him from time to time in the future.

Chapter 9

April 1917

DEPLOYMENT BLUES ASIDE, THERE IS no evidence that Harry had suffered a relapse in his mental health. This no doubt would have confounded Doctor Harkin back in Chiltern Valley who had confidently predicted Harry's mental condition would worsen. It is also interesting to note, that in all of Harry's letters home, and in his diary entries, he makes no mention of his mental health, or epilepsy. It seems Harry was determined to put that part of his life behind him, as though it had never happened. It might also be that he did not want to commit any kind of admission to these conditions to paper. Letters were censored, and Harry may have been concerned that an unguarded word might result in his being sent home. Whatever the reason, Harry never mentions these conditions. He may have been unhappy and moody at times, but never enough to prevent him from performing his duty.

A spot of leave seems to have done Harry the world of good. In a letter to his mother in April 1917 he seems to be in a much happier frame of mind:

"No 6426
Prive H F Withers
18 Reinforcements 24 Battalion
London April 2nd 1917
AIF Lark Hill Salisbury

To My Dearest Mother
Just a line to let you know I am ever thinking of you all. I trust Dear Dad and all are quite well as it leaves me at present. We got four days leave from

Friday last till 8 o'clock tonight. On Friday evening I and eleven other chaps went (to) St Martins Theatre we had complementary tickets issued to us by a young man from the YMCA we were seated in the half guinea seats so you can imagine how we fancied ourselves, and on Saturday there was five drays called at the war club for us, the trip around London cost four shillings. It was a very reasonable trip we left the club at 10 o'clock and came back at half past one for dinner and immediately after dinner we went through St Pauls Cathedral, West Minister Abbey, the House of Lords, the House of Commons and also Tower of London and the King's Stables. There are about a hundred beautiful horses. The harness and coaches are something lovely, the gold coach is over four tons and is pulled by eight lovely black horses. I am sending you a little book called Guide to the Tower of London.

Sunday I went to the Wesley Church which has been built in 1875. After evening service we had the communion service there was something like a hundred persons partook of the bread and wine, and afterwards we went to the YMCA hut and joined in some more singing then finished up about half past ten. I met Harry Clarkson on Saturday he is working in the Church here. Dear Mother it was something lovely to see the jewels in the Tower of London, the crowns are beautiful. In Westminster Abbey there are a lot of old coffins and those with the names of the old Kings and Queens. I saw where the Duchess that died recently was buried and Lord Roberts and in the centre part of the Abbey there is this inscription: Near this place be the remains Colonel Henry Densey his friend surviving Lieutenant General Withers but 2 years and 10 days is at his desire died Nov 1631. I saw the House of Lords where the Kings and Queens and Princes are crowned the three chairs on the throne. I was going to the wax works only it has been snowing so much. The people make a great fuss of the Australians here I think we will go to France in about a couple of weeks. Dear Mother I think I have told you all the news for this time. The last letters I have received was about the end of Feb. I am longing for news from home. Tommie Henderson is drinking a lot. I have some nice mates I was to a meeting at the Salvation Army last Sunday night week, at the close of the meeting there was a young man got converted he had not been in the *meeting till he came out to the front. He gave his testimony afterwards and said he wanted (to) live a new life as he was always drunk and swearing and spending his money. I will close with love to all from your fond son Harry. God be with you. My best for Jesus"*

Harry mentions going to the theatre in the company of eleven other soldiers. This perhaps provides a key to the improvement in Harry's mental health, and incidentally the mental health of all his comrades…mateship. Mates look after each other, they share experiences, they listen to one another's problems, and they jolly each other along when the going gets a bit rough.

Clearly Harry would have liked to have maintained his mateship with Tom Henderson, but it seems Tom was not that interested in what Harry had to offer. In this letter Harry again shows his commitment to his faith, going to church, taking communion, and visits to the YMCA. However, it seems young Tom is interested in a wilder form of spending his time. Tom had also committed an all too familiar crime for AIF soldiers undergoing training at Lark Hill…in that he absented himself without leave for a period of one day. For this offence he was fined three days' pay and awarded a further three days confined to barracks. Worse was to come.

Harry was no doubt greatly impressed to learn that a Withers was buried in Westminster Abbey, and that that particular Withers had been a general. However, his paraphrase of the inscription, including the year of Colonel Desney's death, is slightly incorrect. The actual inscription reads:

> *"Near this place lyes the remains of Collonell HENRY DESNEY who surviving his freind and companion Lieutenant Generall WITHERS but 2 years and 10 days is at his desire buryed in the same grave with him. Obit 21 die Novembris 1731"* [47]

The War Club to which Harry referred in his letter was probably the "War Chest Club". A number of clubs had been established in London specifically for Australian troops on leave in the city. These were designed

---

[47] https://www.westminster-abbey.org/abbey-commemorations/commemorations/henry-withers-henry-disney

to provide the Diggers with a home base, accommodation, good food, and a quiet secure place to rest. The War Chest Club was situated across the road from the AIF Administrative Headquarters in Horseferry Rd, and it provided accommodation for 800 men. Another Digger, Arthur Moore, recorded that the War Chest Club provided the best feed in London, and that for the cost of one shilling he got fed, a bed for the night, and he could sit and read a newspaper. [48]

Harry's comment regarding the cost of goods and food is a little ironic, for in 1917 the AIF Diggers were in fact the best paid of all the British Empire troops. Enterprising businesspeople soon raised the price of the goods they presented for sale, to ensure they received a share of the Australians' monetary advantage. The British Tommies were loud in their complaint that everything from a cup of coffee to the favours of a lady of the night, had become excessively expensive.

For all that, the Diggers remained popular figures. Indeed, Harry's observation as to the popularity of the Australians in London was not unique. Twenty-five-year-old former farmer, Archie Barwick, a member of the 1st Battalion AIF and veteran of Gallipoli witnessed a spontaneous example of this esteem. While waiting to board a train in London, he saw troops from Britain and Canada arrive home from the front. These troops were greeted by a feeble cheer from the waiting public. However when an Australian unit arrived the crowd responded extatically, cheering and clapping, some of the public even attempting to carry the Digger's rifles for them. [49]

In spite of the positive feelings of many of the British population had toward the Diggers, Harry was still susceptible to the blues and in the 2nd of April letter to his mother, he wasn't able to resist complaining regarding the scarcity of mail. However, perhaps his leave and a letter he received from home in early April, promoted a slightly happier frame of mind. He quickly

---

[48] London and the First World War 20-21 March 2015 Institute of Historical Research, University of London Imperial War Museums
https://www.sl.nsw.gov.au/sites/default/files/3._elise_edmonds_-_london_and_the_first_world_war.pdf
[49] Op. cit.

responded to this letter, but notes in a postscript at the top of the page that he is responding to a letter dated 2nd of February:

> "No 6426
> Private H.F. Withers
> 24th Battalion, 6th Brigade
> A.I.F Salisbury Lark Hill
> Lark Hill
> 9/4/1917

PPS Remember me to Will, Alice, Nell, Jack, Kiss the little ones from me. Ask Wal to drop a line. Love to all xxxx]

Dear Mother,

Just a line to let you know how pleased I was to receive your letters and also the post card from Violet. I am glad also to know you have had no trouble in getting my pay. Dear Mother we are all doing well here now as we are getting accustomed to the cold climate, but I don't think we will be here much longer as there is a draft of men leaving for France this evening. We have just arrived back from dinner I have not had a dinner worth talking about since I left home. Everything is very dear here. I thank you for the post card I will have to finish this later when I come from parade this evening as the whistle has gone to fall in. I met Harry Clarkson in London he is returned from France and is now working at the YMCA in London. Dear Mother I trust you are having a better time over there than the people here. It seemed strange to see the women working on the railway stations and also on the trams, and also other duties where men employed. We are to go to Buleford a distance of six miles to have a review before the King. I understand there is to be seventy thousand Australians on review. Today we have had our gas helmets on. They fit right over the head there two glasses to see through and a tube to breathe through. This paper is the piece which Violet sent me I thought I would give it another voyage home. I have plenty of writing paper I thank Violet all the same. I wish for you all to number the letters which you write to me, so I shall know if I am receiving them all. I am sorry to hear of Uncle Harry having to go under another operation. Dear Mother let me know how things are in general and how the people of the valley are. The farmers here are busy ploughing Wal would go mad if he had to put the crop in like they do here, almost every paddock you see three or four teams in each paddock. They use single furrow ploughs some only two horses. You mentioned May Henderson says of me losing my teeth. I have a good plate now. I have been talking to Tom Henderson today he looks very well, he is not in the same company as me but his lines are only about a hundred yards distance. It is dreadful to see the drinking that goes on in the canteens. There is one thing with these canteens, we can get hot meals for about one and three, or cakes or buns and a cup of cocoa or tea for a penny and the same for cocoa or tea. You should see the rush when the whistle goes for mail for this is the thing we long for. There are a lot of the boys sorry that they ever left Australia as this is not the game is cracked to be. I will close with love Dear Mother and Dad and all your loving son Harry F Withers

PS. The letter I am answering was dated Feb 2"

It would seem Harry had either written to May Henderson (possibly Tom Henderson's sister), or Tom had mentioned Harry's dental work in a letter home. On this occasion Harry does not name Tom as a drinker, however he is clearly unhappy with the amount of alcohol consumed by some of his comrades. There are other aspects of life in England that displeased him, particularly the climate and the food, although he likes the tea and buns. On the positive side, he had received mail from home, and that at least pleased him. On the 14th of April a more positive attitude is continued in a letter to his father:

"No 6426   (PS Write soon Love to All)
Prive H.F. Withers
D Comp 24 Battalion 7 Reinforcements
Lark Hill
AIF Lark Hill Salisbury
14/4/17

To my Dear Farther,

Dear Dad, just a few lines to let you know I am well trusting you are all well. I feel rather tired it is now by five o'clock, just come in from tea two slices of bread and jam and some dripping is a great meal. We were out on a route march this morning with full packs on. We left at 9 o'clock and arrived back at 12 o'clock. This is such a miserable day raining and a very cold wind blowing. I am on the emergency Company there are about fifty others and about the same number out of other companies. We have to be in readiness of an alarm being given. I think there will be a draft very soon for France so this may be the last letter I will write home from here. The farmers are busy ploughing and sowing here, and there is some of the crops quite green. There are some men I understand are to go back to Australia. I gave your address to one chap by the name of Bruster. He has been to Chiltern but prior to enlisting he lived in Beechworth. Aeroplanes are quite common here it is nothing to see seven or eight machines in the air together for there is an aerial school

While I went on leave I went to see Mrs Tregeus give a lecture in the YMCA on Monday evening which was very interesting. The place was crowded. Last night I went to a very fine concert in our mess hut, the hut holds about three or four hundred. The performers came from Bristol the concert was arranged by YMCA. I have never been to better concerts in my life than I have since I have been in camp. Dear Dad I trust you and the boys are doing well, wheat and stock must be very dear over here I hope there will never be the shortage there as there is here. I went through the gas chamber yesterday. The chamber is a small place it just holds thirty-one standing close together. We went in the chamber with gas helmets on and had to stop in there about two minutes. The gas is about ten times stronger than the Germans use so you can imagine what is like. When you write do not forget to let me know how the people in the Valley are how the church and Sunday School is. I long to be back I Australia although I am looking well and having a pretty good time here. Dear Dad how did Uncle Maynard get on after the operation. I was sorry to hear of Bill McIntosh death, also Alf Smiths. Tell them at home not to forget to write often, as there is nothing so interesting here as to hear from those I have left behind in Australia. This is been a great trip for me. I have enjoyed the visits around London and also the stopping places on our way over here. I think that there is little more to tell this time so I will close. From your fond <u>son</u> Priv H. F. Withers. Love to <u>all</u> xxx

May God bless and keep and prosper you and watch over you all till I return is my prayer."

While Harry was enjoying a better frame of mind, life back at Ullina Station had taken a tragic turn. On the 21st of February 1917 Alex Withers, William and Margaret's eldest son, died in the Corowa Hospital in New South Wales. Alex had been ill for some time, a fact which Harry had noted in his early March letter to his parents. It is estimated that Harry might have received word of his brother's death in late April 1917, at the earliest. However, mystery surrounds whether or not Harry was in fact advised of his brother's death. Given Harry's mental health issues of the past, it may be his parents decided not to mention his brother's death for fear of sparking a relapse of the condition.

Back in Australia, news of Alex's death was no secret as the following letter indicates:

"Dear Mr & Mrs Withers & Family

I received a letter from Emily Rowe a few days ago informing of the news of poor Alex's death.

I had not heard he was ill, I therefore was surprised to learn the sad news & I want you to know how much I feel for you in your loss & in your sorrow, but you will know so well where to go for comfort and consolation, with the knowledge that Alex is at rest, is with God, & you will see him again, You will miss him very much from his accustomed place & will long for his touch of the vanished hand & hear the sound of the voice that is still. I know just how you are feeling my friends. The Lord be to you all that you need is the prayer of yours in sympathy love E.C. Coates.

PS. Have you heard from Harry. Had I known he was in camp I would have visited him & gone to see him off – I heard he had sailed for the front – Mr Coates & Flossie join in sympathy with you all – write when you can I would like a letter – your twice friend as of old EC Coates[50]*"*

It seems unlikely that in the letters Harry received from his family and friends that no mention was ever made of Alex's death. However, it also

---

[50] E.C Coates may have lived in Melbourne, as the mention of Harry in the letter suggests a visit might have occurred had Harry's location prior to his embarkation been known.

seems unlikely that if Harry knew of Alex's death, that he would not have expressed his grief in letters he sent home. Yet save for his letter of the 9th of March 1917 where he expresses sympathy at Alex's suffering, Harry makes no further mention of his brother in any other letter.

Was there a family conspiracy to conceal Alex's death from Harry? Did a letter or letters regarding Alex's death fail to reach Harry? Ships carrying mail were sometimes sunk, and the impact on the deployed soldiers and their people at home was immense.

For example, on the 5th of January 1917 one Digger, Arthur McPhail Kilgour was dismayed when he learned his Christmas mail had been destroyed when the ship carrying it had been torpedoed. On the 21st of July 1917 Kilgour recorded that at least five ships carrying Australian mail had been sunk, and another two carrying mail back to Australia had suffered the same fate. [51]

Coupled with these disasters, the mail system in general had a poor reputation among the Australians. Numerous letters and parcels to and from Australia simply disappeared or were extremely late. On the 4th of January 1915 another Digger, George Makin, complained that he could not understand what the authorities were doing with the soldiers mail, and that bad feeling was sure to follow if the situation was not addressed.[52]

As time went by, the situation hardly improved. In January 1916 Australian Nursing Sister Olive Haynes while serving in the Middle East, was certain her parents did not receive half the letters she wrote to them. Then in April that same year, following her redeployment to France, she complained that the delivery of Australian mail was extremely slow and that some Australians had not received any mail for months [53]

Another alternative is that the letter, or letters, Harry sent home regarding Alex's death were either destroyed in transit, or were received at home, but were too painful for his parents to retain. At this distance in time, it is unlikely these questions will ever be satisfactorily answered.

Not long after Alex's passing, death also impacted on another section of the extended Withers family:

---

[51] https://sydneylivingmuseums.com.au/ww1/arthur-mcphail-kilgour-1896%E2%80%931941
[52] https://www.awm.gov.au/articles/blog/so-far-home-sending-and-recieving-mail-trenches
[53] Ed Margaret Young "We Are Here Too" Published by Margaret Young 2014, p 138

"Ardveinnie
Edderton
Ross Shire
Mar – 18-17

My Dear Cousin

It is with deep regret I have to write this few lines Dear Cousin I may tell you that my husband died on the evening of the 6th of this month. He suffered for a long time he never came out of the chair till he died and he died very peaceful with good wishes for everybody.

Dear Cousin I hope this few lines will find you well also all your people. I may tell you that I am not keeping very well myself since some time, but I am glad to say that all the rest of us is well at present. Dear Cousin this is a very trying time with the war and no word of it being finished we are all busy about here getting the land ready for the seed we have very good weather but very cold.

Now Dear Cousin I hope this few lines finds you well also all the rest of yours also Mr & Mrs Withers and family. Love to everybody not forgetting yourself & hoping to hear from you

Your loving cousin Mrs West"

The letters sent by Harry's family and friends during the war, have not survived. By the time Harry received the news of Mr West's death he was in France. The Wests, however, were to play an important role in Harry's future.

Chapter 10

Training

THE TRAINING PROGRAM FOR AIF infantry soldiers was planned to be of 14 weeks duration. By the time Harry arrived in England, a tough and exacting training program had been established. The basic concept of the training syllabus was to ensure the deploying soldier was of a standard that would enable him to be swiftly assimilated into the battalion to which he was assigned. The program did not claim to produce a completely trained soldier, indeed once he arrived in France, he was immediately subjected to a further period of depot training before being cleared to march into his battalion.

A major aspect of training at Lark Hill could best be described as physical fitness. Forty-eight hours of the total syllabus were devoted to this aspect of training. Some of this involved stretching and limbering up exercises, but a considerable portion of the allocation was devoted to numerous route marches. The dictionary defines a route march as: "a march for troops over a designated route, typically via roads or tracks". This definition belies many of the aspects of the activity. Generally, the soldiers were required to carry their rifles and full kit, referred to as "marching order", and has been previously discussed this amounted to a considerable weight of equipment. However, aside from the weight, at least for the first few route marches the trainees undertook, there were other discomforts to trouble them. Their feet grew hot and sweaty from the march, boots that may have hitherto been reasonably comfortable, rubbed their feet and caused painful blisters. Equipment straps chaffed and rubbed at shoulders and backs. Perspiration drenched their clothing and stung the eyes. Then when they finally came to a halt the icy winter winds turned the sodden clothing to ice. The men would be torn between the desire for rest, and the desire for continued movement to enable them to warm up again.

Harry seems to have been impressed by the route marches, and as a man used to physical activity and sport, he may even have enjoyed them. Certainly, from February through to April, they gave him something to write home about. By the end of April 1917 Harry must have been fairly fit, and he would have been confident that his boots and equipment were not going to let him down.

Another facet of the Lark Hill training regime was parade ground drill. The Encyclopaedia Britannica defines drill as the:

> *"...preparation of soldiers for performance of their duties in peace and war through the practice and rehearsal of prescribed movements. In a practical sense, drill consolidates soldiers into battle formations and familiarizes them with their weapons. Psychologically, it develops a sense of teamwork, discipline, and self-control; it promotes automatic performance of duties under disturbing circumstances and instinctive response to the control and stimulus of leaders."*[54]

However, in 1914 the relevance of parade ground drill on the modern battlefield was being challenged. The Secretary of State, Lord Kitchener, was not a believer stating:

"Never mind the drill: teach them to shoot, and do it quickly". [55]

However, this observation of Kitchener's was never truly implemented in either the British Regular Army, Kitchener's Volunteer Army, or the AIF, and drill remained an important aspect of the training syllabus.

The AIF, however, lacked sufficient experienced drill instructors to adequately staff its English based training camps. As a result, British sergeant majors were seconded to the AIF to act as drill instructors. In April 1917 AIF Sergeant Eric Evans recorded in his diary his experience of this arrangement.

---

[54] https://www.britannica.com/topic/drill-military
[55] https://trove.nla.gov.au/newspaper/article/198637717

A British sergeant major had put Evans and his fellow Australian through their paces on the parade ground. Evans stated the sergeant major was typical of an old Imperial soldier, giving orders in a very loud voice, but that off the parade ground he was a very decent fellow. [56]

However, in spite of a grudging respect for that particular sergeant major, Evans held a less complimentary opinion of the value of some of the parades the men were obliged to attend, and of certain senior officers scheduled to inspect the men on parade, who failed to attend when the weather turned cold. [57]

It is hard to judge how Harry felt about parade ground drill, however his ability to endure being roared at by a sergeant major, is another indication that he is no longer the anxiety filled person of the past. Maybe his militia experience stood him in good stead, and he simply accepted the fact he had to drill and attend parades. He may even have been good at it. In one letter to his parents, he indicated that he had been chosen on parade for a special treat in the shape of half a dozen scones. It is likely his selection to receive such a prize would be either due to a good turnout, or for smart drill movements, or both. Regardless of various opinions as to the value of parade ground drill, it remained an important part of AIF training, and Harry seemed to have negotiated its associated trials quite well.

Physical fitness, teamwork and discipline were important aspects of Lark Hill training, but perhaps the most important was musketry. However, no muskets were involved, the outdated title referred to skill at arms training with the Lee Enfield Mark rifle. This weapon was the main firearm used by the British and Empire forces during World War One, and therefore the rifle used by the AIF. Every member of the AIF had to be proficient in weapon's care; rapid loading; aiming; range practices from 100 - 500 yards; judging distances; fire control and range movement. Generally, eight weeks of the training course was devoted to this training and the standards achieved for those deploying to the Western Front were

---

[56] http://books.publishing.monash.edu/apps/bookworm/view/Australians+in+Britain%3A+The+Twentieth-Century+Experience/137/xhtml/chapter06.html
[57] http://books.publishing.monash.edu/apps/bookworm/view/Australians+in+Britain%3A+The+Twentieth-Century+Experience/137/xhtml/chapter06.html

extraordinarily high[58]. A trained rifleman could achieve what was referred to as the "mad minute", firing twenty to thirty well-aimed rounds in sixty seconds[59]. This training standard had transposed on the battlefield to a deadly capability, leading the German forces to believe that the British were armed with machine guns.[60]

Harry makes no mention in either his letters or his diary of his training with the rifle. As a bushman he was probably well used to handling a weapon and so his training with a rifle would be nothing new to him, and therefore hardly worth reporting on.

Closely allied to rifle training was bayonet fighting. By 1917 the limitations of the bayonet as a weapon in trench warfare had been recognised. In the close confines of a trench pistols, grenades, home-made clubs and entrenching tools were more easily employed than a long rifle with a bayonet attached. However, bayonet fighting continued to form an important part of the Lark Hill syllabus. The reason for this was supported by the belief this training instilled self-discipline and promoted an aggressive spirit and a mentality of closing with the enemy. Bayonet training also had a value in physical fitness training. The Lee Enfield rifle with bayonet fixed weighed a little over ten pounds. This weight could be well employed by an instructor to increase a trainee's arm and upper body strength as they adopted the various bayonet fighting positions. Then there was the bayonet assault course, several hundred metres of obstacle strewn ground, with straw dummies set up at regular intervals. The soldiers were required to run (referred to in the army as "double") through the course, pausing only to bayonet the straw dummies, before charging on. Around 36 hours of the syllabus was devoted to this form of training.

In his 9th of March letter to his mother Harry also mentioned "bombing". This was training in the use of hand grenades. Grenades had first come into use in the 17th century as hollow iron balls filled with gun powder and were

---

[58] http://unsworks.unsw.edu.au/fapi/datastream/unsworks:36626/SOURCE02?view=true
[59] http://bulletin.accurateshooter.com/2017/10/mad-minute-marksmanship-the-one-minute-lee-enfield-drill/
[60] https://medium.com/war-is-boring/the-303-lee-enfield-was-a-british-tommy-s-best-mate-d7f18ece0e88

employed by specialist troops known as grenadiers. By World War One, bombs or grenades, had become more widely used by infantry soldiers although initially these weapons had a distinctly improvised appearance. At Gallipoli, Australian troops made their own grenades from empty jam tins packed with scrap metal and explosives. By the time Harry arrived at Lark Hill, the Mills Bomb, a self-igniting grenade with built in safety features for the thrower, had been introduced.[61] Safety features aside, the grenade remained for many a trainee, a fearsome weapon. They were first trained with inert grenades and then, in a validation of that training, they were required to throw three live grenades. In spite of the training, for some the transition from inert grenade to live grenade proved to be a terrifying and sometimes a fatal experience. One Digger, a Private Stephens, wrote home of his experience in this regard explaining to his readers that bombing was a rather dangerous aspect of training, and that some of the trainees were unnerved by the weapon. He mentioned one poor unfortunate that was killed during training, and how that death had badly shaken those who had witnessed it. However a Sergeant-Major on the scene had settled the men encouraging them to forget the incident, and to get on with their training, which apparently they did.[62]

Twelve hours of the syllabus were devoted to bombing, but Harry does not seem to have been inclined to report further on his participation in that training. Nor does he mention training with the rifle grenade which enabled a Mills bomb to be fired from a Lee Enfield rifle. Wiring and entrenching were also part of the syllabus, but Harry chose not to write of these either. It was probably difficult for a former farm labourer to enthuse about erecting a fence or digging a ditch.

He makes a brief reference to the Lewis machine gun. The Lewis Gun was a light machine gun and by 1917 every AIF infantry section boasted its own Lewis Gun greatly boosting the section's fire power. Trainees in 1917 were required to fire this weapon as part of their course, but those soldiers destined to be specialist Lewis Gunners when deployed, undertook specialist training.

---

[61] https://www.thoughtco.com/history-of-the-hand-grenade-1991668
[62] http://books.publishing.monash.edu/apps/bookworm/view/Australians+in+Britain%3A+The+Twentieth-Century+Experience/137/xhtml/chapter06.html`

Another aspect of training at Lark Hill was gas training. The first large scale use of chemical weapons occurred during World War One resulting in an estimated 90,000 fatalities. As a result, training for gas attack counter measures was taken extremely seriously and the training undertaken at Lark Hill, required Harry and his mates to be schooled in the correct use of their gas marks, and in the behaviour expected of them should they be subjected to gas attack during their time at the front. In his letter to his father dated 14 April 1917, Harry provided a brief, if a little dramatic, description of this aspect of his training. The gas chamber certainly impressed him however, whilst the Lark Hill instructors may well have told Harry and his comrades the gas used in the training gas chamber was "ten times stronger than the Germans use", this was almost certainly *not* the case. The most widely used gas employed by the Germans and the British was Mustard gas. Mustard gas was lethal if inhaled, and debilitating if it came in contact with the skin as it caused large painful blisters. Whilst both sides issued their troops with gas masks, neither side had developed a suit that could effectively protect the soldier's skin. With this in mind it is unlikely that Australian trainees were exposed to a gas of even greater lethality, and it may be assumed that a far gentler vapour was used at Lark Hill, possibly Tear Gas which had been available since 1914. By telling their trainees that the gas chamber contained particularly lethal gas, the instructors at Lark Hill provided the trainees with confidence in their gas masks.

At the end of their initial training the Australian Digger was a well-rounded soldier capable of fulfilling many combat roles. Some were then allocated to specialist roles in the artillery, mortars, or as heavy machine gunners. As for Harry, it seemed he was destined to be a rifleman. He appears to have been underwhelmed by his training at Lark Hill and is keen to deploy to France. In a letter to his mother dated the 24th of April he was more interested in reassuring his mother of his continued religious convictions, than in any aspects of his daily military activities. However, he indicates that he has learned a little of his likely destination once he crossed the Channel:

No 6426
Prive H.F. Withers
A Company 24th Battalion
A.I.F Lark Hill Salisbury
24/4/1917

Dearest Mother,

Just a few brief lines to let you know that I am well and also to let you know that I may be going to Etaps France. I understand that we will there for three weeks before going to the front but I will be there before you get that's if all is well. Dear Mother I went to a lovely gospel meeting yesterday in the Open Air Mission hut which is a lovely comfortable place which is welcome to soldiers. The size of the hut is about as big as the Valley Church. Around the walls there are lovely pictures and paintings and texts at one end of the building there is a counter where refreshments are served after the meeting which closed at half past nine. There are numbers of men deciding for Christ throughout the various camps. Sunday morning after the service there was a communion service in which about eight men and the Dr partook of the bread and wine. The Doctor is a very fine young man and a happy Christian.

I have not much news but I thought it as well to write a letter before going to France as I have been told that we will not be able to give much information from there. Tom Henderson is on draft also tomorrow evening. The boys in my hut are all busy writing to their parents. I have a nice young man for a mate by the name of McRae he used to live in Beechworth. Dear Mother I trust that you and Dad and all are well. I would be pleased if Wal would drop me a line. Most of the farmers have got their crops on about here. There is one party ploughing with a tractor engine. I will have to draw this letter to a close as I have a lot to get ready tomorrow. So I shall be ready to get away with the draft tomorrow evening. Kindly remember me to the Murrays & Rowe, Mr Cooper, also Nellie, Jack, Will, Alice also give my love to Rene, Violet, Ruthie and kiss the little ones for me. I will close with love to you my Dear Mother and also Dad from your fond son Prive A.F. Withers"

Tom Henderson was to precede Harry's departure for France by almost a month. "Etaps" the destination in France to which Harry referred, is in fact Etaples. Formerly a fishing village, in 1914 the British Army had established a series of large training depots around the village, in order to hone the skills of troops before they moved to the front. For a time, the AIF made use of one of these depots, and Tom Henderson and Harry were destined to undertake their final training at this establishment. According to Harry's letter, he believed that he would almost immediately follow Tom to France, however his departure was not as imminent as he believed.

Chapter 11

A Man of Faith

HARRY'S CHRISTIAN FAITH IS EVIDENT in most of his letters, particularly those written during his time at Lark Hill. To his family this would come as no surprise for the Withers family had a long tradition of worship and service in the Methodist Church, and Harry had been brought up in the strict values of Methodism.

Methodists are part of the Protestant tradition of the worldwide Christian Church, and their core beliefs are of orthodox Christianity. Methodist teaching has sometimes been summed through four particular ideas known to Methodists as the "four alls".

1. All need to be saved – this need is tied to the doctrine of original sin;
2. All can be saved – they believe in Universal Salvation;
3. All can know they are saved – Assurance provided by the teaching of Jesus; and
4. All can be saved completely – the belief in Christian perfection.

The Methodist Church emphasises Bible reading, preaching, and the sacraments, especially Holy Communion and Baptism which they believe were instigated by Jesus[63]. In addition, hymn singing is a lively feature of a Methodist service, and something that Harry seemed to particularly enjoy.

The Methodist ethos also encourages evangelism and mission and while Harry does not provide any examples of his own actions in this regard, he

---

[63] https://www.bbc.co.uk/religion/religions/christianity/subdivisions/methodist_1.shtml

certainly gives the impression that he was greatly impressed by those who followed this particular calling, writing to his parents that:

> *"...at the close of the meeting there was a young man got converted he had not been in the meeting till he came out to the front. He gave his testimony afterwards and said he wanted (to) live a new life as he was always drunk and swearing and spending his money..."* [64]

The founder of the Methodist Church, John Wesley, stressed the importance of personal morality, and often warned of the dangers of gambling and drinking in his sermons. Toward the end of the 19th century the Methodist Church became involved in the Temperance Movement, so it is little wonder Harry took a dim view of the behaviour of some of his fellow Diggers and the amount of alcohol they consumed. Nor was he above naming names of Chiltern Valley men who were over-indulging in the demon drink, men like Tom Henderson. One wonders if Harry's parents passed on his concerns to the Henderson family. He was also keen on providing advice to those at home regarding their religious responsibilities, and he maintained a keen interest in his church back home in the Valley.

Interestingly, at this stage of his army career there is no mention of Harry having any involvement with women while he was in England. It would seem he spent his free time sight-seeing or attending church services. However, there may have been a more earthly reason for his abstinence from matters of female company. The fear of venereal disease.

Venereal disease was a major issue for the AIF and the one certain way of avoiding that affliction was celibacy. This was not the case for many of his comrades. Indeed, a World War Two saying that was applied to American servicemen in England and in Australia was actually coined in World War One, and it referred to Australian soldiers. The Diggers were very well paid in comparison to the British Tommies. This gave the Diggers a distinct advantage in the competition for female companionship and led to the British press coining the phrase "over paid, over sexed, and over here".

---

[64] Letter from Harry to his mother dated 2/4/1917

While Harry was at Lark Hill, his enthusiasm for the Church seems to have grown even stronger. There is a hint at this strengthening in the letters he sent home, in his use of blessings, quotes from the scriptures, and reports of his own attendance at church services and the YMCA. Was this a sign that he had undergone an evangelical experience at Lark Hill? Possibly, Harry was most impressed by the religious work of a Harry Clarkson, a church worker who may have been known to Mrs Withers. He was also enthralled by the number of men *"giving themselves to the Lord"*[65]. In addition, the letters he penned home from Lark Hill, often included the use of a blessing of the recipient:

> *"...God bless and keep you all till we meet again".*[66]

and:

> *"...May God bless and keep and prosper you and watch over you all till I return is my prayer..."* [67]

And yet again:

> *"...For the Dear Lord knows all about our troubles he will guide and keep us. I pray that God will bless you all abundantly..."*[68]

So perhaps, in the vernacular of evangelical believers, Harry had been "born again".

It is also possible that at this stage of Harry's military career, his religion provided him with a reason for the war, and motivation for his participation in it. The war fostered an ecumenical spirit among many soldiers. However, many lost confidence in religion once they were exposed to the bloodbath of the front line. For those men and women, fatalism as opposed to faith provided a form of spiritual comfort.[69] It is also interesting to note that in all of Harry's correspondence regarding his religious beliefs, he seems particularly careful to impress his mother. Perhaps Margaret Withers was the power within the family on matters of faith. Even in expressing his love and

---

[65] Letter from Harry to his mother dated 7/5/1917
[66] Letter from Harry to his mother dated 14/4/1917
[67] Letter from Harry to his father dated 18/3/1917
[68] Letter from Harry to his father dated 6/5/1917
[69] https://encyclopedia.1914-1918-online.net/article/religion_australia

hopes for his father he defers to his mother. Or maybe, William Withers was a little less devoted than his wife and younger son, but if this was the case, it in no way inhibited Harry from assuring his father of his religious zeal, or of trying to lift his father's spirits by reminding him of God's grace and of praying for him too.

Harry did not limit his place of worship to the Methodist church. He was it seems prepared to join in both YMCA and the Salvation Army activities. However, it seems he thoroughly enjoyed his association with the YMCA in England, and later when he arrived in France.

In the earliest months of the war the YMCA had established a series of social centres or "huts" for the use of the troops. By 1916 the number had grown from the original 250 huts to 1,500. The huts were located in training camps, garrison and transit centres, railway stations and in every theatre of fighting across Europe and the Middle East. The huts provided library facilities, games, meals, free hot drinks, and showers. Some huts were large establishments with individual rooms to cater for the various activities provided. Others were small structures, some even tents, but regardless of size or construct, the YMCA hut provided a place where individual soldiers could simply enjoy personal contact either with other soldiers, or with the staff.[70] Harry made great use of the YMCA facilities and clearly enjoyed the Christian worship aspects of the service provided.

Harry was also greatly impressed with the evangelism of the Salvation Army section at Lark Hill. By 1917 the Salvation Army was widely recognised as "Christianity with its sleeves rolled up", but to the troops they were commonly referred to as the "Salvos". Theologically Salvationists were closely aligned with the Methodist Church, however it differed in organizational structure and practise. A peculiarity of the Salvos was that the clergy assumed military rank such as "lieutenant" or "major", and the ordinary Salvationists were referred to as "soldiers of Christ", a title that Harry would have readily identified with.

Throughout his training at Lark Hill, between his worship at the Wesley Church, the YMCA and the Salvation Army, Harry seems to have been able

---

[70] https://www.ymca.org.uk/about/history-heritage/ymca-and-ww1

to maintain a simple, happy, faith in his God. He shows no doubt that with God's blessing, he would return safely home. All too soon that faith would be tested to its very roots.

Chapter 12

May 1917

BY MAY 1917 THE DEPLOYMENT blues seem to have caught up with Harry again, but this time the reason was frustration. Harry was now near the end of his Lark Hill training course and a change, any change, so long as it took him away from Salisbury Plain would be welcomed. Instead, he was forced to wait while others around him were moved away for one reason or another. His postcard to his sister Renee hints that he feels being in the infantry is a major disadvantage, even during a parade:

"Priv H.F. Withers   6/5/17
No 6426
D Company 24th Battalion
A.I.F. Rollestone Salisbury

To My Dear Sister Renee,

Just a line for I know you long to hear from over the sea. How is Roy and Frank Smith around home. I should like to know any of the boys who are at the war their address. Dear Renee you may wonder I do not write often but really there is nothing fresh to write about. You can notice the dark streak opposite the Artillery well that is the Infantry. Dear Renee do drop me a line I long to hear from you and to know how things are over there. I have no more news so will close. From your loving brother Priv H.F. Withers."

There is also the longing for news from home, plus the desire to make contact with any of the lads from Chiltern who had enlisted. In addition, the impression is gained that he has a certain amount of time on his hands as he waits to deploy. The same day that he wrote to Renee he also penned another brief note to his father.

> "Priv H.F. Withers 6/5/17
> No 6426
> D Company 24ᵗʰ Battalion
> A.I.F. Rollestone Salisbury
>
> To My Dear Father
>
> Dear Dad just a few lines to let you know I have not forgotten you. I hope you are enjoying good health and that everything is going on well. I have seen some of the best herds of Shorthorne Cross they were real pictures to look at I counted in one herd between fifty and sixty and they were all about the same colour. Dear Dad I trust you will keep cheerful and not worry to much about me. For the Dear Lord knows all about our troubles he will guide and keep us. I pray that God will bless you all abundantly. Dear Dad remember me to Wal the girls, Nellie, Jack, & Alice from your fond son Harry Withers."

The impression here is that Harry knows he will soon be in France, and he is trying to reassure his father that all will be well. It may also be Harry is once again reassuring his father, that he remained in good mental and physical health, with no sign of any relapse into his former conditions.

That same day, in yet another postcard to his mother, he expresses his frustration at the delay in his deployment:

> "No 6426
> Lark Hill
> Salisbury
> 6/5/17]
>
> Dear Mother Just a line to let you know I am well. I have a slight cold otherwise I am splendid. We are to shift camp from here one day during the week. We are going to another camp about a couple of miles distant. The name is Rollestone I expected to have been in France by this. I was picked with two drafts but did not go. There was another picked Friday so I missed that also as I was on guard over the prisoners in the clink. I was speaking to two men who was on the ship that was sunk the Ballarat. They said that the

submarine followed them for some time before it torpedoed the boat. The weather is lovely and warm as its spring here now. You would not think one was in the same country as when we came here. I will close with love."

The new camp Harry refers to, Rollestone Camp, was located close to Fargo and Lark Hill, and used by AIF training battalions from 1916[71]. He also refers to the sinking of the *SS Ballarat*. The *Ballarat* was a troopship engaged in carrying Australian troops from Melbourne to England, when on 25th of April 1917, in the English Channel, she was torpedoed by a German submarine. Remarkably none of the 1752 people on board were killed. [72]

On the 7th of May, Harry wrote another postcard to his mother. This is a communication that smacks of a desperation to talk to his mother, to give her comfort, but also to gain a measure of comfort for himself. Harry is reading the signs, the move to Rollestone Camp is almost certainly the first step in his journey toward France.

"Priv H.F. Harris   7/5/17
No 6426
D Company 24th Battalion
A.I.F. Salisbury Rollestone

To my Dearest Mother

Just a few lines to let you know that I am well, trusting this note will find you all well. I have been very busy today as we shifted camp from Lark Hill to Rollestone. The weather is very warm and the plains are looking lovely and green. I went to a meeting in the Salvation Army Hut and there was five conversions. This makes a total of forty six in three weeks. There are a lot of men giving themselves to the Lord. Dear Mother I will close now with Love from your fond son Priv H.F. Withers love to all."

On the 11th of May he is back at Lark Hill again, frustrated and wishing he was either home, or in France.

"Priv H.F. Withers No 642   11/5/17
D Comp. 18 Reinforcements 24 Battalion
A.I.F. Lark Hill Salisbury

---

[71] https://anzac-22nd-battalion.com/training-camps-england/
[72] https://www.awm.gov.au/collection/C175198

To My Dearest Mother & Dad,

Just a line to let you know I am well also to let you know that there is a draft leaving for France tonight. I am picked as a standby that is if any of the men fail to turn up well I shall have to go. The boys that are going have drawn 24 hours rations consisting of a tin of bully beef and some biscuits. We have all been examined by the Doctor and passed fit but one young chap who has a weak heart is to go back to Australia. The weather is getting very warm now. The places which were white with snow are now looking lovely and green also the crops look well Tommie Henderson left for France last week. Dear Mother I trust you are all well I am ever thinking of you all. We get up at six o'clock of a morning, make up our beds and go for a two or three mile march and as soon as we get back it is a rush for a wash and grab our dixies and off to the mess hut for breakfast of stew or porridge and bacon. After breakfast we get a few minutes and then it is about time to fall in for parade at nine o'clock. We have a lot of men out of our company some have gone to France during the last week, some have joined the signal school about a couple of miles away, others have joined the Lewis gunners school, and also some have gone to Perham Downs another camp about twenty miles away. So you see we are getting scattered all over the place. We have been told this morning that we are to be ready to pack up as those who are (to) remain are to go to another camp about two miles distant at Rollestone. I wish this war was over I am getting about sick of it. Well I shall have to get a wriggle on and have a bath and change my uniform in case I shall go away this evening. Has Frank Smith arrived home yet? Violet mentioned of him going back. Dear Mother how are the boys? Emily Rowe mentioned that the harvest thanksgiving service was very good this year at the Valley and the Church attendance was about the same. I was glad to know dear little Ruthie is doing so well at school. I would like to know Jack Mitchells address or any of the boys from the Valley. Just fancy poor Bill McIntosh getting killed. Is Rennie still working in the Glen? I would like to know. I think it would be better if she could get work elsewhere, as it must be a hindrance to her Christian life. Dear Mother the men are making jokes over the biscuits some are writing their names on them others are putting *photographs in. Well Dear Mother I think this is all the news for this time, hoping this will find you all in the best of health. Wishing Dad many happy returns of the day for it is his birthday on the 9th. From your ever fond son Priv H.F. Withers. Love to all write soon. Remember me to all my friends at the Valley. Love to all. May God bless you and keep you all until I return is my earnest prayer."*

These delays in Harry's deployment should not be seen as evidence that the AIF had concerns regarding his suitability for the front line. Many other Diggers suffered similar delays and frustration, often leading to individuals going Absent Without Leave...never, it seems a thought in Harry's head. However, just why Harry was returned to Lark Hill from Rollestone and then directed to get ready to go back there, is one of those military mysteries. What is clear is, he has had enough, and the impression may be gained he rather wished it was he who had been found to be physically unfit and returned to Australia. Curiously that option was in his own hands. It will never be known what might have transpired had he presented the medical authorities with evidence of his previous mental health issues and epileptic condition. Instead, he resorts to the comfort of his faith, and seeks to encourage those at home to do the same.

Those next days for Harry, must have passed at snail pace. Then on the 13th of May, the pace suddenly increased to a gallop. He was at last included in the draft for France. He gave the move a brief mention in his diary:

> *"...We left Salisbury for Boulogne France 13 May and stopped one night in tents. The next morning we all marched to Étaples a distance of 18 miles..."*

Harry's bland description of his journey across the English Channel belies the actual danger associated with that undertaking. In its effort to starve Britain into submission the German Navy attempted to blockade British ports. To this end they deployed submarines, surface vessels and sea mines. Over the course of the war, over 700 British and Allied merchant ships were sunk off the English peninsular known as Start Point. During the period 1917 to 1918 at least 35 British or Allied ships were sunk in the

English Channel alone.[73] The month before Harry made the trip across the water on the 20th of April, two British destroyers had engaged and defeated six German motor torpedo boats, and on the 25th of the same month the troopship the *SS Ballarat* had been torpedoed and sunk. However, Harry's draft was lucky and the vessel he sailed on arrived safely at its destination.

Harry had arrived in France. However, he was yet to arrive at the fighting. His diary entry records his initial destination as the French fishing of village of Étaples.

---

[73] http://www.salcombemuseum.org.uk/rw_common/plugins/stacks/armadillo/media/SalcombeMuseumDisplay2017.pdf

Chapter 13

Étaples

IT WOULD HAVE BEEN UNDERSTANDABLE if Harry believed his departure from Lark Hill heralded the end of his training and that he was now ready to fight. The army, however, held a different view. Across the Channel the British Army and the AIF had established several training camps the purpose of which was to further hone the skills of those recently arrived in France. Back in April in a letter to his mother and a few weeks prior to his deployment to France, Harry hinted that his primary destination in France would be Étaples.

Before the war Étaples was a small fishing port located about 15 miles (24 kilometres) south of Boulogne-sur-Mer. Aside from commercial fishing the port had attracted artists from around the world, who painted idyllic sea scapes and scenes of fishing trawlers. However, in 1914 the British Army established a large training depot close to the village, and in 1916 the AIF began to use the facility to train its soldiers prior to their deployment to the front. All newly arrived reinforcements, and those who had previously been evacuated from the front due to wounding or illness, were required to complete the Étaples training course, prior to posting to a battalion.

The Étaples training course had an evil reputation. Training operated on a "bull ring" method which saw troops moving from one form of training to another. The training was physically demanding and intense, and included gas warfare, musketry, bayonet fighting and long sessions of marching at the double (running) across sand dunes. The trainees were required to spend a minimum of two weeks at Étaples, and many men reported that they looked forward to arriving at the front if only to escape the torment of the camp instructors. [74]

The camp instructional staff, most of whom were members of the British Army, were rumoured to have never served at the front and were contemptuously referred to by the trainees as the "canaries". The feeling of disdain for the Étaples staff, was not limited to members of the AIF. The famous war poet Siegfried Sassoon wrote a poem titled "Base Details" in which he expressed the contempt infantry veterans had for the officers and NCOs who staffed Étaples:

> *"If I were fierce, and bald, and short of breath,*
> *I'd live with scarlet Majors at the Base,*
> *And speed glum heroes up the line to death.*
> *You'd see me with my puffy petulant face,*
> *Guzzling and gulping in the best hotel,*
> *Reading the Roll of Honour. 'Poor young chap,'*
> *I'd say—'I used to know his father well;*
> *Yes, we've lost heavily in this last scrap.'*
> *And when the war is done and youth stone dead,*
> *I'd toddle safely home and die—in bed."*[75]

Whether the rumour regarding the staff was true or not, there was considerable tension between staff and trainees, so much so that in September 1917 the tension bubbled over into a mutiny. Harry had completed his stint at Étaples in May 1917, so he was well away from the camp when the mutiny occurred.

In fact, so too were most members of the AIF who arrived in France after Harry. This was because in 1917 AIF and Canadian Forces logistic managers became aware of an anomaly in their use of their respective training camps in France and England. The Canadian training camps in England were located to the east near Folkestone, and their training camps in France to the southwest at Le Havre. The majority of the AIF training camps in England were located in

---

[74] https://anzac-22nd-battalion.com/training-camps-france/
[75] https://allpoetry.com/Base-Details

the southwest, and in France the AIF depot camps were on the eastern coast. The line of transport for AIF reinforcements went from Southampton in the southwest of England, to Étaples on the north-eastern coast of France. This meant that ships carrying Canadian and Australian reinforcements to their respective French training establishments often crossed paths in the English Channel. This rather ludicrous situation was inconvenient in time and exposed the respective transport ships to increased risk of attack by German submarines. Sensibly the logisticians of the two dominions agreed to swap their French training establishment locations. As a result, by June 1917 the majority of Australians completed their final training at Le Havre, leaving Étaples to the Canadians and New Zealanders. [76] Harry's intake would have been on one of the last courses run at Étaples for the Australians and he provided a brief note in his diary regarding the nature of the course:

> "...we were in this camp for ten days during which we put in at the Bull Ring where we had to go through a course of bayonet fighting and gas and bomb throwing and guard drill..."

On arrival at Étaples each new intake was issued with new weapons, gas masks, any lost or deficient equipment was replaced, documentation brought up to date, and medical inspections carried out. Then the training began. All drafts were tested in musketry, bombing and bayonet fighting, and passed through a gas chamber. Only when the trainees had completed this training and judged to be of a suitable standard to join their battalions, were they moved forward to the front. Those who were not considered to have reached the desired standard were retained at the camp for further training.

During his first week at Étaples, Harry found time to pen a brief postcard to his mother dated 23 May. In it he makes no mention of any stress he may have felt, other than his desire for more mail:

> "No 6426
>
> Priv H.F. Withers   23/5/17
>
> 24*th* Battalion A.I.F.
>
> France

---

[76] https://anzac-22nd-battalion.com/training-camps-france/

To My Dearest Mother

Just a line to let you know I am well trusting you and all are in the best of health. We left Salisbury on the 13th for England and arrived here in France on the 15th. Dear Mother I met Priv W. Oats from Chiltern last evening. The first time I seen him since we met at Chiltern when he was home on his final leave. The day I enlisted he left for the Front. Dave Harvey went to the front a few days ago. The weather is getting very hot here now,. I have not had any letters for some few weeks I am longing to hear from home. I will draw to a close. Kindly remember me to all my friends also give my love to all at home. From your fond son Priv H.F. Withers."

This appears to be the only correspondence he wrote during the Étaples course, so it may be assumed he had little spare time. It is interesting to note that other than his desire to receive more mail, Harry makes no complaint regarding the training or the instructors in this postcard. Perhaps given the intense physical focus of the course, the sportsman in Harry may have in fact enjoyed the course. If he did, he was not alone, for in spite of the reputation for harshness Étaples had gained, numerous soldiers found the course most beneficial. One such man, Gerry Evans, a Military Medal recipient and member of the 9th Battalion AIF, was most enthusiastic regarding the nature of the training he received there. He was complimentary regarding the English non-commissioned-officers who trained his draft in drill, and the relevance of the physical training, weapon training, gas training, and bayonet fighting courses. He also seemed to have enjoyed the obstacle course, and was clearly impressed by the testing nature of the various obstacles involved. In summary he claimed to have received greater value from his two weeks at Étaples, than he had from his six months of training in Australia.[77]

In his 23rd of May postcard, Harry mentions meeting two Chiltern Valley men William Oats and David Harvey, both of whom were at Étaples when he was there. Private William Oats, number 4207, was like Harry, a reinforcement undergoing final training before going on to join his battalion, the 29th Battalion where he arrived on the 25th of May 1917. On the 11th of October 1917, Oats was wounded by shrapnel and evacuated to England for

---

[77] Op. cit.

treatment. His wounds proved to be of a serious nature, and he was evacuated to Australia and on the 18th of May 1918, he was discharged from the AIF as medically unfit.

Number 4199, David Harvey was another reinforcement undergoing final training. However, in his case his destination would be somewhat different than Harry and William Oats. Harvey was a baker in civilian life, and the AIF needed bakers to serve in its front line kitchens. As a result, Harvey had been allocated to the 2nd Australian Field Bakery and he served with that unit until the 6th of July 1918, when he contracted influenza and was evacuated to England. After his recovery Harvey remained in England, and in February 1919 he married an English lass by the name of Lily Barker. The couple were repatriated to Australia in July 1919.[78]

Soon enough it was time for Harry to move toward the fighting. On the 2nd of June 1917, having achieved all the required Étaples training standards, he was posted forward to join the 24th Battalion.

---

[78] https://recordsearch.naa.gov.au/SearchNRetrieve/Interface/ViewImage.aspx?B=4735906

Chapter 14

24th Battalion 1915 to 1917

HARRY CAUGHT UP WITH THE 24th Battalion at the French village of Warloy, where he was officially taken on the Battalion's strength on 2 June 1917. In his notebook he recalled his journey from Étaples to reach the Battalion:

> "*After finishing our course we left for Albert where we had dinner after 5 hours of travelling. Soon after dinner we were marched a distance of about seven kilometres to Warloy here we remained about a fortnight...*"

Harry's brief comment regarding life at Warloy gives the impression of inactivity; however, this observation conceals a bitter truth. The Battalion had recently suffered a severe mauling at the Second Battle of Bullecourt, and was at the time of Harry's arrival, beginning the process of rebuilding and retraining.

The 24th Battalion had a proud history. A Victorian unit, it had been raised and deployed in a hurry. The original troops were mustered at Broadmeadows Army Camp in the first week of May 1915 and sailed for Egypt at the end of that week. The men would hardly have had time to say farewell to loved ones, and a great number of them would never return to Australia.

The 24th Battalion's first commanding officer was Lieutenant Colonel William Walker Russell Watson. Watson was a dentist by profession; however, it seems he harboured a lifelong passion for the military. In 1886 aged just eleven, he joined the militia as a bugler. Ten years later he gained a commission as a lieutenant, and twelve months later promotion to captain. Through his diligence he earned a reputation as an exceedingly capable officer. In 1900 he volunteered for service in South Africa, where he served with distinction. On his return to Australia, he continued his service in the militia, and prior to the commencement of World War One he had attained the rank of lieutenant colonel. In 1914, when war was declared, he applied for a commission in the AIF and was appointed commanding officer of the infantry Battalion within the Australian Naval and Military Expeditionary Force tasked with seizing German Pacific Territories. On his return to Australia, he was appointed to command of the 24th Battalion AIF. During the next two years Watson would gain a reputation as one of the better AIF battalion commanders. He was respected by his troops and was intensely loyal to them. However, he gave short shrift to anyone he judged to be shirking their responsibilities. [79]

On landing in Egypt, the Battalion undertook a rigorous training program from July through to August 1915, before deploying to Gallipoli on 4 September 1915. For the next sixteen weeks the Battalion shared duty with the 23rd Battalion at Lone Pine. The fighting at this location was so intense the battalions were rotated daily, to enable some respite.

In March 1916 the Battalion moved to France and entered the line at Fleurbaix near Albert. Through July and August of that year the Battalion took part in the major offensive around Pozieres and Mouquet Farm. At Pozieres during the night of 7-8 August, a shell burst in an abandoned gun pit that Lieutenant Colonel Watson and his headquarters had occupied, killing everyone except Watson. He suffered shell shock and was evacuated for treatment and did not return to the Battalion until October 1916. The European winter of 1916-17 was particularly bleak, and the Battalion worked hard, alternating between time in the trenches at the front and labouring tasks close behind the lines. It was during one of their periods at the front that the Battalion used white nightshirts as a means of camouflaging their patrols as they moved across the snow-covered no-man's-land. Harry and his fellow trainees had arrived in England at the tail

---

[79] http://adb.anu.edu.au/biography/watson-william-walker-russell-9008

end of that winter and whilst their living conditions were far from good, at least they had huts to sleep in. The men at the front in France during that time lived in appalling conditions, often knee deep in freezing water and mud. Harry had indeed been fortunate to have missed those early drafts to join the Battalion.

In May 1917, while Harry was subjected to the harsh training at Étaples, the Battalion took part in the successful second battle of Bullecourt on the Hindenburg Line. Success is a relative term, as is participation, for the 24th Battalion's involvement in the battle lasted just twenty-four hours. On the 3rd of May the Battalion had advanced for five hundred metres beyond the Hindenburg Line to a point close to Reincourt; there it was outflanked and after heavy fighting was forced to retire. During this fighting the Battalion suffered approximately eighty percent casualties. The after-action report of this battle lists the Battalion casualties as two officers killed in action, with a further two listed as wounded and missing. Thirty-five other ranks were killed in action. Nine officers were wounded in action, and 221 other ranks wounded in action and 116 other ranks listed as missing.

The Battalion was then withdrawn from the action to rest and regroup. It would take a considerable time and a huge effort, to reinforce and retrain the unit before it could be returned to the front line. It was at that time, having completed his Étaples training, that Harry joined the Battalion.

Poor Harry, he probably believed that once he reached the Battalion the training would be finished. However, under the circumstances the Battalion needed all the training it could get. In fact, even if the Battalion had not been engaged in rebuilding itself, the reality of life in a professional army is that training never stops. In 1917 the larrikin ways that had characterised the AIF Digger were gone, and the 1st AIF had become a professional organization.

The Battalion's war diary provides a litany of training activities undertaken during that first month that Harry spent with the unit. Infantry minor tactics were revised, route marches were undertaken, bayonet fighting practice, and the inevitable CO's parades and inspections. Then in July, the Battalion was moved by train to a camp at Bapaume where the training continued unabated.

In late July 1917, the Battalion got a new CO. The original CO, Lieutenant Colonel Watson, had been promoted and moved to England to command a brigade. The new CO was Lieutenant Colonel William Edward James.

Before the war Lieutenant Colonel James was a farmer, and like his predecessor in his spare time had also served as a member of the militia. In May 1915 James joined the AIF with the rank of captain and was appointed as a company commander in the 24th Battalion. Prior to his promotion to lieutenant colonel, James had been serving as the second-in-command of the 24th Battalion.

Harry would have been most impressed with James, as the new commanding officer was a Methodist by faith and a Rechabite by persuasion. As such James completely abstained from alcohol. However, Harry would have been a little disappointed to learn that James was not evangelical in his beliefs. For with the exception of his immediate family, James did not impose his views regarding the evils of alcohol on others. However, James had a reputation as a fine judge of men, and his personal standards of sincerity, bravery and readiness to help anyone in need, inspired in his men great affection and respect. [80]

In a letter to his mother, Harry makes no mention of his new CO, however this may well have been a wise move. Letters from the Western Front were censored by junior officers of the Battalion. Harry's platoon commander would almost certainly have censored Harry's letters. Any mentions of troop movements or locations, or battle plans were expurgated, but praise or censure, of a superior officer was also frowned on.

"To my Dearest Mother
France July 11th 1917

Just a brief line to let you see I am ever thinking of you all over the seas. You may think me very slow at writing well I trust you will not be anxious as it is not always convenient to write, again there is little to write about for you know the life of a soldier is not all beer and skittles as the saying goes for it is about the same day in day out. You must find it very quiet not that

---

[80] http://adb.anu.edu.au/biography/james-william-edward-6825

Nell and Jack and the little ones have gone to Ararat to live. I got a letter from Nell since she went back with Maggie. I have not seen Tommie Henderson for some time as he is in a different battalion to me. I was sorry to hear of Wal losing the horse he bought. The mine must be in full swing now. How is Mr McRowe after his accident. I had a letter from Emily some time ago, also one from Grace Maynard she mentioned Nelly going to stay with Lilly till Xmas. How is uncle after undergoing the operation. Dear Mother I have little more to say for this time and will draw to a close. My address the same. I have sent a PC[81] to Jack Mitchell but I have not got an answer yet. Dear Mother keep the home fires burning and keep smiling till we meet again. Give my love to Dad and all at home, from your fond son Priv H.F. Withers D Comp 24 Batt A.I.F.

Love to All XXXXX"

Harry appears to be well across events at home so the mail must have caught up with him again. Poignantly, he has at last written to Jack Mitchell, unaware that four months previous to the date of his letter, his brother-in-law had been killed in action.

Harry had little time to ponder the lack of response from Jack Mitchell, for the new CO had no intention of slackening the Battalion's training program. He continued to hone the fighting skills of his men. However, he also proved to be a man of compassion. On the 27th of July 1917 he marched the Battalion back to the scene of the recent battle at Mouquet Farm where a memorial service was conducted for the Battalion dead.

That memorial service was the last Battalion activity Harry would be involved in for some time. On the 28th of July he reported sick and was diagnosed with Trench Fever, a highly contagious rickettsial disease transmitted by lice. He along with several other Battalion members suffering from the same illness, were evacuated to a field hospital.

No doubt Harry was missed by his mates in the Battalion. However, life in the Battalion itself would hardly have missed a beat, as it continued to train and ready itself for its inevitable return to the line.

---

[81] Postcard

Chapter 15

Sickness and Recovery

THROUGHOUT THE AGES DISEASE HAS always stalked the soldier. Given the right circumstances sickness could claim many more casualties than even the most violent and aggressive enemy. The first real attempt to address this situation occurred during the Crimean War. However, the improvements made at that time had done little to improve the lot of the ordinary soldier in World War One, when disease of one kind or another caused the majority of casualties. Trench Fever was just one of the illnesses that confronted those at the front. The filthy living conditions in the trenches were ideal habitat for mice and rats which bore the lice and fleas that carried the disease.

Lice were a perennial problem for the armies of both sides. Harry was unlucky in two ways. First, not everyone who was lousy contracted Trench Fever, though thousands did. Secondly, he had yet to enter the front line and was therefore yet to be fully exposed to the filthy conditions in the trenches. It must therefore be assumed he became infested with lice at one of the camps to which the Battalion was assigned, possibly at Bapaume, or he picked up his population of lice from some of the other members of the Battalion. There is evidence to support the former of these theories. The Battalion war diary entry dated for the 15th of June records the unit's arrival at a camp near Bapaume, and the entry for the next day indicates the Battalion moved to a "better cleaner site". One can only assume the first site was pretty grim, for survivors of the Battalion were used to front line conditions. They must have been very pleased with the new camp site, for the entry for the 16th also recalls "a half holiday". In addition, the overnight stay at the first, dirtier, camp almost fits with the incubation period for Trench Fever of around fifteen to thirty days, and with the date Harry reported sick. However, regardless as to how Harry became lice infected, the resulting disease made him very sick.

Once the disease presented, a victim might expect to suffer reoccurring fevers that typically lasted for five days, leading to another name for the disease… "five-day fever". Along with a high fever came severe headache, pain on moving the eyeballs, soreness in the muscles of the legs and back, and frequently excessive physical sensitivity, especially of the skin. It was a moderately serious disease although lethal cases were rare. It is estimated that from 1915 to 1918 one third of all British troops and one fifth of all German troops had at some time suffered from the disease.[82] This was a worrying statistic for commanders on both sides, and in an effort to ensure the victims were quickly returned to duty, treatment centres were quickly established. Harry mentions his experience with Trench Fever in his diary:

> "Just before the Battalion left here I was sent to hospital. I left the hospital at Beu Farm after 5 days in bed with trench fever. From Beu Farm a number of us to CCS[83]. I remained here one night the following morning I with several others were carried to the Red Cross train on stretchers. The train left here for Rueon. From the train at Rueon Station. We were put in Red Cross cars and taken to the 1st Australian General Hospital. In this Hosp I remained 11 days. …"

It is interesting to note his reference to four or five days in bed at various locations, and it may be assumed this was because of the recurring nature of the disease.

Some of the place names Harry uses in his diary entries differ from official spelling and/or names, for example Bus Chyer. This might be his error, or it could be that he was using names the Diggers themselves had given to particular places. For example, they referred to "Ypres" and "Wpres".

---

[82] ancienthistorylists.com/world-war-1/top-10-diseases-that-were-spread-in-world-war-1/
[83] Casualty Clearing Station

Harry gives his illness a rather casual mention in a letter to his mother dated 10 August 1917:

"Convalescent Hospital
Rouen France 10/8/17

To my Dearest Mother

Just a few lines to let you see and all at home are not forgotten by me. I have been in Hosp since the 23rd last month. I left the Battalion on the date mentioned I had trench fever and was twelve days in bed. I am up and feeling much better now. I have not seen anything of Priv T Henderson for over a month and I don't think there will be any chance of meeting him over here again. I met Priv C Vance from Chiltern in hosp. This is an awful country for rain we don't get much benefit from the sun. I don't know how France got the name of sunny France. I am sending you a P Card there was not many to choose from France. Dearest Mother I trust you all at home are quite well. I am to go out of this hosp tomorrow. I have been at some good concerts at the Y.M.C.A. Have you heard from May and Nell lately. It is some few weeks since any mail has come for me. Dear Mother there is very little to write as news is a bit scarce. How is Wal and Arthur getting on with the work. Are the young horses working quietly. Did Uncle get over the operation all right. Is Mr James in Chiltern yet. I never met his brother. I have not heard from JJ Mitchell. I will draw this brief note to a close. From your ever fond son Priv H.F. Withers."

He hardly elaborates in a separate letter to his sister Margaret dated 14 August 1917:

"To my Dear Sister Maggie

Just a line to let you see you are ever in my mind although so many thousands of miles apart. You have thought no doubt that I had forgotten you but this is not the case I should have written sooner no doubt only for my having been on the move so much during the last few weeks . I have not been too well for I have had Trench Fever. But I am getting very much stronger now. Dear Maggie I trust you are all well. Have you heard from home of late. I am forwarding you a P Card as a small souvenir from France. Things are rather quiet here at present, but I shall write all being well again in a day or two. I have seen Private C. Vance from Chiltern whilst in Hosp. I have not seen Priv T Henderson for some time and I don't think I shall have a chance of meeting him here again. Dear Maggie I have very little to write about so you will have to excuse this little news. Be sure and drop a line I long to hear from you and all my friends in dear old Australia. I shall draw to a close with love from your fond brother Priv H.F. Withers. Address same as before. Love to all."

Harry's brief mention of Tom Henderson in this letter is telling, and he is apparently displeased with his friend. There is a hint of this displeasure in the change in his method of reference. Tom is no longer referred to as "Tom" or "Tommie", but instead as "Priv" (Private) T Henderson. A look at Tom Henderson's army record provides a probable reason for Harry's change in attitude.

Almost as soon as Henderson had arrived at the 22nd Battalion he absented himself without leave again, this time for twenty-six days, a period of time that came dangerously close to desertion. Interestingly, he was not captured by the Military Police, but turned himself in to his Commanding Officer (CO). There was little the CO could do for him, it was his second offence, and the length of time he was absent could mean only one thing…General Court Martial. Henderson was found guilty and sentenced to one year in gaol with hard labour. He was then moved back to England to begin his sentence. However, someone, possibly his CO, intervened on his behalf. His sentence was suspended, and he was returned to his Battalion, albeit somewhat under a cloud.[84] Harry probably felt Private T Henderson had let the Chiltern Valley men down, but it seems he drew the line at detailing the miscreant's deeds to the family.

The second Chiltern Valley man mentioned in these two letters, is Charles Vance. In civilian life, Number 7062 Private Charles Vance had been a porter with the railways, stationed at Chiltern Valley. He had enlisted at Melbourne on the 3rd of November 1916 and sailed for England on the *Hororata* with the same draft as Harry, and Tom Henderson. Thereafter, their paths separated as Vance was allocated to the 8th

---

[84] https://recordsearch.naa.gov.au/SearchNRetrieve/Interface/ViewImage.aspx?B=5338713

Battalion, joining that unit in France, on the 21st of May 1917. Like Harry, Vance was only in-country a short time before he fell ill. His army record records that he had reported "sick" and was admitted to hospital, on the 28th of July 1917 and that his illness lasted until the 6th of August 1917. No other details of his affliction at that time are recorded. However, he may have been a victim of Trench Fever, like Harry, or perhaps influenza, a disease that would later plague the whole of Europe. In any event it would seem that Harry and Charles Vance renewed their acquaintance just prior to Vance being returned to the 8th Battalion. Harry does not appear to have been particularly enthusiastic about this meeting, perhaps both men were still feeling the impact of their illnesses, or perhaps they had nothing much to talk about.

Harry's prediction that he was unlikely to meet Tom Henderson again, was to prove tragically correct, and could also have been extended to Charles Vance, as he was not to meet either man again. Vance returned to his Battalion, and in October 1917, at the Battle of Menin Road, he received a gunshot wound to the left thigh, and was again hospitalized for a time. He returned to duty but in June 1918, he contracted influenza and was once again placed in hospital. Again, he recovered and returned to duty, but on the 25th of August 1918, at the Battle of Hamel, he was killed in action. He is buried at Harbonnieres, France[85].

Number 6350 Private Tom Henderson did not reoffend. On the 17th of July 1918 during a sustained German chemical attack, he was overcome by gas and evacuated for treatment. He returned to duty five weeks later, but on the 29th of September at the Battle of St Quentin, he too was killed in action. He is buried at Peronne, France. [86]

Harry recovered from Trench Fever and was given a choice as to his next move. He could spend time at the Number 2 Convalescence Detachment, or he could go directly to the new AIF Training Depot at Le Havre. It is somewhat amusing to note he chose the Convalescence Detachment rather than the camp at Le Havre. Following its relocation from Etaples, Le Havre was now the

---

[85] https://recordsearch.naa.gov.au/SearchNRetrieve/Interface/ViewImage.aspx?B=8397331
[86] https://recordsearch.naa.gov.au/SearchNRetrieve/Interface/ViewImage.aspx?B=5338713

AIF's Base Depot training establishment in France.[87] It would seem Harry's experience at Étaples had left him with no desire to return quickly to that kind of training environment. He recorded his recovery process in his diary:

> ".. After leaving this hospital[88] I put in another four days in bed at No 2 Con Camp. From here I had the choice either going to the base at Le Harve, or going to a Con Camp at Bus Chyer went to latter place. About three weeks here..."

Aside from any desire to avoid the training depot for as long as possible, the transfer to the Convalescence Detachment was probably a very good choice as it gave Harry time to fully recover from his illness. However, even though he was convalescing he was expected to carry out some duties as he recovered. Again, his luck was in, or was it the fact that Harry was a more mature, steadier soldier than many of his younger comrades, for he was selected to a position of relative responsibility. He recorded the nature of his duties at the Convalescence Detachment:

> "...The Australian Sergeant Major got me a job as MP[89] which job lasted some six weeks..."

Eventually the time came for him to return to active service. To do this he first had to pass through the course at the AIF Base Depot at Le Havre. There was no avoiding this fate and Harry records his experience in his diary:

> "...From here a number of us was sent to the Base. The first day we were to get all shortages of clothing. The next day we marched a distance of about three miles. After having our gas helmets on for a time we went through the gas chamber. From this chamber went and made a ring and had half an hour with our masks on. Soon as the half hour was up we were marched back to camp..."

In the slightly sanitised version of an old army saying, Le Havre was "the same stew…different gravy", to that served up at Etaples. Harry passed the course and was ordered to re-join his unit.

---

[87] https://anzac-22nd-battalion.com/training-camps-france/
[88] 1st Australian General Hospital
[89] Military Policeman

Chapter 16

October 1917

BY OCTOBER 1917 THE 24TH Battalion was once again battle ready. In September the Battalion had taken a largely supporting role in the fighting at Menin Road and Polygon Wood. At the end of the month, it was withdrawn from the line and billeted at the Cavalry Barracks in the Belgium town of Ypres from where it prepared for its part in the Third Battle of Ypres. It was not a long wait. This battle was in effect a continuation of the Battle of Passchendaele. On the 4th of October 1917 the Battalion moved to take up its position in the assault. However, as it moved to the start line, it was heavily shelled by German artillery. Two officers were killed, and forty other ranks were either killed or wounded. In spite of this tragedy the Battalion crossed the start line on time and began to advance toward its objectives. During this advance the German force's machine-gunned the Battalion formation, however the Battalion reached its first objective, taking numerous German prisoners in the process, and forcing the enemy to withdraw. The Battalion had paid a heavy price for its victory with a further four officers and forty-five other ranks killed in action and another five officers and one hundred and eighty-four other ranks wounded.

The Battalion then consolidated its position, and the next day it faced considerable enemy activity and in the face of this and the number of casualties suffered, it could not continue the advance. At this stage, the Brigade Commander decided to relieve the Battalion, however as the

Battalion manoeuvred to complete the relief, a further nine officers and fifteen other ranks were wounded, and one man was listed as missing.

Being relieved from the point of the advance did not mean the Battalion could rest, and after some rapid resupply and reorganization, various detachments of men were sent to support other units in the line. During this work a further twelve casualties were suffered.

On the 9th of October the Battalion was back at the front of the advance where it encountered a number of enemy strong points. These enemy positions were overcome, and in the process six enemy soldiers were killed, five taken prisoner, and a machine gun captured. However, once again the cost to the Battalion was a heavy one. Five officers and thirty-one other ranks were killed, four officers and seventy-three other ranks wounded. The Battalion consolidated its newly gained position and then on the night of the 10th of October it was again relieved and placed in the support line. By the 27th of October, in bright sunshine, it moved back to the Ottawa Camp near Ypres. It was there, on that date, that Harry re-joined the Battalion.

Harry's journey to accomplish this involved quite a hike and he provided a brief description of the trip in his diary, however the date he records is at odds with his army record:

> "...The next morning we left the base and to train at Le Harve after about two hours marching in the rain. Before entraining there was a number of us put on guard over the men's Packs and storage till the train left at 9 o'clock. After travelling all night and up till four o'clock next day we disembarked at Hazelbrook. From Hazelbrook camp we went to Ypres. We spent several days there before going into the line. The first time on Oct 4th..."

By rough calculation this would mean Harry must have arrived back with the Battalion on approximately the 1st of October. This would mean that he took part in the recent battle involving the Battalion. However, according to his army record, he arrived back at the Battalion on 27th October 1917. This is not to suggest Harry was deliberately falsifying the dates he recorded in his diary. It is clear that Harry wrote much of his diary entries well after events. It is even likely that he did not begin to keep a diary until perhaps late in 1918. Writing at that distance in time, without the benefit of accurate data to refer to, even under the best of circumstances, was likely to give rise to error. The conditions under which Harry would have made his diary entries were far from ideal. Whilst it is most likely he wrote while he was out of the line, he would have been extremely tired, perhaps suffering from shock at things he had seen or done. Under such conditions he can be excused for not being absolutely correct with some of the dates he recorded.

A letter he wrote to his father on 25 October 1917 supports the theory that the dates recorded in his diary for his return to the Battalion are incorrect:

"To My Dear Father

Just a line to let you know you are not forgotten by me and that I am well. I received your letter today which was dated 27 August and was delighted to know all are well. The autumn is about finished now and winter commences next month. We have not had much hot weather one would almost wonder how the crops ripen the weather is turning rather wet and cold. I have not met any of the men from the valley or district yet. I do hope the railway strike will soon be settled. I have heard that the mice have been playing havoc with wheat which is a great pity in these times of stress and trouble. I am pleased to know the work at the mine is going ahead. It is alright having Mag and Jack up home again as it will be company for dear mother. I am ever thinking of you and how I should like to have a meal with you all again. Just fancy having no cows to milk for months. I am pleased to hear you have plenty of feed for the stock. It is taking Frank Smith a long time to get well. I expect to be at the Huns long before you get this note. I think this is all for this time. All being well will write again. From your fond son Privt H.F. Withers

I will wish you all a Happy Xmas   Love to Mum and all"

It would seem that as of 25 October, Harry had yet to be involved in the fighting. Indeed, it appears he was more concerned with his father's fight against a mouse plague, and the railway strike.

The mouse plague of 1917 was one of the largest plagues ever experienced in Australia. The wheat belts of Queensland, Victoria, South

Australia and Western Australia were impacted, starting in around February and finally receding in June.[90]

The railway strike Harry referred to was in fact a general strike of Australian workers. The strike had begun on the New South Wales railways and tramways, in response to a new way of monitoring worker productivity. The original strike soon spread to the rest of Australia as thousands of workers came out in support. The strike lasted for six weeks and cost the workers around $159 million dollars, and the economy about $805 million dollars in today's money.[91]

In another letter to his mother, of which only the last page remains, it would seem the Battalion was still at rest and that Harry has probably had a share of a cake. However, while he has received mail from others, he is clearly disappointed not to have received any from home:

"...The men just received a beautiful cake from a lady friend in Melbourne Albert Park. I received a letter from Grace Maynard yesterday and was pleased to hear that all were well at home when Grace wrote she mentioned of Rene being down to see them also of Rene going out home and that Sandy won the prize at a dance at Lilliput I understand he was dressed as a tramp. I am pleased to hear that uncles foot is just about well again. A number of the men have got sore feet and one or two with trench feet. One thing the men get good treatment from the Doctors and the RMC. The men are busy writing to their people and friends. I have not received any letters from home this last two or three weeks. Dear Mother I have not much news but I trust this note will find you and Dad and all well at home. Kindly remember me to Mag Jack Nell Jack Will Alice and all my friends I must wish you all a happy New Year. Be sure and write Love to all from your fond son Priv H.F. Withers"

For the 24th Battalion and the newly returned Harry the remainder of October was taken up with foot washing and inspections, specialist training and rehearsals for their return to the line. However, while Harry may not have been involved in the Battalion's operations of early October, November would see a dramatic change in his fortunes.

---

[90] https://www.google.com/search?client=firefox-b-d&q=mouse+plague+in+australia+1918
[91] https://dictionaryofsydney.org/entry/great_strike_of_1917

Chapter 17

November 1917

THE NOVEMBER BATTLE THAT WOULD embroil Harry, and the 24th Battalion was actually the third and final part of what was to become known as the Battle of Passchendaele. This series of battles had commenced in July 1917. In the middle of that year the over-strained French armies had mutinied and as a result the British forces had to assume a greater role on the Western Front, a situation that gave Field Marshall Sir Douglas Haig the opportunity to act unilaterally. On the 31st of July he launched a major offensive, attacking from the British line at Ypres. The attack was planned to bring the war to an early end by driving the Germans from the surrounding high ground and advancing onwards to reach the Belgian coast. In spite of appalling losses on both sides, and often in terrible weather, fighting continued until November 1917.[92]

The Australian infantry divisions had joined this battle in September 1917 and immediately employed a systematic, step by step, approach to the battle. This meant in effect the Australian infantry selected achievable objectives, always within the protective range of supporting artillery. On achieving an objective, they would consolidate their gain, before once again pushing forward.[93] On the 7th of November the 24th Battalion resumed its role in Haig's offensive and moved back into the line to relieve the 19th Battalion.

---

[92] https://www.awm.gov.au/articles/blog/battle-of-passchendaele-third-ypres
[93] Op. cit.

Harry had arrived at the fighting, and if ever there was a situation that could have caused a relapse in his mental health, this would have been it, but it seems he endured the battle as well as most. Even so he must have been extremely grateful that his time in the line, did not involve the mass attack that had typified the Battalion's recent operations. Instead, for the next six days the 24th Battalion would attempt to conduct an aggressive patrolling program across no-mans-land, right up to the German positions. As a result, for the first two days of the Battalion's time in the line, patrols were the main activity.

It is likely that Harry participated in some of these patrols. Fresh from training he would have been a logical choice to be included on a patrol. On the one hand his inclusion in a patrol would give him a taste of "the real thing", providing him with experience that would stand him in good stead in the future. In addition, including Harry in a patrol, enabled a man who had had longer periods in the line, the opportunity for a rest from the tension associated with patrolling no-man's-land. There is, however, no mention in Harry's diary of any patrols he participated in, and the censor would no doubt have prevented his writing home of the experience.

However, aside from the Germans, a familiar, secondary foe was about to be encountered again…rain. On the 8th of November it began to rain. Showery at first, but by the 10th of the month it was raining heavily. In the 24th Battalion's section of the line, patrolling had to be reduced in order to apply maximum effort to repairing trenches, and dugouts that began to flood and collapse.

In fact, the earth had turned to unstable mud, and the Battalion war diary refers to the repair work as "Salvage". This work would have been extremely tiring. The mud in the trenches was often of the consistency of thick soup that sucked the existing duckboard paths beneath the surface, making movement along the trench an exhausting task. The solution was to bring in more duckboards in order to replace the sunken paths. Work parties had to carry these heavy wooden constructions from the rear positions to where they were required, a dangerous and tiring task. Where the glutinous muck entered dugouts, it rendered these dwellings unliveable until the muck was removed. However, excavating the mess proved to be all but impossible with a shovel, and the best way of removing it was either by bucket or pump. The pumps used were generally piston driven and of a design able to deal with glutinous materials such as mud, as well as water. The downward stroke of the piston filled the pump chambers with the unwanted fluid, and the upward stroke forced the fluid out. Hoses or pipes were used to direct the fluid out of the trench. The power source for these pumps was provided by a soldier operating a handle which drove the piston up and down. This labour-intensive system was extremely tiring for the individuals operating the pump.

Where pumps could not be operated, or where pumps alone were insufficient, soldiers had to use buckets to salvage their trenches. However, to empty an ordinary bucket over the top of the parapet, placed the soldier wielding the bucket, at great risk should he show any part of himself above the parapet. Snipers on both sides of the line were ever watchful for the unwary. To mitigate this risk, buckets were manufactured that had the appearance of a giant soup ladle. A bucket device connected to a long wooden handle enabled the user to empty water and mud over the trench top in relative safety. This method was particularly tiring, and probably more than a little frustrating, as the user struggled to control the heavy bucket at the end of the long handle. [94] [95]

In spite of this change in work focus, some patrolling continued. On the morning of the 9th a fighting patrol consisting of two NCOs and twenty other ranks, and supported by a Lewis Gun, ventured into no-man's-land. This patrol probably had the task of dominating the section of no-man's-land to the Battalion's front, but not to actually attack the German positions. That same afternoon a reconnaissance patrol of two officers also departed the Battalion trenches. Both of these patrols returned unharmed, having found no sign of the enemy. Then on the night of the 10th, two more fighting patrols of similar size, were deployed. Again, the patrols returned safely having found no sign of the enemy. At some stage early the next day two corporals from B Company, were killed and an officer slightly wounded.

---

[94] https://www.awm.gov.au/collection/C1342340?image=4
[95] Ed. Sir John Hammerton, **The Great War I Was There**. London Amalgamated Press Ltd, p 881

The unit war diary is unclear as to how these casualties occurred but the possibility of a gas attack is hinted at. The other entry in the war diary of note is "*Rain – heavy*".[96]

The rain was to have a massive impact on the overall Battle of Passchendaele, for it had turned the whole battlefield into a treacherous swamp. Vehicular movement was impossible, the much-vaunted tanks were disabled by the mud, and movement by foot restricted to duckboard paths. Those unfortunate enough to fall into the worst of the mud, simply disappeared into the morass. In spite of this, the Australian battalions had managed to take the Passchendaele heights, but the effort left them totally exhausted. Unable to advance any further, the Diggers had to be relieved.

On the 11th of November, the 24th Battalion was relieved by a British unit, and were then retired behind the line. The next day the Battalion moved further back from the line arriving at their new camp at 4 pm. In what must have been a massive understatement, the war diary records:

"men much fatigued"[97]

By the 15th of November, the last of the Australian units had also been relieved, mainly by Canadian troops. The AIF Divisions had suffered 38,000 battle casualties during this battle, a staggering number that included 12,000 dead or missing.

For the remainder of the month as the Battalion recuperated from the battle, it returned to a daily schedule of training, work details and organized sport, activities that typified time out of the line. Given the huge number of casualties, the AIF Divisions as a whole, now found themselves in a similar position to that faced by the 24th Battalion back in May, after the Second Battle of Bullecourt. Reinforcements, time and training were the only cure for the kind of damage the Australians had suffered. So far as the 24th Battalion was concerned it would be January 1918, before the unit was returned to the line, and March 1918 before the AIF Divisions as a whole, took part in another major battle.

On the 19th of November Harry found time to write to his father, and

---

[96] https://www.awm.gov.au/collection/C1342340?image=4
[97] https://www.awm.gov.au/collection/C1342340?image=5

other than a reference to a new friend he had made, he provides no news of the battle or the conditions under which it had been fought:

> "Belgium
> 19/11/17
>
> To My Dear Father
>
> Just a line in answer to your ever welcome letter which I received by the mail this evening and was delighted to hear from you and to know all are well. Fancy having such a wet season. I am pleased to know you have plenty of feed for the stock you must have a good percentage of lambs. I am glad to know that diamond has such a nice foal. I have not met Bill Grace or any of the Valley boys. I am sure Mr Rovegreen must be pleased to have Stan back again. It is a good thing Frank Smith is improving I am pleased to know Ruth and Jackie are growing up such strong children. I have not heard from Nell or May for some time. It is nice for Mum to have Mag and Jack so close. How is the meeting at the Valley and who is the minister. I have a nice mate a young fellow by the name of Moss from Beechworth he is a salvationist. Dear Dad I will draw to a close with love to all from your fond son Harry. I wish you all Happy New Year. Address the same."

It is interesting to note that Harry's usual practise of using his letters as a vehicle to proclaim his own faith and to encourage others in theirs, is somewhat lacking. Perhaps, like many other front line troops, his experiences since re-joining the Battalion had created an element of doubt as to the good intentions of a heavenly father.

It seems the CO of the 24th Battalion believed that by keeping his men active, they would be less likely to brood over their past losses. The Battalion's war diary for the remainder of November records a strenuous program drill, tactical schemes and sports. However, there was time to catch up on a variety of administrative issues. On the 24th of November, a Court of Inquiry was conducted into the men listed as "Missing" after the May 1917 Battle of Bullecourt. This court was presided over by Captain Ellwood MC, the members of the court being Lieutenants Ball, and Irving.[98] Every AIF

---

[98] https://www.awm.gov.au/collection/C1342340?image=6

battalion was required to conduct official inquiries into those listed as Missing In Action. Was the man killed? Was he wounded? Might he be a prisoner of the Germans? Some of these questions could be answered through communication with the Germans. Both sides exchanged the names of those who they held as prisoners, and those of the dead who had been identified. However, this data was not always available, and the Courts of Inquiry had to rely on the witness statements of men who had been with, or near to, the missing man. After listening to several witnesses for each of the missing, the court would decide if a finding of killed in action could be recorded, or if the man would continue to be recorded as Missing In Action. For the 24th Battalion, reliving that terrible twenty-four hours in May 1917, must have been a harrowing experience. However, for the families of the missing, if their loved one was lucky, the Court of Inquiry may have found that the missing man was in hospital, or a prisoner of the Germans. For those who were unlucky, a recording of Killed In Action might have provided their family at home some closure.

Chapter 18

December 1917

IN THE FIRST HALF OF December 1917 the Battalion activities continued to focus on training. The route march continued to play an important part in toughening the men, as did bayonet fighting and drill. These activities were interspersed with rifle range shoots, specialist training, sports, games and church parades.

On the 10th of December the Battalion war diary records that another Court of Inquiry was conducted. This time into the loss of cardigan jackets. The cardigan jacket was a knitted item of clothing, popular among the troops, and it would seem a significant number allotted for the Battalion's use had gone missing. Several possibilities for this loss come to mind. The Digger is a resourceful fellow, and it would not be beyond the realms of possibility, that one of them had purloined the cardigans and sold them on the Black Market. Special police units patrolled the rear areas in an effort to control the seamier side of the war. Stories abound of large numbers of Allied troops, many of them deserters, who inhabited particular areas behind the line, from where they conducted all manner of nefarious activities. A British Special Branch officer, E.T. Woodall, wrote of a raid on one particular den of iniquity:

> "...The same evening the Provost Marshal and I, with a large posse of men, raided the headquarters of one old lag we were after, an outlying tool-house in a spare plot of ground near Paris Plage Lighthouse. We discovered a veritable

> *Aladdin's Cave of stolen stuff. My old lag and his pals, all absentees, had stolen goods to the value of thousands of pounds, taken from various camps in the neighbourhood…"*[99]

Was the loss of the 24th Battalion's cardigans yet another case of theft that might be attributed to behind the line criminals? Mr Woodall also explained that the Military Police were almost powerless to act against some of the larger criminal organizations and in fact "turned a blind eye" to crimes and criminals they could not prosecute. Numbers of these criminals avoided apprehension throughout the war and were cunning enough to wait in hiding until British and Commonwealth authorities adopted a more lenient view of their wartime activities before returning home.

With regard to the 24th Battalion's missing cardigans, another possibility was that a large number of members of the Battalion conspired to obtain an extra issue of the popular item. However, it is more likely that the Battalion's quota of the items simply became lost in the vast supply system that existed behind the lines. In any event it is unlikely the outcome of the case of the missing cardigans will ever be known as the findings of the court are not recorded.

It seems that Harry wrote only one letter during this period.

> *"In the Field*
> *17/12/17*
>
> *To My Dear Mother*
>
> *Just a line to let you see you are not forgotten by me. No doubt you have wondered how you have not heard from me sooner. One of the reasons is I have not received any mail and have been waiting for some news from home before writing. I have not got any mail so am dropping you a line which I trust will find you all in the best of health as it leaves me at this present time. I have been waiting anxiously for news from home also the parcels which Vi said Rene was sending. I got the letter about two or three weeks ago but the parcels have not come to light. The weather has been keeping good until this morning when the snow commenced to fall we had two light falls previous to*

---

[99] Ed. Sir John Hammerton, The Great War, I Was There, Volume Two, London Amalgamated Press Limited, p1260

this. I have not met any of the Valley boys yet. No doubt Rene heard of Jack Wilkinson getting killed. We had a good number of men and officers killed but not so many as one would expect in the face of shells and bullets. It is no fun with the shells screeching over one's head and bursting all around. I am fortunate in escaping any injuries in the previous three stunts.

The country throughout Belgium and France is terribly battered about also the village of Ypres which was a very fine town before the war is now in ruins and also every village is the same where there has been any fighting at all. This is obviously the worst fighting I've been in give me Australia once I return I shall never want to leave again. I wrote to Grace Maynard yesterday. How are all at home. I trust you my dear mother and Dad and all the rest are well. I suppose the boys are busy harvesting. Private Tipping one of my mates knows a young fellow who was in the same machine company as Jack Mitchell. He is going to write to him and see if he can find out anything about poor old Jack. I will have to draw to a close as I want to try and get some sleep. I will drop a line again. I trust you will have Happy Xmas and New Year this is my wish to all and I hope I will have the same and that we will not be in the line. Love to all from your fond son Harry.

My address the same. Be sure and write and kindly ask a favour of Vi Rene or anyone I should be pleased to hear a line. Love to all"

Harry's reference to the condition of Ypres was an understatement. When he arrived at the town it was a battered ruin. Neat and well-maintained houses that in days of peace had housed happy citizens had been reduced to piles of broken masonry and rubble. The Cathedral of St Martin, part of which dated back to the 13th century, the centre piece and pride of the town, was a shapeless mess. The level of destruction Harry witnessed seems to have had a marked impact on him.

Harry's use of the word "stunt" was World War One Digger talk for patrols or attacks made against the German forces. Thus, it may be assumed that the "stunts" Harry refers to in the letter are activities he undertook while in the line, almost certainly in the form of patrols.

In the same letter, Harry states that the fighting he has recently experienced was bad, and he referred to his own luck at not being wounded or killed. In addition, he suggests that the "we" had suffered a significant number of casualties, a statement that may lead to some confusion. If by "we" he is referring to the Battalion, then his statement is incorrect as the Battalion's casualties could be considered as light. However, if he is referring to Australian casualties in the overall Battle of Passchendaele, then his statement is tragically correct. During that battle the AIF suffered around 38,000 casualties.

This letter reveals a number of other interesting aspects of Harry's life at that time. He was always at pains to advise his parents of his health, and in this letter, following his recent bout of Trench Fever, news that he was fit and well must have been a comfort to his mother.

Harry's letter also indicates that he is suffering a relapse of deployment blues. He is upset that he has not received letters from home. Clearly, he is worried for his family's health, and there is the hint that as they have not written to him, he won't write to them. But of course, he has relented and written anyway. It is obvious he is thinking of home and the nature of the work being done there at that time of year, and his declaration that on his return to Australia that he will never leave again, speaks of a deep yearning. Interestingly, he writes of "when" not "if" he returns home. Even with this indication of a continued positive approach to his own life, this letter demonstrates that Harry is now fully aware that life at the front is very different to anything else he had experienced, and that it could be tragically temporary.

However, it is the deaths of two Chiltern Valley men that has greatly affected Harry, particularly that of his brother-in-law Jack Mitchell. To find that for almost ten months, he had been trying to contact a dead man must have been a troubling shock. Yet Harry would have been fully aware that he was living in a world where life was cheap and death a common commodity. His pure and worshipful view of the way life should be, was being challenged by everything he saw about him. His sad observation regarding the destruction of the Belgian towns and villages indicate a deeper, more earthly concern for his fellow humans. In this letter too, there is a lack of religious greeting or encouragement and the closest he comes to expressing a matter of faith, is to wish all at home a happy Christmas, and he concludes the letter with a hope, not a prayer, that he will not spend his Christmas in the line.

At least that part of Harry's Christmas wish list came true. The Australian Divisions remained out of the line. In theory they were at rest, however in practice their days were far from free. By the middle of December, in addition to unit training and sporting activities, the Australians were required to provide a considerable number of men for work parties within the Australian area of responsibility. The work focused on repairing defences, building and rebuilding the duckboard pathways enabling soldiers to move about the marshy areas, and assisting in tunnelling work. The 24th Battalion carried out its share of this requirement, and soon Harry found himself working in a much different environment to that which he was normally accustomed.

On the 26th of December, Harry wrote to his sister Violet, and he is clearly in a better frame of mind. He had spent an enjoyable Christmas, and he reports his engagement in tunnelling work:

"Dec 26th 1917

To My Dear Sister Violet

Just a line to let you know I am quite well. We spent a very happy Xmas considering we are so close to the firing line. A number of us are working down a mine. Xmas Eve I was on work with two other men at top of the shaft. The mine was meant to blow up the enemy. The enemy did not advance far enough so there are three shifts working. This week I am going below working on the pump pumping water. It will take some time before the explosives are taken out. We are billeted in a big dugout which place holds some two thousand men. The electric light is on day and night. Our Xmas dinner consisted of Roast Beef, Rabbit, Vegetable, cabbage, potatoes, soup, plum pudding and sauce. Today on the ordinary rations.

The snow has been falling very heavy yesterday and today. The ice has not melted on the shell holes for over a week. Fritz is still sending over some shells as well as plenty of other big shells. The men are pleased as each man was given a very nice little box as a Xmas gift sent to us by the Australian comforts fund. Each box was nicely packed with different articles of a pocket handkerchief, boot laces, cigarettes, pipes, lollies and other articles. I have been looking forward to a parcel from home, but have not received any yet. I have not had any mail since October and only a post card then but that was very acceptable.

Dear Vi I think there is very little more to write about just now but will write again. Kindly remember me to Mag, Jack, Nel, Jack, Will, Alice and all my friends at the Valley. Dear Vi tell the other girls not to be disappointed if they don't get a letter for it is not convenient to write at all times. Never-the-less I am ever thinking and praying for you all. I will close with love to all from your brother Privt H.F. Withers

All my love to Ruthie and the other little ones

He is still upset at the lack of mail he has received from home, but Christmas and the tunnelling work seems to have had a positive impact on him. Interestingly, a happier Harry has returned to his faith, as he advises his sister that he prays for her and the rest of his family. The new job had given him something different to write about and had possibly contributed to his more positive state of mind.

Tunnelling may seem a strange battlefield activity, however tunnelling, or mining, was an age-old war fighting method, revitalised during World War One. Tunnels could be dug beneath the enemy positions, then packed with explosives and detonated. Tunnels could also be used to shelter troops or to move them unseen to a point of tactical advantage without exposing them to the dangers of no-man's-land. 1915 had been a time of constant underground warfare as British and German troops strove to gain the ascendency of the subterranean battle space. Australian tunnellers were first deployed on the Western Front in May 1916, as a Mining Battalion, however soon after that battalion's arrival in Europe, it was split into three separate tunnelling companies, and one repair company. The members of the tunnelling companies were drawn from men who had in their civilian lives, experience in mining. The Australian tunnelling companies met with considerable success, but perhaps their greatest success was at Messines, where on 7 June 1917 a mine beneath the German positions at Hill 60 was detonated with devastating impact.

A number of tunnelling companies, including the 1st and the 2nd Australian Tunnelling Companies, had been deployed to the Messines sector. The major tunnelling project in the sector was the excavation of a large tunnel complex at Hill 63. Hill 63 was near the remains of the Belgian village of Ploegsteert, referred to by the Diggers as "Plug Street". The plan was that where these tunnels passed beneath the German positions, the tunnels would be packed with explosives, and at the appointed time, detonated. The explosive caches were referred to by code names including "Hyde Park" and "The Birdcage", that are mentioned in Harry's diary. However, as the Germans had been forced to withdraw from their Hill 63 positions, the explosives beneath Hill 63, were never detonated. Instead, the tunnel complex was converted to provide reasonably safe accommodation for troops resting after their stint in the line. The Diggers' name for this accommodation tunnel was the "Catacombs". The accommodation areas within Hill 63 were seen by British and Australian leaders as essential for preparations for the coming spring offensive. Therefore, any delay in the work was unacceptable. Tunnelling, however, was of course an extremely labour-intensive occupation, and to ensure the work was kept to schedule, infantry units were required to provide work parties to help with work in the tunnels. This was a common practise during most of World War One tunnelling operations. Infantry work parties would be detailed to assist the professional mining organizations engaged in the operations. The infantry were essentially beasts of burden, engaged in digging, carting away spoil, and in pumping or carrying water away from the tunnel working areas. This was the case at Hill 63, and Harry was one of the one hundred 24th Battalion men detailed to help with the tunnelling work. However, it is important to note that the members of this work party had not been transferred to the tunnelling company, merely attached for duty. In addition, the tunnelling company the men of the 24th Battalion worked with was not an Australian tunnelling company, but a British one, the 184th Tunnelling Company of the Royal Engineers. Harry made further reference to his tunnelling work in his diary:

> "...Twenty-five men chosen out of each to join the Tunnelling

Company. We were at the Tunnelling Company camp and remained eight days. From here we left for the Catacombs on the corner of Hyde Park corner on the way to Messines. The first day after arriving at the catacombs there was nine of us to go and work at the bird cage and worked night shift till Xmas Day and on Boxing Day we changed on to afternoons. Wednesday 27th in morning stopped in bed till dinner time. After dinner in motor bus to Romarin to the baths got back to Catacombs at Four o'clock. Had tea then went to work at bird cage. 28th went to work as usual. Fritz shelling ridge and woods both whilst we were going to and from work. 29th went to work as usual. In afternoon Fritz plane came over the cook house while we getting our tea and came down on hill 63.

Lille and Armentiers, Messines are all in vision from the top of hill 63. 30th went to work in Bird Cage. Fritz shelling ridge about one hundred yards away. Nothing else of importance to mention."

For all that, work beneath Hill 63 seems to have been a pretty good job. It was probably warmer underground, for as Harry recorded, conditions above ground during this period, were extremely cold. However, it was probably a good deal safer in the tunnels than in the trenches and dugouts. German counter tunnelling units were not active in the area so there was little risk of attack from that quarter, and while underground Harry and his work party mates were relatively safe from enemy artillery fire. Not entirely safe, for there was always the risk of cave-in or equipment failure leading to any number of industrial accidents.

Why was Harry picked for the tunnelling task? Perhaps he volunteered. Another possibility is his home town's association with the mining industry, and perhaps his platoon commander assumed Harry had some mining experience. It might also have been assumed that as a farm labourer in his civilian life, that Harry would have some experience with pumps, a task he records as being the nature of the work he was employed on while he was with the tunnelling company.

Once again there is no indication that the front line experience, or the underground work, has had any kind of adverse impact on Harry's mental health, or of his having experienced an epileptic seizure. Either event would almost certainly have led to his evacuation to a medical facility, and a recording of the event included in his medical documents. As a result, it is probably safe to assume that Harry's Traumatic Brain Injury had indeed healed.

For the remainder of the Battalion work above ground continued. Reinforcements began to arrive, replacing some of those who had been killed or wounded. During December the war diary records eight officers and ninety-five other ranks joined the Battalion, and at the end of the month the total Battalion strength is recorded as forty-five officers and eight hundred and seventy-five other ranks.[100] Soon, all too soon, the battalion would be ready to return to the line.

---

[100] https://www.awm.gov.au/collection/C1342341?image=8

Chapter 19

Jack Mitchell

HARRY MENTIONED THE DEATH OF Jack Mitchell to his parents in his letter dated the 17th of December 1917. That death had a deep impact on the Withers family as a whole. Before the war, Jack was employed in the mining industry at Chiltern, and in 1909 he had married Grace Withers, Harry's younger sister. Jack and Grace had one child a daughter they named Ruth, but sadly Grace had died in 1912 when her daughter was only two years old. After Grace's death, Jack's mother assisted in caring for young Ruth, but when Jack enlisted in the AIF this situation must have become more complicated.

Sometime after Jack's deployment to France, the Withers family began to take more responsibility for the child, particularly the Withers eldest daughter Margaret Stewart, who accepted the role as Ruth's guardian. In recognition of this assumed responsibility, Jack Mitchell was to make financial allotments to the Withers family, from his pay.

After basic training, Jack had embarked for Egypt in December 1915, thus missing the Gallipoli campaign. Initially he was allocated to the 14th Battalion, but on his arrival in Egypt, the AIF was undertaking a major restructure, and he was at first transferred to the newly raised 46th Battalion. Then in March 1916 he was again transferred, this time to another newly raised unit the 12th Machine Gun Company. Considerable training in his new role followed. This took place in the desert around the Suez Canal. With his training in his new role complete, on 2nd of June 1916 along with the rest of the 12th Machine Gun Company, he embarked on the "*SS Kingstonian*" bound for France.

Three months after the 12th Machine Gun Company's arrival on French soil, the Company took part in the battle of Pozieres, where Jack played an active role. From that time, save for brief periods of rest, Jack and the 12th Machine Gun Company, were almost continuously in the line, providing vital fire support to the infantry battalions.

Where Harry appears to have struggled with some aspects of army life, Jack seems to have been a natural soldier, and he was soon identified as a potential leader. In Harry's defence it should be noted that an infantry battalion was roughly eight times the numerical strength of a machine gun company. It was therefore somewhat easier for a soldier's strengths and weaknesses to be seen in a smaller unit. It should also be noted that Jack's promotional prospects were greatly enhanced by the casualties among the NCO's and SNCO's in his unit. Conversely, Harry's illness reduced his chances of being in the right place at a time when a promotional position may have become available. Jack on the other hand seems to have remained fit and healthy, and to have created a good impression within his unit.

During this time Jack wrote at least one letter to the Withers family. One letter, of which only the final pages have survived, was possibly addressed to his father-in-law, William Withers. That letter was probably penned in late September 1916 and in the surviving fragment, a little of Jack's character is illuminated:

"...The French religion is very peculiar. There is big iron crosses all over the place and Christ nailed to it, & so far as I can see they worship it. It is a great insult if you attempt to damage it. The Germans have blown a lot of them down, they have even bombarded Cemeteries & rooted up the bones and dead bodies, & blown the head stones all over the place.

Goodbye

From Jack

You didn't tell me who won the premiership

Remember me to Bill & Alice

How are they progressing at the little church remember me to Mr Cooper & Miss Lappin. Tell her we often have a service at the back of the Firing line & how we sing & enjoy, we owe a lot of thanks to the Y.M.C.A."

As a matter of interest, Fitzroy won the 1916 Victorian Football League premiership, defeating Carlton by 29 points. However, Jack's letter reveals more than an interest in the football results.

Jack, it seems, was ready to get on with the war. Clearly the Protestant upbringing he had received placed him at odds with Catholic France, and he also reveals a dislike of Germans and their attitude to the war. The dislike of all things German was not an uncommon aspect of life within the British Empire at that time. Anti-German sentiments had resulted in British Royalty changing their surnames from, "Saxe-Coburg-Gotha", to "Windsor". It was also responsible for numerous anti-social activities directed against people of German heritage and their interests. It would seem that so far as Jack was concerned the whole reason for fighting the war was to ensure what he perceived as German brutishness was prevented from spreading across the world.

Jack's enthusiasm for soldiering paid off, for on the 22nd of August 1916, during the Battle of Pozieres, he was promoted to the rank of lance corporal and wore the single stripe on his sleeve denoting that rank. By the 22nd of January 1917, after further time in the line, he had been promoted to the rank of corporal and wore two stripes on his sleeve, and on the 31st of January he was promoted to the rank of sergeant and wore three stripes. With each promotion came greater responsibility, and more pay. In a letter to his sister-in-law Nell [101] dated 26th of January 1917, it is clear that the extra money was going to be most welcome.[102]

"Fighting Germans   *26 – 1- 17*

France

Dear Nell,

Just a line to answer yours of the 21st Nov also the photos'. I was quite delighted when I got them, they were delivered to me in the firing line and I almost forgot I was at the war for the second. It is awfully cold here now, the ice is a couple of inches thick, I see some of the boys skating on it. I suppose you never heard of any one going for water in a bag, but it is so here now

---

[101] Nell is Ellen Withers. "Nell" appears to be the name the family used in addressing her.
[102] SGT J.J. Mitchell Army Record.
https://recordsearch.naa.gov.au/SearchNRetrieve/Interface/ViewImage.aspx?B=7980590

when the men go for water for the cooks they have to take bags and carry back ice, the water is all frozen into hole of ice & they have to use a pick & shovel to break it up & push it into the bags, everything freezes over night & we nearly freeze to death during the day. I am quite well but the cold takes some matching; a lot of the boys have trench feet; and it is no joke to get them; I am pleased you received my cable, I was quite surprised when I received it couldn't work out what was wrong.

You say that you haven't heard from the mata for a couple of pays to know whether she is getting the money, Well I can only suggest that she must be getting it alright otherwise you would soon hear from her. Well Nell I have been promoted again to <u>Corporal</u> so if I'm capable of holding it there will be some more money coming through for Ruthie; Corporals pay is 10/- a day So I will probably draw 2/- a day for myself & 3/- a day more will go to Ruthie. If it comes through like that you can send the mata an extra shilling a day & two more for Ruthie, but it maybe a little time before I get it through. As I am nearly due for leave to Blighty & I may drain a little extra for that occasion; I am anxious to see England. Has Ruth received the three parcels I sent her since the broaches. I am glad to hear that Bill and Alice are busy making horses and carts, I am afraid they will all be wanted after next spring. I am sort of dreading it coming

Remember me to them both. I had a letter from Greta; you say she was inquiring after one, she must have had a letter shortly after she wrote to you. I sent her a photo of the boys and the guns and she said Jackie picked me out immediately. I am sending you another snapshot taken by one of our officers, showing how we shoot down German aeroplanes if they come too close, or rather how we <u>try</u> to shoot them down, they get very cheeky at times. I suppose you can easily pick me out there also, I am Lance Corporal in the photo, or what they call Number 1 on the gun. I fire the gun and am responsible for the care of it. Of course now I have practically nothing to do with the gun, only when we are in the firing line I am in charge of the gun teams.

Mr Maynard must have had a bad time with his foot, it will be hard luck for them if he loses his foot; there will be enough cripples in Australia without him

Well Nell I suppose you have heard about the fate of poor Peart & Forsyth. J Peart was killed & Forsyth was invalided home to Australia. I was quite downhearted when I heard the news, there was also five or six other Canbelego boys killed. The Germans are getting them gradually but they will get their deserts next spring I hope; I would like to meet Harry very much, I hope he gets on alright, <u>But don't let Wall come</u> remember me to poor old Dad I often think of him; he's a Briton to part with his two sons, if Wal has left by the time you get this & even offered his third. But then of course he was always a Britain; How is Mum getting on, tell them to cheer up for I don't think there will be any war left after next Spring, if so don't worry over us too much for we died for you all, & to save our country from these cruel hounds of Germans. I could tell you many things Nell that would I am sure astonish you, but I must not say too much or you might not get this letter at all, so it is better to be sure than sorry. We used to hear a lot about the cowardly things the German used to do before we left Australia, and sometimes we used to doubt it; thinking they could not be so cruel. But now we know from experience and to our sorrow that he is a cowardly fighter; they pour bullets into our boys until they get up close & then they throw up their hands and surrender and the boys don't get a chance to get their own back, or revenge the death of their mates. But we have them winged now. So watch for good news in a month or two.

Now I think I have told you enough this time Nell, I hope this will find you all well. I pray to God to spare one, that I may return to you all safe and sound. Now goodbye and give my love to all I remain your Fighting Brother Corporal J.J. Mitchell 3833 M.G. Coy"

Jack and his mother appear to be at odds, possibly over the responsibility of caring for his child Ruth. It would also seem that they may have clashed over money in the past.

His comments regarding the conduct of the German soldiers, is a little ironic. The German Army employed their machine guns in much the same way as the Australians and the British. Machine guns were sighted to the flanks of defensive positions. From these positions the guns could fire at an attacking force right up to the moment when the enemy were upon them.

The choice then for the machine gunners was bleak. They could try to withdraw to a new position, they could fight until they were killed, or they could try to surrender. Soldiers on both sides had no love for machine gunners, and as a result they were often not given any opportunity to surrender, a harsh reality of warfare that very possibly led to Jack's death on the 11th of April 1917.

In a way it seems Jack had a premonition of his own death, when he admits to Nell that he is dreading the spring. In spring the countryside would be dry enough for the next major offensive to commence, and Jack knew there would be more casualties, and it must have been in the back of his mind that he could well be one of them. Clearly, he is determined to continue to do his duty, however, he also bluntly states to Nell, that Wal, almost certainly Harry's younger brother, should remain at home and that the Withers family had done enough for King and Country.

Jack was keen to catch up with Harry, but at the time he wrote to Nell, Harry was still in training at Lark Hill. Sadly, Harry and Jack were never to meet in France, and it is particularly poignant that when Harry wrote to his parents in May 1917 asking for Jack's address, Jack was already dead.

Jack was at first listed as missing. The 12th Machine Gun Company was committed to the fighting at Bullecourt when the German forces mounted a strenuous counterattack forcing the Australians to withdraw. In the confusion of the withdrawal the Company could not recover three of its guns and Jack had been engaged in rendering those weapons inoperable before they fell into enemy hands. It was during that work that he disappeared.

There was possibly only one thing worse than receipt of word that a loved one was missing, and that was notice of his, or her, being killed in action. Missing was so… uncertain. Was the missing soldier dead, or was he a prisoner of war? When the Withers were advised that Jack was missing, several representations were made to AIF headquarters for news regarding his fate. These representations were unsuccessful and, in an endeavour to seek an answer to this quandary, the Premier of Victoria, Sir Alexander Peacock KCMG MLA, was contacted seeking his assistance in ascertaining Jack's fate. Where the Withers may not have been satisfied with the speed and nature of the army's response to their inquiries, the Premier received a swift response to his inquiry:

"22 May 1917

> Dear Sir,
>
> I have to acknowledge the receipt of your communication of the 14th instant, concerning the case of No 3833 Temporary Sergeant J.J. Mitchell, 12th Machine Gun Coy. Who is posted missing since 11.4.17, and regret that so far, no further responses have come to hand.
>
> Next of kin will be promptly advised of anything further received.
>
> Yours faithfully
>
> Major
>
> Officer i/c Base Records[103] "

No doubt the Premier passed on this inconclusive statement to the Withers family, who in turn could do nothing but wait, and hope.

The AIF was generally thorough in its investigating the probable fate of those listed as missing in action. However, the tempo of battle dictated when those investigations could take place. In Jack's case, it was not until July 1917 that the 12th Machine Gun Company began its inquiry to establish his fate, and that inquiry did not conclude until the 4th of November 1917. The statements provided by witnesses to the action where Jack disappeared are particularly relevant:

> "Statement made by No. 1783 Pte F.E. O'Connor 12th M. G. C.
> re No. 3833 T/Sgt Mitchell J.J. 12th M. G. C.
> Missing 11.4.17
> The above named T/SGT Mitchell was in the German trench with me at Bullecourt, but I cannot state whether he was killed or not.
> Dated at V.A.D Hospital, Bedford, this 23rd day of July 1917
> (sgd) F. O'Connor

---

[103] https://recordsearch.naa.gov.au/SearchNRetrieve/Gallery151/dist/JGalleryViewer.aspx?B=7980590&S=28&N=54&R=0#/SearchNRetrieve/NAAMe

Statement made and signed before me.
(sgd) V.S.A, Bell M.O.
V.A.D Hosp
Bedford" [104]

Later in November 1917 the inquiry concluded with the following statements:

<u>"No. 3893. Cpl. Robert Aunger Rowe states:</u>
I am a Corporal belonging to the 12th M.G. Coy. A.I.F and knew Sergt. Mitchell since I went into camp in Sep. 1915. In the attack on Bullecourt on 11th April 1917 we both moved forward to the newly captured position when Sergt Mitchell visited the gun (to which I was attached) several times. Shortly after, we retired and I have seen or heard nothing of Sergt Mitchell since. I firmly believe that he was killed, because as we were very close friends, he would have written to me had he been taken prisoner.(Sgd) R.J.A. Rowe. Corp 3893[105]

<u>No 240. Pte William Harding states:</u>
In the attack on Bullecourt in April 11th 1917, I was a member of the crew of Sergt Mitchell's gun, which took up a position in the Hindenburg Line. During the counter attack were ordered by Lt Duton to move our gun to a shell hole thirty yards in the rear.

Sergt Mitchell was with us at this time. I went away for ammunition and when I returned the Sergt was removing the feed block and lock from the gun. He was alone. I knew the gun was to be abandoned and I retired behind the infantry. I did not see the Sergt leave the shell hole, and as he has not been heard of in the Coy since, I am of the opinion that he must have been killed by machinegun or shell fire' (Sgd) W.H. Harding Pte 240[106]

---

[104] https://recordsearch.naa.gov.au/SearchNRetrieve/Interface/ViewImage.aspx?B=7980590
[105] Ibid
[106] Ibid

<u>No. 3518. L/Cpl Arthur William Wall states</u>:

In the attack on Bullecourt in April 11th 1917, I was on Sergt Mitchell's gun, which took up a position in the Hindenburg Line. During the counter attack we were ordered to take the gun to a shell hole thirty yards to the rear. Sergt Mitchell was then with us. Owing to the close pursuit of the enemy we weren't able to retain this position and contiued to retire. During the retirement I lost sight of the Sergeant and have not seen or heard of him since, and therefore I think he was killed before reaching our line.

(Sgd) Arthur W. Wall L/C 3518 [107]

The Court finds that 3833 T/Sgt Mitchell J.J. was killed in action during the retirement from the Hindenburg Line at Bullecourt on the 11th April 1917(Sgd) A.F. Taylor Lieut <u>President</u>

(Sgd) 2/Lieut Cullimore E.M. <u>Member</u>[108]

I was in command of the 12th Aust. M.G. Coy during the operations mentioned in the above evidence. In my opinion the finding of the court is a correct one.

(Sgd) W.H. Crouch Capt.

O.C. 12th M.G. Coy"[109]

The finding that Jack was killed in action destroyed what faint hope Jack's mother and the Withers family must have clung to, that somehow Jack had survived. Seven-year-old Ruth was left as the only survivor of the tiny family Jack and Grace had started with their marriage in 1909.

---

[107] Ibid
[108] Ibid
[109] Ibid

Harry's parents, Margaret and William Withers of Ullina Station, Chiltern Valley. [110]

Ullina Station homestead, Chiltern Valley[111]

---

[110] Photograph – L Reiss
[111] Photograph – L Reiss

6426 Private Harry Withers[112]

HMATS Hororata the ship on which Harry sailed to war.[113]

---

[112] Photograph - L Reiss.
[113] Photograph – Australian War Memorial

An AIF camp on Salisbury Plain. This camp would have been typical of the accommodation provided for Australian soldiers undergoing their training prior to deployment to France.[114]

Australian soldiers completing a route march at Salisbury Plain. Harry appeared to have enjoyed these activities.

---

[114] Photograph – Australian War Memorial

Members of the 24th Battalion AIF occupying a trench in October 1917. This photograph was probably taken just before Harry re-joined the Battalion after his bout of Trench Fever. [115]

The 6th Australian Light Trench Mortar Battery. Harry joined this unit in June 1918. [116]

---

[115] Photograph – Australian War Memorial
[116] Photograph – Australian War Memorial

A three inch mortar crew in action in France.[117]

The church at Montbrehain after the battle in which Harry was killed. The church was one of the objectives for his old battalion, fighting in this area was particularly fierce.[118]

---

[117] Photograph – Australian War Memorial
[118] Photograph – Australian War Memorial

Harry's grave at Calvaire, Montbrehain, in Plot 1 Row B 4[119]

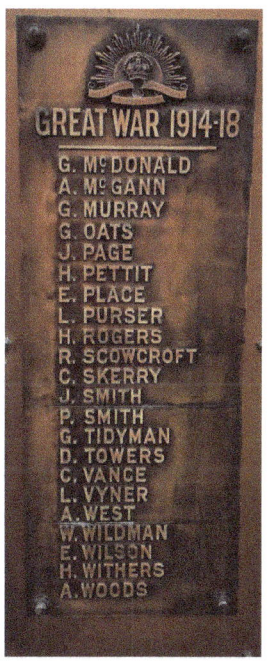

The Chiltern Memorial Gateway plaque erected in memory of those local men who died on active service in World War One.[120]

---

[119] Photograph – L Reiss
[120] Photograph – L Reiss

Chapter 20

The Home Front

BY 1917 THE ATTITUDE OF many Australians regarding the war had changed. The almost frenzied rush to join the AIF, had slowed to a point where enlistments were insufficient to replace the casualties being suffered by the deployed force. This recruitment issue led to two attempts by the Commonwealth Government to introduce conscription, however the majority of the electorate were heartily sick of the war, and both of these attempts failed.

There were other issues confronting the Australian population. Inflation, low wages, industrial action, xenophobia and paranoia plagued the nation. In the majority of cases, it was the poor who suffered most from the impacts of these afflictions. However, there was almost always, someone keeping an eye out for those less fortunate than themselves, particularly if they had a loved one serving overseas. Margaret and William Withers held with this altruistic attitude. Amongst the cards and letters Margaret retained was a letter of thanks penned to her by Lance Corporal E Bottrell:

"County of London War Hospital
Epsom Surry June 19 1917
8am Sunday

Dear Mrs Withers
Your welcome letter to hand a couple of days ago, was pleased to receive

it as I hadn't heard from Aust for a good while, but of course my letters had gone over to France and had to come back to England. I had a letter or two from my wife the same day and she told me that she got a very pleasant surprise one day when she came home to find a bonzer load of wood in the yard, for which I thank you very much, it is very nice to know that those I've left behind are not without friends.

I hope very soon to be home and thank you personally for your kindness. I am getting better slowly but I'll never be the same again. Im still spitting up blood and black lumps, I think it's the gas right enough and Im terribly short of breath and get very little sleep at night. I hope Frank Smith is doing well the wife told me that he was poor, well dear Friend I think that is all for the time, so hoping yourself and family are all well I remain ever your sincere friend

Ted
No 1146
L/CPL E Bottrell
D Company
37th Battalion AIF
OAS Abroad
PS

Ive never had the pleasure of meeting Harry or Willie Grail. I've made inquiries but can get no satisfaction and I've written three or four letters to him but had no reply and I also forgot to mention that another Zeppelin was brought down on Saturday that by aeroplane raid was only 15 miles from where I am and the guns and bombs could be heard quite plainly they killed a good many women and children & if a German ever speaks to me in future I shall give him one to go with (they are not civilised)."

A load of wood…a time-honoured bushman's means of providing support to a fellow countryman in need. Clearly the gift was appreciated by the recipient, and by her spouse Ted Bottrell. It may have been that the Withers were supporting another Chiltern Valley family with a soldier overseas. On the other hand, they might simply have seen the gift of the firewood as their Christian duty to help another in need.

Number 1146 Lance Corporal Edmund Bottrell was an interesting character in his own right. A miner at Chiltern Valley, he had enlisted in the AIF at Wangaratta on the 7th of March 1916. Of dark complexion with dark hair, he was five feet six inches in height and weighed 136 pounds. Unlike Harry, Bottrell was a married man, and at the time of his enlistment he and his wife Vera had two children a daughter, Dorothy, and a son Edmund.

Allocated to the infantry, Bottrell was posted to the 37th Battalion and he completed his initial training in Melbourne. On the 3rd of June 1916, he embarked on the troopship *HMAT Persic,* bound for England. Three days later as the *Persic* made its way across the Great Australian Bight, Bottrell decided to send his wife a letter. He addressed the letter to "Mrs V. Bottrell, Chiltern Valley, Victoria". However, he did not post the letter in the normal way. Instead, he sealed it in a bottle and threw the bottle overboard. Fast forward thirty-one years. On April the 23rd 1947, the bottle, with letter still inside, was found on a beach around seventy miles from Albany, Western Australia. The letter was in good condition and clearly legible. The finder sent the letter on to the Post Mistress at Chiltern Valley, who in turn readdressed it to a Wangaratta address where Bottrell was then residing in a community hospital. [121]

Back to 1916, Bottrell arrived in England on the 25th of July, and like Harry undertook his training on Salisbury Plains. On the 22nd of November he was deployed to France where he undertook the additional training course at Étaples. There things started to go badly wrong for him. On the 2nd of December he was admitted to hospital with a case of the mumps. His condition deteriorated, and it was not until the 2nd of February 1917 that he finally returned to his unit. In May 1917 he was again back in hospital this time with tuberculosis. He was subsequently evacuated to hospital in England from where he wrote his letter to Mrs Withers.

That was effectively the end of Bottrell's army career. On the 27th of September 1917 he was returned to Australia, and on the 24th of December,

---

[121] https://trove.nla.gov.au/newspaper/article/69594366?searchTerm=&searchLimits=l-publictag=WWI+letter+in+a+bottle quoting the Wodonga and Towong Sentinel (Vic: 1885 – 1954) Friday 6 June 1947 page 3.

discharged from the AIF as medically unfit. He died in 1956.[122]

Willie Grail referred to in Bottrell's letter was another Chiltern Valley man, obviously known to the Withers family. No 6629 Private William Grail, aged 18 years, enlisted in the AIF on the 13th of May 1916, and was allocated to the 7th Battalion. After basic training he embarked for England in April 1917, and deployed to France in October 1917, his deployment having been delayed through illness. On the 6th of July 1918, at the Battle of Hamel, he was severely wounded in action. As a result of his wounds, he did not return to active duty and after recovering he was repatriated to Australia in 1919.[123]

When Margaret and William Withers had delivered the load of firewood to Vera Bottrell, they had already received news of Jack Mitchell's death. Their daughter, Margaret Stewart, had assumed the duties of guardian for Jack's daughter, Ruth, so along with the grief at his death came even greater responsibilities for the child. No doubt the Chiltern Valley Methodist congregation would have offered their support to the Withers family. Jack himself had ensured Margaret and William were receiving some monetary support via an allotment from his pay, and this was increased by the Commonwealth after his death, from four shillings per fortnight to thirty shillings per fortnight. The child herself received an allotment of twenty shillings per fortnight from July 1917. Jack's mother was not forgotten either. She received an allotment of two pounds a fortnight. However, it seems she had few responsibilities regarding her grandchild, or of Jack's final arrangements.

Jack had named Margaret's husband John Stewart as his executor, and the child Ruth as his sole beneficiary. There were insurance policies to be administered, requiring the family to provide proof of death to the insurance company. All of these requirements continued on, long after the war ended and included the receipt of Jack's medals, which were bequeathed to Ruth, and the inscription for his cross marking his grave to be settled. Along with these sad and unpleasant tasks their daily tasks of work, and keeping the

---

[122] https://recordsearch.naa.gov.au/SearchNRetrieve/Interface/ViewImage.aspx?B=3100413
[123] https://recordsearch.naa.gov.au/SearchNRetrieve/Interface/ViewImage.aspx?B=4669655

home, had to continue. These were the sad duties shared with thousands of other Australian families who had lost a loved one during the war.

As 1917 drew to its painful close, the singular hope of the majority of people was that the fighting would cease, and their men and women could return home.

It was a vain hope.

Chapter 21

January 1918

AS THE NEW YEAR DAWNED, Harry was still attached to the tunnelling company. Technically he was out of the line, but he was still within the range of the German artillery, and battle casualties caused by German shells were the focus for his diary:

> "Jan 1st Fritz shelling Plug St Wood also railway line and Dead Horse Corner. Shell exploded on top of dugout and blew it in. One Sergeant died from concussion several other men wounded. 2nd did not leave the Catacombs in morning Band came up and played outside the catacombs. About nine o'clock commenced shelling Messines Ridge, Plug St Wood also Dead Horse Corner. 3rd everything quiet during morning in afternoon a number of Fritz planes were flying very high over our billet. Shortly after the planes left and were out of sight several lots of shrapnel burst near the catacombs also near the soup kitchen wounding three men. 4th very quiet all day till evening the Fritz commenced sending over shrapnel ones 18 pounders and 9.5 shelling very rapidly. Fritz also shelled duckboards near St Eives trench. The snow commenced to thaw today. The ground has been covered with snow since Xmas and the ice as not melted on the shell holes. Some of the men were skating. We also had to break the ice to wash."

This artillery incident Harry observed is not mentioned in the 24th

Battalion war diary, so it must be assumed the incident involved a nearby battalion. However, in spite of German aircraft and artillery fire Harry remained safe in his underground lair. He seems to have enjoyed the work, was well fed and had sufficient time off for a decent rest.

> *"Pea soup for dinner stew for tea. 8th snow falling heavy all day. 9th Nothing of importance to mention. 10th very quiet on our front during morning our guns continued all day. In evening whilst three Engineers and two of my mates were bailing water from new shaft Fritz shelling very heavy. 11th Changed shift from afternoon to day shift had ride back from work on light railway."*

Harry's entry regarding his activities on the 11th of January was to be his last regarding his attachment with the tunnelling company. On the 12th of January 1918 he and the remainder of the work party returned to the Battalion.

The Battalion war diary is very precise in recording the return of the tunnelling work party:

> *"...At 10 am the 2 officers and 100 O/Ranks who had previously been attached to 184th TUNNELLING COY for duty in the forward area re-joined their companies and made preparations for the move..."*[124]

The move to which the war diary refers, took place that afternoon, and it was predictable...back to the front line.

Harry and his tunnelling mates hardly had time to settle back into the Battalion routine, for that same day, the Battalion moved back to the front to relieve the 28th Battalion. The initial part of the Battalion's move to the front was undertaken by train. The British had constructed a light rail system that criss-crossed the area behind the lines. This system transported ammunition, supplies and men...going forward to fight, and then on the return journey it evacuated wounded to the rear for treatment. The trains were pulled by either steam locomotives such as the Baldwin Class 10-12-D locomotive, or by petrol driven motor engines, such as the 40 horse-power Simplex petrol locomotive. It is likely that the train used to ferry the 24th Battalion to its

---

[124] https://www.awm.gov.au/collection/C1342342?image=4

next front line assignment was pulled by one of the latter engines, as in 1917 these locomotives were operating in the Ypres area. These trains did not run to carriages, but instead small low sided trucks served to carry goods, and men. [125] However, in spite of an obvious lack of comforts, many a soldier would have stated that the train "beat the hell out of walking".

Harry was involved in all of the busy activity that accompanied the move and the Battalion's first day in its new position. The Battalion's war diary entries, from the 12th through to the 16th of January, provide an insight into what Harry's life in the trenches would have been like. First the move to the 28th Battalion's location and the procedure followed to swap the two units over:

> "...The two companies A and C for the front line entrained at CONNAUGHT SIDING and at 4 pm the remaining two companies with HQ entrained at the same place...[126]
>
> ...The guides from 28th Battalion were waiting and each platoon was guided into its position without a casualty. Our front line which consisted of posts numbering from 1 to 9 (right to left). These were partially linked up by a revetted trench. No 1 Post was located at V11 d 50.65 and No9 Post at V11 l 1.5 A Company occupied the front line from No 1 Post to No 4 Post (inclusive) and C Company No 5 Post to No 9 Post (inclusive) also Listening Post at V11 l 25-5-50. Our Bn front extended from RIVER DOUVE (exclusive) North to U 11 d 65-00, South B Company were in support in USEFUL LANE and D Company in reserve at SUSIDARY Line near BHQ."[127]

The combination of letters and numbers used in the diary entries to describe a location are map grid numbers. The procedure followed by the 28th and 24th Battalions in swapping places is known as a "Relief In Place". When in contact with the enemy it is a particularly dangerous manoeuvre. The inward and outward movement of the relieving troops must be carefully

---

[125] Ed. Sir John Hammerton, The Great War, I Was There, Volume Two, London Amalgamated Press Limited, pp 1236-1237
[126] https://www.awm.gov.au/collection/C1342342?image=4
[127] Op. cit. also https://www.awm.gov.au/collection/C1342342?image=5

managed, so that the position is not suddenly undermanned and therefore weakened. Communication between both battalion's headquarters is vital, and an understanding reached as to what stage of the relief control of the position passes from the battalion being relieved to the incoming unit. Of particular concern is the need to ensure the enemy does not become aware that a relief in place is taking place, as an attack timed to coincide with the changeover would be likely to succeed. However, in January 1918, the 24th Battalion's relief was conducted without any problems and no casualties were sustained. The war diary records:

> *"...We had completed the relief by 7 pm and a wire to that effect sent to Brigade. The weather was frosty and the ground hard and the men fairly comfortable..."* [128]

Comfort would have been a relative thing...comfortable as compared to a trench full of water and mud or being attacked by an active enemy. However, on the Western Front these discomforts were never far away.

Harry does not reveal which Company he belonged to. At Lark Hill he was allocated to D Company, but there is no reason to assume he was allocated to that company when he arrived at the Battalion. However, regardless as to where he was actually located during this time in the line, he would have been busy. Patrolling began as soon as the relief in place was completed, and it may be assumed that once again Harry would have been required to do his share of this dangerous work. The patrol sent out by the Battalion on the 12th and 13th of January found no sign of the enemy, but this did not mean the Battalion could relax its vigilance. Maintaining the ascendency in no-man's-land was vital, as it protected the Battalion's defensive position and kept open the option for future offensive action.

The 14th of January was also conspicuous for a moment of high drama, as the Battalion war diary records:

> *"...6.40am a hostile patrol of about five men approached our No 2 post and when challenged threw 2 bombs and made off. Our rifle fire was without result and the patrol escaped..."* [129]

---

[128] https://www.awm.gov.au/collection/C1342342?image=5
[129] https://www.awm.gov.au/collection/C1342342?image=7

While the keeper of the war diary would have been shocked at the thought, it is possible, the Battalion's riflemen did not aim to kill the German soldiers in this patrol. By 1918, many men on both sides were heartily sick of the war and killing. As a result, the Australians may have just tried to frighten the German patrol away. If this was their purpose, they succeeded.

In addition to the work of carrying rations and water, other tasks had to be carried out. Patrolling was of particular importance and a series of patrols ventured out from the Battalion's position to ensure Australian dominance of no-man's-land. In conjunction with this work, the trench system had to be repaired and improved and the defensive wire obstacles to the Battalion's front strengthened. The trench improvements and wire obstacle work involved more work parties, first to carry the required stores, such as sandbags, sheets of corrugated iron, and rolls of barbed wire, from the rear to the front.

On the 15th of January a heavy snow fall covered the battlefield. Not so thick that it prevented the Battalion's work, or the delivery of hot meals and the water for foot washing, but it increased the discomfort of living in the trenches. Then on the 16th the snow was followed by another natural event:

> " *heavy rains, a complete collapse of the trench system has taken place…* "[130]

Once again, the ground in no-man's-land turned to marsh making patrolling difficult. Roads and lane ways flooded, the River Douve burst its banks changing from a peaceful stream to a raging torrent. In a further effort to avoid casualties from Trench Foot, fifty-eight pairs of gum boots were issued, certainly insufficient to cater for all the men, but perhaps they were provided to those engaged in repairing the trench system. In spite of the rain and flooding, the Battalion conducted an internal relief in place, replacing the two forward companies, A and C, with C and D companies who hitherto had been occupying depth positions. The weather possibly helped keep the enemy at bay during this activity as it was observed they were suffering in the wet conditions also.

---

[130] https://www.awm.gov.au/collection/C1342342?image=8

By the 17th it was too wet to continue patrolling. The bottom of the trenches held around two feet of mud and water. Foot washing was no longer possible and almost immediately twelve cases of Trench Foot were diagnosed, and the sufferers evacuated. Mud and water had penetrated every dugout and the men found sleep almost impossible. On the 18th, fifteen more cases of Trench Foot were evacuated, but in a piece of good news, a new cook house had been established closer to the forward lines.

On the 22nd of January the Battalion was relieved and returned to the tunnels below Hill 63, not to tunnel, but to rest in relative comfort and safety. Indeed, after life in the trenches the Catacombs must have been pure luxury for all those who were billeted there. In February 1918 Lt Col A.R.L. Wiltshire, CMG, DSO, MC of the 22nd Battalion A.I.F. wrote of the tunnel system in glowing terms, recalling wonderful tunnels and drives, electric light, and bunks for the men to sleep on. One of Wiltshire's men remarked to him that the facility was not unlike conditions on a troopship and all the Catacombs lacked was a propeller. [131]

Wiltshire would have received no argument from Harry, one gains the impression he would have preferred to stay with the tunnelling company for the duration. However, that was not to be, but at least he was able to enjoy the fruits of his underground labour. Perhaps he was able to guide other members of the Battalion around the tunnels.

The Battalion was more comfortable in its underground surround, but it was not immune from the usual rounds of work parties, cleaning and repairs to weapons and equipment. These activities continued until the 30th of January when finally, the Battalion was moved further back to the village of Lottinghen. They travelled by train, arriving in the village on the 31st of the month. The war diary describes Lottinghen as:

> "...a scattered village with a population of 2000 inhabitants. The people are mostly engaged in farming pursuits except for one large cement works which is now manufacturing concrete pipes for the British Army..." [132]

---

[131] http://acms.sl.nsw.gov.au/_transcript/2012/D14087/a3370.htm
[132] https://www.awm.gov.au/collection/C1342342?image=16

It had been a particularly tiring month for Harry and his mates, and Lottinghen seemed to be a place they could rest and recuperate.

When a battalion came out of the line for a rest, a similar procedure was followed. Most times, the battalion would leave the line under the cover of darkness, to march several kilometres toward the rear, before bivouacking at some prearranged location. The men were invariably weary, dirty (in the winter mud encrusted) and unkempt. Most times there would be a hot meal waiting for them, and after finishing their meal, most would simply lie down and sleep. The following day they would rest, then on the following days bathing facilities would be made available, clean clothing issued, and any shortages in equipment addressed. A few short days later that same dishevelled battalion that had wearily left the line, were well clothed, clean, and could turn out on parade as smart as any battalion in peacetime.

Chapter 22

Food and other Housekeeping Issues

HOT FOOD, A BATH, CLEAN clothing and a rest, after any time in the line must have been very welcome. However, as a front line soldier, Harry was probably like most of his ilk, and regarded all those who lived and worked closer to the rear area than the forward trenches, with deep suspicion and contempt. This attitude was particularly directed at the huge logistics organization that existed behind the lines with the single purpose of feeding and supplying the fighting organizations at the front.

Harry, it seems, had little interest in logistics. The closest he came to mentioning the topic was when the lateness of mail annoyed him, and when he complained in his letters about the food. However, whilst he may not have enjoyed the front line cuisine, he was probably better fed while he was with the 24th Battalion, than when he was detached for duty with the British tunnelling company. His diary entry of the 28th of December 1917 suggests food with the British unit was pretty scarce:

"*...The days rations four men to a loaf one small piece of bacon per man*".

Perhaps though, it was the monotony of the diet that really annoyed him. In another entry he recorded:

"*During previous days 2 1/2 strips of bacon for breakfast, pea soup for dinner, and stew for tea.*"

In spite of Harry's grousing, food was almost as important as ammunition on the Western Front. Indeed, tremendous effort was being expended by both sides of the conflict, in an effort to feed their front line troops.

Certainly, General Monash gave these two commodities equal significance stating:

> "...the big question is, of course, the food and ammunition supply, the former term covering meat, bread, groceries, hay, straw, oats, wood, coal, paraffin and candles, the latter comprising cartridges, shells, shrapnel, bombs, grenades, flares, and rockets. It takes a couple of thousand men and horses with hundreds of wagons, and 118 huge motor lorries, to supply the daily wants of my population of 20,000.
>
> With reference to food we also have to see that all the men in the front lines regularly get hot food - coffee, oxo, porridge, stews."[133]

The supply of food as a commodity was a major issue for the logistic systems for both sides, as the respective naval blockades made the import of foodstuffs by sea a dangerous undertaking. By 1918 Britain was supplying thirty million kilos of meat to the Western Front each month. The soldiers' daily rations were meant to include fresh or frozen meat, but often tinned bully beef was the main source of the meat consumed. Vegetables were scarce and dried barley and lentils were often used in the absence of fresh vegetables.

In contrast, German troops were somewhat worse off than their enemies. They were short of butter, margarine, cooking fat, sugar, potatoes, coffee, tea, fruit and meat, even though within the German nation their army was the number one priority with regard to food distribution. In 1917 German soldiers were existing on a fraction of the calories available to their enemies. By 1918 this situation was barely maintainable. In one report on food shortages at the front General Sixt von Armin, the commander of the German 4th Army stated:

> "All troops were unanimous in their request for increased supplies of bread, rusks, sausage, tinned sausages, tinned fat,

---

[133] https://spartacus-educational.com/FWWtrenchfood.htm

bacon, tinned and smoked meat, and tobacco, in addition. There was also urgent need for solidified alcohol for the preparation of hot meals.

In various quarters, the necessity for a plentiful supply of liquid refreshments of all kinds, such as coffee, tea, cocoa, mineral waters, etc., is emphasized still more. On the other hand, the supply of salt herrings, which increase the thirst, was found to be, as a general rule, very undesirable. There is no necessity for an issue of alcoholic drink in warm and dry weather." [134]

In AIF front line kitchens, the meat, in whatever form it arrived at the kitchen, was almost invariably turned into a stew of one kind or another. One recipe used to create a version of Irish Stew was as follows:

*"**Ingredients**: meat, potatoes, onions, pepper, salt.*

***Method**: peel and wash and slice the potatoes, peal, clean and cut up the onions, cut the meat into small pieces. Place a little water in the pot and a layer of potatoes at the bottom, then a layer of meat and onions, season with salt and pepper. Add further layer of meat, potatoes and onions, potatoes should form the final layer. Barely cover the layers with water, stew gently for two hours."* [135]

Another staple meal was soup, often prepared in a fashion similar to the following:

*"**Ingredients**: 1 portion of lentils, ½ portion of oatmeal, 1 portion of mashed potato, 1 portion in all of chopped onion, carrot, turnip, salt and pepper.*

***Method**: Soak lentils overnight then drain. Place lentils in the pot and cover with water and cook for one hour. Add the vegetables and cook for a further half an hour, season with salt and pepper. Sprinkle with oatmeal and add mashed potato. Stir frequently, gently simmer until lentils are soft."* [136]

---

[134] https://spartacus-educational.com/FWWtrenchfood.htm
[135] John Hartly, Bully Beef & Biscuits: Food in the Great War, Pen and Sword Military 2015.
[136] Op. cit.

At times the troops received a ration of bread, however on many occasions the bread was replaced by army biscuits. This item in the rations was rarely popular as it was so hard that it often had to be soaked in water before it could be eaten.

The effort required in moving food and ammunition to the front was immense. When Monash provided his homily on the importance of logistics, he was talking of supplying an army. However, at battalion level, the issue of logistics was equally as important, but addressed by a much smaller number of men.

Within each AIF battalion the man responsible for logistics was the quartermaster, or QM. It was he, who received the battalion's allocation of ammunition, food, clothing, and so on, from the logistic officials in the rear. From that allocation, it was his responsibility to ensure that every man in the battalion received his full entitlement.

Early in the conflict, the static nature of trench warfare presented the QM with some difficult choices when planning and implementing food preparation and distribution. Food caches had to be established in secure areas, often necessitating the selection of a site some distance from the front. Kitchen or cooking sites were ideally positioned out of range of enemy artillery.

Aside from a few clerks, and storemen, the QM commanded a number of cooks. The cooks were hard-working fellows, who faced the unenviable task of preparing a variety of meals from the often meagre rations that were allocated to the battalion. Sometimes their efforts earned the praise of their clients, on other occasions their ire, and certainly early in the war, some cooks were unskilled in the practical aspects of their trade. The old army joke of "Who called the cook a bastard?" and the standard response of "Who called the bastard a cook?" must have had its genesis around that time. However, later in the war, cooks were well trained and were able to provide satisfying bulk meals often under very trying conditions.

Cooking was generally carried out in large vats, or cauldrons, which were heated over open fires. The QM had to be extremely careful in siting the battalion food cache and kitchen.

Food caches and kitchen areas that were sited too far to the rear increased the difficulty of delivering the food safely and in an edible condition. On the other hand, food caches and kitchens sited too close to the forward area ran the risk of being destroyed by the enemy. Smoke produced by cooking fires, and the movement of transport wagons, attracted the attention of enemy artillery observers and hostile aircraft. Once cooked, the food would be loaded into buckets, or rectangular metal cartons referred to as "dixies", for carriage to the front.

The initial part of the food's journey from the kitchen to the front line, was generally performed by a battalion's Transport Section. The Transport Section consisted of a number of drivers, several teams of horses and a variety of horse drawn wagons. In addition to food, the section also moved other stores and equipment required by the battalion. Wherever possible the section would deliver the required commodities as close as possible to the line. Enemy action, and or weather conditions often limited the distance horse drawn vehicles could achieve.

From wherever the transport section could deliver the requirement the final part of the journey to the forward trenches was always achieved by work parties from the battalion, who were tasked to carry the food or other requirements to the forward positions.

Harry may not have believed it, but by 1918 the preparation and distribution of food to the front line had been improved and refined. Along with these tangible improvements, came a realisation by many senior officers, of the importance of feeding their men properly. For example, on taking command of the 24th Battalion, Lieutenant Colonel James had decreed that henceforth every man should receive at least one hot meal a day.[137] This laudable ambition was more easily said than it was to achieve, and it was not implemented without great effort on the part of the QM and his staff. A measure of their success and of the effort involved in meeting the CO's demand is recorded in the Battalion's war diary entry for the 13th of January 1918:

> "Breakfast 7am, Dinner 12 noon, Tea 5pm, Supper (soup

---

[137] https://www.awm.gov.au/collection/C1342738?image=21

and tea) 11pm. These meals were carried forward in large food containers on the men's backs"[138]

Interestingly, the same diary entry overlooked the effort required to cook and deliver the meals to the point where it could be carried "on the men's backs". However, the effort required by those men detailed to carry the rations forward was indeed worthy of note. The cooked food was carried in specially designed containers as described by the QM of the 24th Battalion in the Battalion's war diary entry in August 1918:

"The container was designed to solve the problem of man transport of hot food. It consists of two vessels one inside the other. The outer one is somewhat like a flattened milk can, one side being shaped to fit comfortably on a man's back. It is supported by straps passing round the body. Inside this is a smaller vessel with a capacity of about 4 and a half gallons. The space between the two is packed with asbestos for insulation purposes.

These containers have certain disadvantages. When filled with tea or stew, a container weighs about 65 lbs. This imposes a great strain on a man carrying it, say, a mile under the conditions usually obtaining in the fighting zone. To carry it a longer distance would be beyond the powers of an average man. Besides this, when the container has once been opened any stew remaining in it will sour if the container is again closed up. This problem of a suitable vessel for carrying hot meals a long distance to the front is one not easy of solution. Perhaps the converted petrol tin described by the QM has solved it; but the petrol tin has not so far been tried under server conditions obtaining in winter." [139]

Asbestos and petrol tins to carry food! It all sounds unsafe and unsanitary to modern ears, but this was the way things were on the Western Front.

Later in the war, as the Australian infantry became more mobile, so too,

---

[138] https://www.awm.gov.au/collection/C1342342?image=6
[139] https://www.awm.gov.au/collection/C1342738?image=20

of necessity did their supporting supply system. Again, the QM of the 24th Battalion observed:

> "The forces in support and reserve to the fighting line were moving constantly forward, while fresh divisions were passing through them during the day, making their way up to the front line to carry on the fight.
>
> All these troops were in artillery formation, covering the whole country within view. One could not help thinking of a disturbed nest of ants – with this difference, that the ants, in this case platoons in file, moved in an orderly manner and all in one direction".[140]

The immediate issue for every QM in that great mass of moving formations, was to keep track of their own unit and ensure the unit supplies got to them. This was not an easy task for as the QM of the 24th Battalion noted:

> "Even a Battalion is difficult to find in a countryside swarming with troops".[141]

By 1918 getting food up to the troops was made a little easier by the introduction of mobile kitchens, or cookers. These items were basically a wood powered stove, mounted on a two-wheeled cart axle. It could be pulled either by horse or motor vehicle, to a position close to the forward lines where the food could be prepared. The risks for those who prepared and transported the food remained the same and both cooks and transport drivers were often working under artillery fire, or attack from aircraft. Perhaps if Harry and his mates had been shown the nature of the supply system, and the way their food was prepared and delivered to them, they may have shown greater appreciation for what they received, and of the people who worked so hard to ensure they got it.

There were other aspects of trench life housekeeping of which the troops had a greater understanding. Harry had already suffered one of the results of the often, filthy living conditions...Trench Fever. There were other diseases that stalked the trenches on both sides of the line, but fortunately Harry did

---

[140] https://www.awm.gov.au/collection/C1342738?image=23
[141] Op. cit.

not fall victim to these. Trench Foot was one of these insidious ailments. The condition was caused by prolonged exposure of the feet to damp and unsanitary conditions. The symptoms of Trench Foot were easy enough to detect. The feet became numb and could either turn red or blue in colour. There was also a decaying odour as the tissue of the feet began to die. As the condition worsened the feet began to swell, then blisters and open sores developed which in turn led to ulcerations. Untreated, gangrene could develop, a condition which often required amputation of the feet.

As far as was possible, the Medical Corps, and the officers of every Australian unit, endeavoured to combat Trench Foot infections among the men. It was a disease that could be avoided by personal hygiene, but this was not always possible when the men were in the line. Additional effort was required and in January 1918 while the 24th Battalion was in the line a strenuous program was implemented to combat the disease. The practise of officers and NCOs conducting regular foot inspections was augmented by a program of foot washing. The war diary mentions:

> *"...six cans of hot water were sent forward at 2pm and all men in the line had their feet washed in troughs and were issued with a pair of clean dry sox each...* [142]
>
> *...The feet were also treated with talc powder. The wet sox were collected and sent back to the drying sheds".* [143]

The next day the hot meals and more hot water were again delivered to the forward line with the added note in the war diary:

> *"...fresh sox obtained from the drying sheds at HYDE PARK CORNER..."* [144]

Whilst the socks were apparently "dry" no mention is made as to whether or not they had been cleaned...one can only hope. However, every small comfort Harry and his mates received, every bullet they fired at the enemy, every mouthful of food that sustained them, came at the effort, and sometimes the cost of those employed in the logistic system.

---

[142] https://www.awm.gov.au/collection/C1342342?image=6
[143] Op. cit.
[144] https://www.awm.gov.au/collection/C1342342?image=6

Chapter 23

February 1918

THE BATTALION WAS ENJOYING A well-earned rest in the French village of Lottinghen. Harry provides his own observation of Lottinghen in a card to his mother without actually naming the village. The omission of the village name from the postcard was possibly because of censorship; however he is not so constrained in his diary where in his usual brief style he indicates the Battalion had moved to the village:

"Left Messines and went to Lottinghen for six weeks."

However, in the postcard he at least provides some further detail:

"France
3/2/18

Dear Mother

I received the parcel you and Dad sent yesterday. No doubt I should have received it sooner only for being on fatigue work for about six weeks before going in the line. We were in the line for eight days. The French are busy with their ploughing they are about a hundred years behind the times working on the land. Most of the people are wealthy in the village where we are staying at for a spell. This village has never been visited by Australian troops. I got a great surprise to hear of such a wet season and such awful floods. I trust you have had a good harvest. I will drop the girls a line again. I expect to go on leave to Scotland any day. I will close with love and best wishes to all from your fond son Prte H.F. Withers"

This postcard suggests that Harry is more than a little jaded, particularly at the delay that occurred in the delivery of the parcel his parents sent. He seems to blame the delay on the time he was attached to the tunnelling company. Indeed, the enthusiasm he had previously displayed for the tunnelling work seems to have evaporated, and he now refers to that period of time as "fatigue work". In addition, there is perhaps a little sarcasm creeping into his observations of the "wealthy" villagers and the French farming methods. It is also clear he is longing for his leave.

As Harry alluded to in the postcard, the reason for the Battalion being at Lottinghen is "for a spell". However, as with other periods when the Battalion was out of the line, the time spent at Lottinghen, did not provide a complete break from training. Only leave taken in the United Kingdom could provide that luxury, and UK leave for Harry was still over a month away.

The Battalion had planned a comprehensive program for the month of February which included physical exercise, rifle shooting, specialist raining, sport and some short leave.

On the 1st of February, day one of the Lottinghen "holiday", the Battalion undertook a six-mile route march. Dress for the march was "Drill Order" with rifles, in other words uniform, web belt and rifle. This march would have been conducted as more of a flag waving exercise, to show other troops in the area that the 24th Battalion was in residence and that even though they had recently come out of the line, they were up and about. In addition to the route march, a complete kit check was conducted. The kit check enabled the compilation of a comprehensive list of all shortages and unserviceable items, that had been lost or broken during their last stint in the line. Over the following weeks the supply system, otherwise known as the "Q" system would replace the missing and damaged items. The next day commenced with a period of close order drill…marching and counter marching on the parade ground. The rest of the day was then devoted to an inter-company football competition. The 24th Battalion was a Victorian unit, so the code of football played was Australian Rules. There was also a pleasant surprise in store for all ranks. Day leave was approved for visits to the nearby seaside town of Boulogne. Leave groups had to comprise of one officer and 25 other ranks. For the remainder of the Battalion's stay at Lottinghen, groups of this size made the journey to Boulogne for a day at the beach.

Boulogne was much more than a tourist destination for resting Australian soldiers. As the war progressed the area had developed into a major supply facility, storing food, ammunition, weapons and equipment. Boulogne was also the site of several major Allied hospitals, however, it also provided a relatively stress-free environment for soldiers on short leave.

During its stay in Lottinghen the Battalion was billeted in vacant buildings, and possibly the homes of some French people with spare rooms. The CO was keen that these billets were kept neat and clean and on the 3rd of February he conducted an inspection of the dwellings. These inspections were repeated at various times during the Battalion's stay, ensuring standards were maintained. The 3rd was a Sunday and the Battalion conducted two separate church parades, one for the Protestants which no doubt Harry attended, and the second for the Roman Catholics. Another achievement for the day was the establishment of a reading and writing room at the local school. Perhaps Harry used that room to write the postcard dated the 3rd, to his mother.

On the 4th of February, the Battalion began a program of range practises, to ensure the soldiers maintained their shooting skills. This, like the short leave program, was a rolling program that continued for the duration of the Battalion's stay. Other programs that commenced and continued in the same fashion were physical training, and drill.

The Battalion also began to demonstrate its spirit, or élan to the rest of 6th Brigade. The Brigade had instigated an inter-battalion football competition (Aussie rules) and the competition was taken very seriously. At the 24th Battalion, inter-company football matches were conducted, and Battalion selectors chose the best players from this competition for the Battalion's team. The first game in the Brigade competition occurred on the 15th of the month against the 21st Battalion. The game was played at the nearby village of Harlettes, and the 24th Battalion marched there, with its band playing, and one assumes flags flying, ready for the fray. It was a close game but eventually the 24th Battalion won and returned to Lottinghen triumphant. In the overall Brigade football competition, the Battalion team won its way into the grand final where it met the 22nd Battalion. Once again, the Battalion with its band playing, marched to the place of competition, this time at the village of Selles. In a hard-fought game, the 24th Battalion were too good and ran away with the win, 6 goals 14 behinds to 2 goals 5 behinds.

Prior to the war Harry had been a keen footballer, but it is unclear if he took part in any of the Battalion teams. At the ripe old age of 33, he was one of the older soldiers in the Battalion, so perhaps he limited himself to a supporting role. He may also have recalled his last recorded game back in 1913, when a knock to the head brought on a relapse of the condition caused by the fall from his horse, and judged it was too much of a risk to take to play for the Battalion.

Aside from football, the Battalion's companies and platoons competed against each other in all forms of the training program. On the 24th of February the best platoon in each company then competed for the title of "Champion Platoon in the Battalion" decided at the assault course. A platoon team consisted of one officer four NCOs and 24 men, although one of the teams in the competition was led by a sergeant.

Speed through the course was important, but so was leadership and control. The platoon members had to help each other through the obstacles, the officer and NCOs controlling and leading their men. However, skill-at-arms was the key point the judges watched for. It was no use being the fastest through the course if at the end the soldiers could not shoot accurately or maintain their weapons.

An assault course was then, and is now, generally made up of a series of obstacles, some of which consisted of barbed wire, others of wood or masonry, with the odd pit full of water thrown in for good measure. The obstacles would be spaced far enough apart so that the soldiers moving through the course would be required to run between the impediments, in order to keep a competitive time. At various stages through the course a weapon handling skill would be tested. The 24th Battalion's assault course included, a bayonet fighting section, a rifle range, and a Lewis Gun range.

The bayonet fighting section was probably a series of straw filled dummies which the soldiers had to attack. Judges apparently watched this section of the course and awarded points for the manner in which the dummies were attacked and the way the soldiers handled their bayonets.

The rifle range section was possibly sited toward the end of the assault course. By the time the soldier arrived at this section of the course, they would be breathing heavily from their work negotiating the other sections of the course. In this condition shooting accurately becomes difficult. Unless breathing is controlled the rifle tends to wobble around, and accuracy may be lost. Each man would be required to fire a number of rounds at a target and points awarded for each hit.

The Lewis Gun section of the course was in all likelihood the last stand on the course. The soldiers may not have been required to fire the weapon, and instead would have been tested on stripping and assembling the weapon. A number of weapons were probably placed in a line and the first soldiers to the stand would have been required to strip the weapon. The next men would be required to reassemble the gun and those following to strip the weapon and so on. The judges would check to see that the stripping was sequential and that the weapon would work once it had been reassembled. Those stripping the weapon could make the job of those reassembling easier by laying the parts out in order.

The Battalion war diary recorded the competition in some detail:

"In the afternoon the champion platoon for each company met in competition on the assault course to decide the Battalions Platoon Championship. The contest proved most interesting and instructive and demonstrated the effectiveness of all arms when well used. No 13 Platoon D Company won easily and well merited their victory. C Company were second and complimented by the judges for good bayonet work and control. The following are the detailed scores:

	Rifle	*Bayonet*	*L.G. (Lewis Gun)*	*Total*
D Coy 13 Platoon	*127*	*75*	*122*	*324*
(Lt A Stuart)				
C Coy 10 Platoon	*103*	*100*	*41*	*244*
(Lt R Irving)				

A Coy 2 Platoon (Sgt A.C Westmeat)	99	54	76	229
B Coy 8 Platoon (Lt R King)	72	73	59	204 " [145]

As the month drew to a close the military aspects of the program increased, and specialist training such as gas and first aid training were introduced. By month's end the Battalion had achieved a rest and was once again nearing readiness for another stint in the line.

The Battalion ended the month with a visit to the Brigade bath unit and several concerts which were apparently well received. Harry, however, makes no mention of any of these activities in his letters, and it would appear that he is once again suffering from the blues. A real leave would provide a degree of cure, but that was still two weeks away.

---

[145] https://www.awm.gov.au/collection/C1342343?image=11

Chapter 24

March 1918

MARCH BEGAN WITH MORE BAD weather. The Battalion was still at Lottinghen so they were at least protected from the worst of the elements. Snow and heavy rain forced the postponement of several training activities and inter-company football matches.

By the 4th of March the weather had improved sufficiently for training to resume, but by the 5th, the rain had once again set in, and the platoons remained in their billets. The 5th also brought the news that the Battalion was once again to return to the forward area. The war diary recorded the general feelings as the Battalion prepared to leave:

> *"The rest was greatly appreciated by all ranks and full advantage was taken of the liberal hours to visit neighbouring villages. All the troops visited Boulogne at least once. Football was the chief form of recreation and keen interest was shown in the inter Platoon and inter Company matches and such..."*[146]

Harry must have been disappointed that his leave did not fall due before the Battalion went back in the line. However, it was what it was. On the 6th of March the Battalion boarded the light rail train at Lottinghen and took the slow journey back toward the fighting. The journey was broken at the town of Kortepyp where they camped the night. Then the following morning, after the issue of ammunition and steel helmets, they entrained at Connaught Siding continuing the journey forward, detraining at Hyde Park Corner.

---

[146] https://www.awm.gov.au/collection/C1342344?image=4

They were back in familiar territory, not far from the positions they held in January. The war diary records:

> "...The Battalion has taken over from the 34th Bn 3rd Div AIF the relief being completed by1030pm. Disposition A & B Coys in the front line and Wally Support, C Coy in close support at Gray Track and D Coy in reserve at Avenue Farm. The Bn holds the left of the Brigade sector opposite the ruins of Warneton with the River Douve on the left flank..."[147]

Back in the line, Harry probably wished for a quiet time, this was not to be either. Soon after the Battalion completed the relief in place, its position was shelled by German artillery. One man was killed and three wounded. On the 8th of the month another two men were killed and a further five wounded by artillery fire and the forward trenches damaged. From time to time the Australian artillery responded, shelling the German trenches and their artillery positions. The results of this fire were not known, but after several days of artillery duels the sector grew quieter.

Aside from artillery duels, for the whole of the period that the Battalion remained in the line, vigorous patrolling was once again its major focus. Day and night patrols ventured out into no-man's-land, but most found no sign of the enemy. It would be nice to think that with his leave so close, that Harry might have been spared patrol duties, but perhaps he would just have had to take his chances along with the rest. The 9th of February was a quieter day and Harry found time to write a letter to his parents:

> *"France*
> *9/3/18*
>
> *Dear Dad*
>
> *Just a line in reply to your most welcome letter which I received on Tuesday. I am pleased to know you were well at time of writing as it leaves me at present. The weather is very warm during the day though the nights are cool and of a morning there is very heavy dew on the ground. Most of the crops look very well and grass is a foot high. I am pleased to know you have received my letters and cards. I can hardly imagine you having such a*

---

[147] https://www.awm.gov.au/collection/C1342343?image=11

cool summer and that the grass is green in March. It is fine to think that Reggie is able to assist Wal with the ploughing. Rene mentioned of Wal and Jess living in the cottage. Are you putting the land under cultivation which you got from McGlesson. Has Wal got the young horse broken in yet the chestnut one. Fancy Frank Smith having such ill health he must have got a great knocking about over here and is Reggie home. I have met Jim O'Neil several times he looks well. Has Clive left Australia. George Ashley is over here though I have not yet met him. Edmond must have a bad time now that he is in such a bad state. I must say though I consider the French people are about a hundred years behind the time in many ways. One thing I must give them credit for and that is fine stock they breed both in cattle and horses and for the way they work on the land. Fancy stock dear in Australia I thought stock dear in Scotland young cattle selling at 15 and 16 pounds cattle that you would only give about 2 pound 10 before the war.

Dear Dad news is very scarce. How is Mrs Coates, Rene mentioned of her coming to the Valley. I suppose the Valley is very quiet now that many of the young men and women are married. Is McGleeson still teaching at school. I have not had any mail from any of the Maynards for a long while is Uncle better. I have heard that the Glen is going down fast that there are a lot of houses being removed every day. I will have to draw to a close kindly remember me to Mr Rowe and my friends at the Valley and Glen. I remain your ever fond son Prte H.F. Withers

Love to all. Write soon"

It is interesting to note his reference to cattle prices in Scotland. As he had yet to take his leave, it is assumed he had been communicating with his Scottish cousins, arranging the visit. Cattle prices would be of far greater interest to Harry than news of the fighting.

On the 13th there was considerable excitement when a German patrol was detected on the Australian wire. The enemy was engaged with small arms fire and several killed. On the 15th the high drama of the 13th was replaced by amusement when the Germans deployed a small paper balloon, to which was attached propaganda material. The balloon landed in the Battalion trench, and on examination, the propaganda material proved to be aimed at Irish troops, appealing to them to swap sides. Clearly the Germans were mistaken as to the nationality of the troops who opposed them.

On the 16th the Battalion was relieved again, this time by the 23rd Battalion. Harry had survived and proceeded toward England to commence his leave. His army record provides a brief statement to describe this momentous occasion for Harry:

"16/3/1918 Proceeded on English leave"

Leave was a rather vexed subject for the British and Commonwealth soldiers on the Western Front. Early in the war, leave was hard to get, and no longer than six days in length. The soldier going on leave had to allow around a day's travel to move from the front to England and another to return to his unit at the end of the leave. If, as was the case for Sergeant J. Reid of the Gordon Highlanders, home was in Scotland, more time had to be allowed to travel to and from home. Reid apparently had no notion that he was due for leave, and his battalion's means of allocating same, seemed to have been a fairly casual process. Advised that he was to take six days his journey home involved an initial road trip in a mail cart, a rail journey to Boulogne, a ship across the channel to Folkestone, another train to London, a taxi ride, and then a longer rail journey to Scotland. This complex journey used up a considerable amount of his six days leave. However, at least he was able to enjoy three days with his family before making the same journey in reverse, back to the fighting. [148]

As the war progressed leave became better managed, and members of the AIF who having spent the required time in the line, were entitled to 28 days' leave in the UK. This length of leave out of the line gave the soldier time to relax, and to live a more "normal" life. However, it also heightened an existing issue for the authorities; that of soldiers absenting themselves without leave, like young Tom Henderson. For soldiers on leave from France this amounted to illegally extending their leave. However, for others who were waiting to deploy, they simply broke the bounds of camp and did not return.

By September 1917 this problem had become so bad that the

---

[148] https://www.iwm.org.uk/history/voices-of-the-first-world-war-home-on-leave

commanding officer of UK Depots, Major General J.M. McCay announced that all future cases of AWL exceeding 14 days would be tried by court martial. This decree would have been a consideration in Tom Henderson's court martial decision. He also made an impassioned plea to the troops, in which he claimed those who went absent without leave were aiding the Germans, and that the absentees were betraying their mates in France.

McCay's appeal met with limited success, for the numbers of absentees was steadily increasing. In January through to May 1918, forty-four Australian soldiers had deserted, and one thousand four hundred and thirteen were listed as AWL[149]. Many of these men should never have been enlisted, for they were never likely to have accepted army discipline and training. Others, however, were men who having seen the horrors of the front, simply decided the way to survive the war lay in failing to return from leave. For numerous soldiers faced with an imminent return to the front, this must have been a consideration.

It was one thing to have the thought, another to get away with performing the deed. The AIF Military Police waged a constant battle against absentees. In October 1917 "The Times" reported a raid by AIF Provost on the Phoenix Hotel, a London public house of low repute. During the raid the publican was arrested and charged with four summonses alleging aiding and abetting deserters. In addition a number of Diggers whose leave passes were invalid were also apprehended, and eight others listed as deserters were also found and arrested.[150]

It is doubtful, however, that Harry harboured any such thoughts. Whilst he was often lonely, and disillusioned, he maintained a strong sense of duty to his country and to his battalion. He badly needed his leave, but at the end of it, he would return to the war.

Harry planned to spend most of his leave in Scotland, where he would visit his cousins, the Wests. To get there he would have followed a similar track to that outlined by Sergeant Reid…light rail, or perhaps a motor

---

[149] http://books.publishing.monash.edu/apps/bookworm/view/Australians+in+Britain%3A+The+Twentieth-Century+Experience/137/xhtml/chapter06.html
[150] Op. cit.

vehicle, from the battalion to Boulogne. There he would take a ship bound for Folkestone, then train to London. A taxi or perhaps a bus might have taken him from Victoria Station to Kings Cross. From there he probably caught the train to Perth, and from that city perhaps the Highland Railway to Edderton. The journey probably took him three days to accomplish.

After the destruction of France and Belgium the journey into the Scottish Highlands must have been a pleasant experience for Harry. This was then compounded by the warmth of the welcome he received. He was not alone in his enthusiasm for Scotland. Many Australian, Canadian and American soldiers chose Scotland as a leave destination over London and other English centres. For example, in October 1917, in a letter to her mother, Nursing Sister Olive Haynes clearly enjoyed her time in Scotland:

> "...Well here we are, up in Bonnie Scotland – and it is a bonnie place too – no place like it..."

Then again:

> "...Here I am back in London. We did love Scotland so. It is quite different from England – the people are so hospitable and homely, more like ourselves..."

Harry wrote enthusiastically of his Scottish experience to his sister Maggie:

"Edderton Scotland
24/3/18

Dear Maggie

Just a few lines to let you see you are not forgotten by me. I have been out walking with Matthew West having a look over the hills and the different properties. This morning Willie West and Mat and myself went to Church and I saw the old church where Grandmother McKenzie used to go. I went into Tain yesterday a town about seven miles and I went and saw a Mrs Ross a first cousin of Mums. There are different families of the Ross's. The people are very kind they cannot do enough for one. I got a great surprise to think I have so many relations. Wednesday is my day to go back to London. The next morning we have to leave for France I must say I do not like the idea of going back. Dear Maggie you must excuse me for not writing often, I should do so if it was not for the censoring of the letters one hardly knows what to write about as they are particular in censoring. I saw yesterday a house where Sir Walter Raleigh and Mary Queen of Scots used to live also Carnegie Estate. I have seen the old battlefields where the English and the Scots fought. I have seen many old history spots. Well Mag I have plenty of Lassies here as there is no other Australians here. There are a few other soldiers but they are Yanks and Canadians. The weather is dull and misty rain is falling. The train passes close to the door so I must hurry and get Mrs West paper. I have told you about all for this time so will ring off with love to Jack Mum and Dad and all at home. From your fond brother Prte H.F. Withers

Write soon Love to All"

It is interesting to note that in this letter Harry hints at an interest in the fairer sex. At the age of thirty-three he was by no means past such matters, however, so far as the AIF was concerned Harry was at the older end of the spectrum. Fifty-seven percent of the AIF were aged twenty-five years or younger, and eighty-one percent were unmarried. Unsurprisingly these statistics occasioned a lively interest in female company. This is not to suggest that all of this interest was immoral, some eight thousand Diggers met and married British women, and most returned with them to Australia. However, in the major cities of Britain, the well-paid Diggers were often easy targets for "good time girls" [151]. If Harry had ever shown an interest in this kind of a lady, he certainly would never have written home about it. Yet when his up-bringing and core values are taken into account, one must conclude he would never have involved himself in the bawdier type of male to female interaction.

For Harry, and many others in his demographic, social interaction with females was a well ordered, steady, process, with strict rules governing behaviour. Rarely would a well-bred young lady consent to an un-chaperoned date. The use of first names was considered an over familiarity, and only allowed after a respectable period, and then only with

---

[151] http://books.publishing.monash.edu/apps/bookworm/view/Australians+in+Britain%3A+The+Twentieth-Century+Experience/137/xhtml/chapter06.html

the lady's permission. If one reads between the lines of this particular letter of Harry's, one is brought to question… is his mention of "Lassies" a veiled indication to his sister, Maggie, that he had found a girl who interested him?

Further evidence that Harry had met a lassie that had sparked his interest is found in the next letter he sent to Maggie:

> "London
> 28/3/18
>
> Dear Maggie
>
> Just a line to let you know I arrived back from Scotland to London after twenty-five hours in the train. I have seen some of the most beautiful country anyone could ever wish to see. I had a lovely holiday in Scotland everybody is so kind no matter where I would go there would be some man or lassie who would invite me out to lunch. But if I get another chance I shall be up in dear old Scotland again. When I was getting Willie and Matthew West and Barbara each gave me halfcrowns I did not want to take it but they would have me take it. Mrs West and Miss Anderson were broken up when I left they stood waving till I got right out of sight so you can see the welcome I had. London is very quiet and the streets are dark at night as they are afraid of air raids. Well dear Mag I am leaving for Dover in the morning thence by boat (to) Calais France. Word as been going all around to get all men back to France and all leave is stopped for a month I shall be back on the old diet again tomorrow a small piece of bacon for breakfast stew for dinner and bread and jam for tea or else rice. I will close as it is bed time. From your loving brother Prte H.F. Withers"

It is assumed that the Barbara he mentioned is a cousin, or a person he considered a child, as this would excuse his use of her first name. Mrs West was his hostess, and she was clearly fond of him. But who is Miss Anderson and why would she be so upset at the departure of a man who, until a few short days ago was a stranger?

There is no mention of Miss Anderson in Harry's next letter from Scotland, this one sent to his mother:

> "Elderton Scotland

26/3/18
Mrs William Withers
Chiltern
Chiltern Valley Rd
Victoria
Australia

Dear Mother

Just a line to let you know I have not forgotten all at home. I write often but you know the letters are all censored and one hardly knows what to write about. I am leaving here for London tomorrow & the next day I leave Victoria Station by train for Dover. Thence by boat to Calais France, and then back to my battalion. We have been in the line near Messines I do not know if we are going in the same place or not. I will close with love to all from your fond son Prte H.F. Withers"

He could have told his mother about Miss Anderson, but apparently chose not to. One wonders if Maggie concluded her brother had a romantic interest, and whether she told their mother.

Aside from the obvious enjoyment in visiting Scotland, meeting his relations for the first time, and perhaps a romantic interest, there is another aspect regarding his frame of mind that is confirmed in the letters he wrote whilst on leave. Harry is a changed man from the naïve fellow who first wrote home from Lark Hill. This is not to suggest he has ceased to believe in God, although that could have been the case, however, contradicting that possibility is evidence of his attendance at church while staying with the West family. However, from November 1917, his letters were devoid of the religious salutations and blessings that populated his earlier correspondence. The reason for this would seem obvious. Harry had now seen and done things that would have severely tested the nature of his strongly held faith. Perhaps he wondered why God could allow such horror, death and devastation to exist. It would seem that from the moment he completed his first stint in the line, he had developed a realistic, even cynical, view of the world and God's place in it.

Chapter 25

April 1918

THE DAY HARRY'S LEAVE COMMENCED the battalion moved into the shelter of the Catacombs beneath Hill 63. It remained there until the 23rd of March when once again it had returned to the line where it remained until the 1st of April 1918. That period in the line is recorded in the war diary as being relatively quiet, and no casualties were recorded.

After being relieved, this time by a British unit the 1st Wiltshire Regiment, the battalion was moved to the south, past Calais and Boulogne, to Millencourt on the Somme. Much of the journey was undertaken by bus, a novel mode of travel at the time. The main objective while at Millencourt was rest, and this they did for just on a fortnight. The war diary records, almost in amazement, acres of green fields. However, this happy state could not last and on the 12th of April the battalion returned to the line, this time at a position approximately 1500 yards to the west of the ruins of the town of Albert.

From their new position battalion members could see the famous tower of the "Leaning Virgin". Before the war, a statue of the Virgin Mary graced the top of the town's Basilica, however in 1915, the Basilica, along with the rest of the town had been damaged by shell fire and the statue of the Virgin slumped to an almost horizontal position. Soldiers on both sides believed that when the Virgin fell the war would end. Believers in this superstition were able to claim some justification, for later that month the statue fell, and by November the war had ended.[152]

---

[152] https://www.worldwar1postcards.com/5-the-leaning-virgin-of-albert.php

Harry's army record notes he re-joined the Battalion on the 13th of April 1918. The Battalion war diary recorded the day as:

"...cloudy and was quiet except for light shelling of one area – no damage was done. Work on trenches and shelters continued and good progress made. Some of the forward posts are protected by "concertina" wire. Owing to practise SOS shoot by the Artillery no patrols were sent forward. Enemy snipers were active but caused no casualties." [153]

Concertina wire mentioned in the diary, was a barbed wire obstacle erected from large coils of wire that could be shaken out to a long length, like a concertina. These coils could be laid out and then built on by other concertinas to form a high, wide, barrier of wire. However, like all wire obstacles the concertina was vulnerable to artillery fire, and if not protected by machine gun or rifle fire, vulnerable to being cut, or moved away by enemy soldiers.

The diary also mentions a "practise SOS shoot by the Artillery". Defensive positions were more often than not supported by the guns of artillery batteries. Infantry in the position would assess the most likely directions and areas from where an enemy attack might materialise, and they would register these areas as targets for the supporting artillery. The abbreviation SOS hints at the Morse Code distress signal "Save Our Souls", however in artillery parlance the abbreviation stands for "emergency fire task". During World War One should an enemy attack threaten a position, the infantry could call for an SOS task via a telephone, or sometimes by a series of agreed coloured flares. However, before an SOS target could be confirmed by the artillery, the target had to tested, so that the maximum effect might be achieved. Testing also ensured the artillery did not bring fire down on friendly troops.[154]

For a man just back from a restful leave, the combination of a friendly artillery SOS test fire, the enemy's light shelling and sniper fire, might have put Harry's nerves on edge. On the other hand, this combination of noise and threat, may have served to ease him back in to front line life.

---

[153] https://www.awm.gov.au/collection/C1342345?image=7
[154] artilleryhistory.org/documents/artillery_abbreviations.pdf

On the 14th the Battalion recommenced its patrolling activities, including an abortive attempt to raid the German trenches. During that attempt one man was seriously wounded. The next day the enemy apparently tested their own artillery SOS line. This must have been a noisy event for the Battalion, but as the shells fell to the front of the German positions, and not on the Battalion's positions, no damage or casualties were caused. However, luck was about to turn against the Battalion. That night the Battalion was relieved, but during the relief in place the German artillery shelled one of the Battalion's company positions wounding six men.

The Battalion returned to its billets at Millencourt, where save for minor administrative issues, they rested. In this happy state, and in warm sunshine, they remained until the 19th of April. They were due to return to the line that night, but as preparations were being made, the enemy shelled the billets causing a number of casualties. This unfortunate incident did not hamper the return to the line and the Battalion had completed its relief of the 23rd Battalion by 9.30 pm.

The 20th proved to be an active day. The Australian artillery heavily shelled the German line, and in retaliation the Germans heavily shelled the Battalion positions. During this response one of the original members of the Battalion was killed. The war diary also recorded the final demise of the "Leaning Virgin", German artillery fire had finally toppled the statue.[155] During this violent activity Harry wrote a letter to his father:

"France
20/4/18

Dear Dad

Just a line in answer to your ever welcome letter which I received a few days ago, I should have answered sooner only for being in the trenches. We are having a good share in the line. We had five men killed a few days ago and four wounded. One of my mates who went on leave to London has been killed he was married so he leaves a wife and two young children. I got a great surprise to hear of you having such a wet season I was sorry to hear that the crops yielded so poorly. The country about here looks very

---

[155] https://www.worldwar1postcards.com/5-the-leaning-virgin-of-albert.php

good now the grass is about a couple of feet high and there is a lot of ground fallowed and a good many acres under crop and swedes this is what the people mainly feed their sheep and stock on. And they fatten alright on them. I am pleased to know you got a good price for the quarry paddock. I can't get over Andy Bennet buying sheep for he would not have them on his mind at one time. I was pleased to hear that Nellie and Jack and the little girls were well when you wrote you said you wished this dreadful war was over so does everyone here. We had a good number of men gutted when I was away on leave. Fancy Mr Barttell being so ill. The war has done a great deal of damage to a lot of villages it is surprising the lot of nice houses which are deserted when Fritz commences to advance and commences shelling. Why some people clear out and leave everything they possess except the cloths they are wearing. I have not much news so you will have to excuse this brief line and scribble as I have some letters to write and the day is getting on. I will now close with love to you and all at home

From your fond son Prte H.F. Withers

Love to All

I will be glad of a line from anyone anytime

Once again Harry's version of the Battalion's casualties appears to be at odds with the Battalion war diary. However, on this occasion, he may have provided details missing from the war diary. The "several casualties" suffered on the 19th mentioned in the war diary when the billets were shelled, may well have included some who were killed. In addition, by the time Harry put pen to paper, he may have been privy to news that some of those recorded in the diary as wounded, had died of their wounds.

Reading this particular letter and knowing that the enemy had heavily shelled the Battalion position, the image may be gained of Harry sheltering in a dugout, furiously writing about home and family, in an effort to take his mind off the enemy bombardment. One can also detect a growing maturity in Harry's communication with his father. In his earlier letters his salutations to his father are extremely formal, almost reverent. In this letter it appears Harry is communicating with an equal. He is still respectful and loving, but the impression is gained he had become much more at ease in his relationship with his father.

The next day, the 21st, brought a new terror…gas. Luckily the Battalion had not been directly targeted, however, the wind blew the residue of the gas from the area of the intended target, across the Battalion's position. Most members of the Battalion did not resort to their gas masks, but it was unpleasant to say the least. On the 22nd, the enemy's tempo of activity increased, and a heavy artillery barrage was unleashed onto the Battalion, resulting in five casualties. Again, the war diary does not record the nature of these casualties. The increase in enemy activity continued the following day with more shelling and a further gas alert. This time all members of the Battalion donned their respirators. The following day the shelling diminished, but at one stage an aircraft bearing British colours strafed Battalion headquarters with machine gun fire. An investigation of the incident found that the aircraft had been previously captured by the Germans and used against the Allies.

On the 25th the Battalion was once again relieved, and no doubt thankfully, returned to the billets in Millencourt. It was ANZAC Day, and the Battalion conducted a brief remembrance service. In addition, the Battalion band travelled by train to Abbeville where a concert was provided at the 8th Australian Casualty Clearing Station.

The Battalion was now at rest, although on several occasions over the next four days it provided work parties to improve wire obstacles at the front. Of course, Harry could have been involved in these activities, however if he was, he made no mention of it in his diary, and if he wrote any letters home at this time, those letters have not survived. It can only be surmised that he would have taken his turn with whatever work was conducted, and that he enjoyed the rest from the line. The officer charged with entering the war diary entries certainly seems to have appreciated the changed conditions, for he records green fields, flowers starting to bloom, and birds singing. In this buoyant mood came further good luck…the Battalion was to move further to the rear for a brief, but no doubt well-earned rest.

Chapter 26

May 1918

ON THE 2ND OF MAY the Battalion moved further back from the line to Pont Noyelles, where they were billeted in the almost deserted village. They marched to this location, the band playing them on their way. This display was well received by locals they passed along the way, with cheering and clapping. The war diary noted the local attitude to the war:

> *"...The industry and optimistic hopefulness of the villagers is very striking, they can still be seen ploughing and cultivating in front of the defences and in many cases under shell fire..."* [156]

One gains the impression the war diarist held a more pessimistic view of the future.

For the next week the Battalion remained in billets at Pont Noyelles, alternating between periods of rest and training. There was a Divisional attack being planned and on several occasions the officers were called away to reconnoitre the area over which the Battalion would have to pass in the attack. Then on the 9th of May the Battalion returned to the line.

Patrolling and work strengthening the Battalion posts immediately commenced, however, aside from a few incidents, one in which an Australian Stokes Mortar destroyed a German minenwerfer, or light mortar, their time in the line was relatively quiet. On the 15th of the month the Battalion was again relieved by the 23rd Battalion and moved to support

---

[156] https://www.worldwar1postcards.com/5-the-leaning-virgin-of-albert.php

trenches. The war diary entry for the 16th of May recorded the situation:

> *"HQ in cellar of chateau, C & B Coys in Ballarat Line, A & D in Tasmanian Line in D28 and J10 respectively. Baths were arranged by collecting all the tubs in the village and using the hot water system of the chateau. Clean clothing was also issued. A cellar containing large supplies of red wine discovered. A guard mounted to protect it and liberal issues made daily to Companies".* [157]

The old Harry would not have approved of the issue of wine. However, maybe the "new" Harry had a more open-minded view of the consumption of alcohol… maybe not. Perhaps he was one of the guard mounted to protect the precious liquid.

The 19th of May was the day the AIFs 6th Brigade would attack the German positions at the town of Ville sur Ancre, to clear the enemy from the town and the high ground to its south. The nature of this attack was to follow the highly publicised and successful, AIF tactic known as "Peaceful Penetration". This tactic was hybrid between trench raiding and patrolling. However, it could be argued that the attack on the 19th of May was anything but "peaceful". At 2 am the attack began under the cover of a heavy artillery bombardment. This was the signal for all the elements of the Brigade to advance. The 24th Battalion's part in this battle more closely resembled the concept of peaceful penetration. The Battalion's first task was to use bridges that had been specially constructed by the Engineers to cross the Ancre River to the north of the village. This part of the operation had to be achieved by stealth. The Battalion's second task was to destroy a number of enemy outposts located on the opposite river bank. However, a problem was encountered before the attack commenced. The war diary records a worrying situation:

> *"1.40 am Engineers report that third bridge over Ancre erected but fourth bridge not in position owing to action of enemy. Two sappers wounded in operation"* [158]

This situation might have been disastrous. However, after some initial

---

[157] https://www.awm.gov.au/collection/C1342346?image=8
[158] https://www.awm.gov.au/collection/C1342346?image=9

difficulty the Battalion crossed the river and quickly overcame the German outposts in the area. The other battalions in the Brigade did not fare as well.

To the south the 21st Battalion met stubborn resistance, and the 22nd Battalion, charged with conducting the main assault, suffered very heavy casualties. At the height of the 22nd Battalion's attack, all the officers were either killed or wounded, and a sergeant, Sergeant Ruthven, assumed command of the Battalion. Under Sergeant Ruthven's inspired leadership, the 22nd Battalion fought on and gained its objectives. For his actions Ruthven was awarded the Victoria Cross, the first awarded to a member of the 6th Brigade. [159]

Having achieved their individual battalion objectives, the 21st, 23rd and 24th Battalions were ordered to clear the village of the enemy. By 4.40 am the German garrison surrendered. In one of the sad ironies of war at 9.15 am the German artillery commenced shelling Ville sur Ancre, killing and wounding many German prisoners who were being held there.

The 6th Brigade operation was judged to be a great success. Australian casualties at 418 killed and wounded, were considered to be light, and German casualties were around 8oo men, plus the loss of a considerable number of machine guns and other heavy weapons. So far as the 24th Battalion was concerned the cost of its success was one officer and three other ranks wounded.

The next day the Battalion moved to Bonnay where it formed part of the Divisional Reserve, and once again had the opportunity to rest. The war diary records the 21st of May, as a most profitable occasion:

> *"All ranks spent the day building new and improving old shelters and succeeded in making themselves comfortable in Bomb Gully whose steep banks were very convenient. The number of beds and mattresses in use is surprising – these are 'temporarily loaned' from absent civilians of neighbouring villages and help to make rest most restful."* [160]

The name of the gully in which the Battalion had taken up residence,

---

[159] https://www.gov.uk/government/case-studies/ww1-australian-vc-recipient-william-ruthven
[160] https://www.awm.gov.au/collection/C1342346?image=11

"Bomb Gully", may have had its genesis in a variety of ways, however, so far as the 24th Battalion was concerned, the name was derived from the bombing activities of German aircraft. The keeper of the war diary found aerial bombardment was not to his taste:

> "...Every night ten to twenty bombs are dropped near us mainly in the battery position near the river. Sometimes however they come close and it is very unnerving to hear the swish of the bombs as they fall – generally a succession in a straight line at 50 yds interval but sometimes four or five at a time..."[161]

Harry's diary records little of this. In a brief and a little confused account of his activities in May, he makes no mention of the attack, or any of the related activities:

> "Having our rest we went into reserve for two weeks and after three weeks in front line we were at Millencourt four and a half kilometres from Albert then we came out from Albert we went for a rest at Berteaucourt 12th May 1918 Sunday. In the morning we went on parade to church in the afternoon I went for a walk to St Ledger and got back after having eggs and chips for tea 13th Monday we went out to another parade ground and formed up for a gas lecture and inspect our box respirators. When we were in the midst of our drill the rain came on. We were then formed up and marched back to camp and dismissed and had dinner. At half past 2 we were lined up for parade but it was still raining so we dismissed once more. In the afternoon rained too much to go on parade. Went to pictures in evening at Y.M.C.A.
>
> 14 Tuesday went out through the town to the parade ground for physical training the first drill we had was physical exercise after this we had instruction on the Mills Bombs. After this bayonet fighting then formed up for the march home for dinner."

Again, Harry's record of events differs from the Battalion war diary, and

---

[161] https://www.awm.gov.au/collection/C1342346?image=13

the impression that he has written, or updated, his diary at some time well after the events he mentions, is maintained. He is correct that the Battalion's first rest area was Millencourt, but unless Harry as an individual, had managed to spend time at Berteaucourt, he was mistaken as to the Battalion's other resting locations. Perhaps by excluding reference to the battle of the 19th and 20th he was trying to block the memories of the event from his mind.

On the 26th of the month, a momentous occasion for the AIF took place. General Birdwood was replaced by the newly promoted Lieutenant General John Monash as the General Officer Commanding the Australia Corp. This appointment would have ramifications for the way the AIF would fight the remainder of the war. However, save for several officers attending a farewell for General Birdwood, the Battalion remained at Bonnay for the rest of the month. As was usual, the Battalion activities alternated between rest, sport and work parties. Whilst they were technically out of the line, they were still within range of the enemy artillery, and aircraft. On the 27th of the month, D Company took the air war to a new level by capturing an enemy aircraft. Surrounding units all tried to claim they had shot the aircraft from the sky. However, the aircraft showed no sign of battle damage and when closely inspected was found to have run out of petrol.[162]

On the 30th of the month, in a frightening demonstration of power, German artillery ranged in on the Battalion position, firing high explosive shells. Amazingly the result of this bombardment was one man, a signaller, wounded.

The time of rest was almost over for the Battalion and the next day they began to prepare to relieve another unit in the line. Tragically as the relief in place progressed, a German shell impacted on a road used by the relieving battalion, killing three men, and wounding another ten men. This tragic event did not prevent the relief in place concluding by 11.30 pm. The Battalion was back in the line; however, some doubt must now be expressed regarding Harry's exact whereabouts.

---

[162] https://www.awm.gov.au/collection/C1342346?image=12

Chapter 27

June 1918

AT SOME STAGE DURING JUNE 1918 Harry was once again detached from the 24th Battalion. However, this time he was attached to the 6th Australian Light Trench Mortar Battery. The first indication of this move is contained in a letter to his mother dated the 28th of June.

"France 28/6/1918

Dear Mother

Just a few lines in my spare moments to let you know I still think of all at home. I was pleased to hear all were well when Violet wrote. Vi's letter came to hand on the 24th. Dear Mother the weather is keeping lovely and warm and the country looks lovely and green. Some of the crops look well and others are badly in need of rain. The vegetable crops also look well. Dear Mother one of the Battalions in the Brigade have just held the sports which were really good. Corp Cunningham or Frank as we know him by was second in the diving, one man was dressed up as a swagman and another was acting as Charlie Chaplain. When the men are out of the line there is cricket and football and cricket played a lot which games are greatly appreciated by the men. Violet said you would like to know the Battalion colours well I am not with the Battalion. Well the Battalion colours were red and white diamond. I have been attached to the Light Trench Mortars which I like better than the infantry for the infantry is the same old thing day in day out but the mortars are interesting indeed. I have not heard from the Maynards for a long while you might kindly remember me to them and all my friends at the Valley. By all accounts the Glen is very quiet now that so many people have left and so many homes have been removed. Violet mentioned of Mr Coates calling in to see you. Dear Mother I will close for this time hoping these few lines will find you, Dad and all in the best of health. Love to all from your ever fond son

No 6426 Prte H.F. Withers

Australian Imperial Force 6th ALTM Bty

France

Dear Mother my address is as the present No 6426 Prte H.F. Withers 6th Australian Light Trench Mortar Battery AIF France

I have to ring off this time hoping to hear from you soon

I remain your fond son

Prte H.F. Withers

Give my love to Dad and all xxxxx"

Harry seems to be quite happy with this detachment and clearly holds his section commander, Corporal Frank Cunningham in high regard. Unfortunately, Corporal Cunnigham's army record is not available and so it is not possible to provide any background detail regarding him. However, once again there is a difference between Harry's official army record and the letters he wrote home. Harry's army record shows that he was officially detached from 24th Battalion to the 6th Australian Light Trench Mortar Battery (6th ALTMB) on the 14th of September 1918. However, the letter to his mother and other letters written in June, July, and August suggest he was with the mortar battery well before this. How could this be?

Harry's suggestion to his mother that he was finding infantry work repetitive, and that he wanted something new, would hardly be a sufficient reason for any kind of unofficial detachment. Yet the reason for his move from the Battalion may well have been as simple as being that he was in the right place at the right time. However, before delving further into how Harry became a mortarman, a little about the mortar as a weapon, and a broad understanding of the place the 6th ALTMB had in the 6th Brigade's order of battle, is required.

The mortar was not a new weapon, having existed in one form or another for centuries. Essentially it was then, and remains today, a short tube, or barrel, designed to fire a projectile at a steep angle, greater than 45 degrees, so that it falls more or less straight down on top of an enemy. The weapon fell out of favour after the Napoleonic Wars but returned to relevance in the trench warfare of World War One. During that conflict, the weapon's firing characteristics provided a distinct advantage, as the mortar crew was able to fire the weapon from the comparative safety of the bottom of a trench.

World War One mortars came in three types: heavy, medium and light. On the Allied side, the heavy and medium mortars were assigned to the artillery, however light mortars were considered to be an infantry weapon. Both sides employed mortars, indeed at the beginning of the war, the Germans held a considerable advantage in mortar (minenwerfer or "mine thrower") technology and use.

On the Allied side of the line there were a variety of light mortars in use, however the weapon used by the 6th ALTMB, was the Stokes three-inch mortar. The design of the Stokes Mortar was simple, yet extremely effective. The entire system weighed in at 108 pounds, and it fired a 10 pound 76.2mm high explosive (amatol filled) cylindrical projectile out to 800 yards, though its effective range was closer to 750 yards. The smoothbore launch tube held an elevation limit of 45 to 75 degrees. The design comprised of a baseplate, launch tube, elevation controls, bipod and the projectile. For transporting, without accounting for ammunition, the weapon was designed to be broken down into three primary components … the barrel, baseplate and bipod. A trained crew could fire between twenty-two and twenty-five rounds per minute if required, but generally the rate of fire was around six to eight rounds per minute. This lesser rate was generally held to, as a higher rate of fire could cause the barrel to overheat, which could result in danger to the operators.

A mortar of its very nature cannot be aimed directly at a target, and instead provides what is termed as "indirect fire". The mortar point of impact for the mortar projectile is determined by the power of the propelling charge, the elevation of the barrel, and the direction the weapon is pointing.

In the AIF, the Stokes Mortar was the weapon commonly employed in the "light mortar" role. The weapon was generally operated by a team of three men. The Number One in the crew was responsible to lay, or aim the mortar, through the use of a known fixed point, or zero line. He would then set a bearing on which to align the weapon, using a clinometer and range of tables to set the elevation for the weapon.

The Number Two on the mortar crew loaded and fired the weapon.

The Number Three on the crew kept the supply of bombs up to the mortar. On the order to fire he would adjust the charges to match the range and elevation required to engage the target. He would then remove the safety pin from the fuse before passing the bomb to the Number Two. The planning range for the Stokes Mortar was 800 yards, however, its maximum effective range was closer to 750 yards.

The mortar came into its own when employed in groups, or batteries, so that the bombs delivered onto the target covered the immediate target area. On the Western Front the mortar was the ideal weapon for softening up a target prior to an infantry attack, or for providing more immediate supporting fire during a battle, than the distant supporting artillery could generally provide.[163]

On an organizational level, Stokes Mortars were organized into batteries of two sections each of four weapons, with one battery under command of each infantry brigade. This gave the brigade commander considerable choice as to how his mortars might be employed. He could either use the battery as a whole, with all mortars firing from a single location, or he could allocate a section of mortars to work with and to directly support his infantry battalions.

The 6th ALTMB had initially been raised in Egypt, during the AIFs expansion after the Gallipoli campaign. Thereafter, wherever the 6th Brigade fought, so too did the 6th ALTMB. Initially the 6th ALTMB had obtained its authorised strength from volunteers coming across from infantry battalions, in much the same way as Jack Mitchell's 12th Machine Gun Company had been created. However, as the war went on, while some reinforcements were received from the new drafts arriving from Australia, much of the batteries'

---

[163] https://www.militaryfactory.com/smallarms/detail.asp?smallarms_id=651

manpower requirements were provided by the infantry battalions within the brigade to which the battery was assigned. This was not considered to be a huge impost on the battalions, as a light mortar battery's authorised strength was fifty-one men in total. However, some infantry commanders objected to depleting the strengths of their rifle companies to man the mortar batteries. This feeling was strengthened by a routine requirement for the infantry to provide work parties to carry additional mortar ammunition from the rear to the firing points. No doubt those same commanders would have complained bitterly if their supporting mortars were unable to fire. Nevertheless, the feeling was there, and at times the light mortar batteries became a political "hot potato". For example, on the 6th of June 1918, the 6th Brigade war diary recorded the following:

> "A reply came from Division today to our proposal to amalgamate the medium and light trench mortar batteries. Corps could not consider it, transport was given as the main difficulty. They also stated it had been carefully considered at the time medium mortars were organised and was turned down definitely then."[164]

It would seem that either Commander 6 Brigade wanted to increase his indirect fire power capability by this amalgamation, or he was tired of the infantry having to maintain the trench mortar battery's strength.

The life of a mortarman may have appealed to some on the basis they were less likely to be required to advance across no-man's-land. However, while mortars were generally fired from the cover of a trench, the life of a mortar crew was not without considerable risk. If a firing point was detected the enemy would bring counter battery fire from their artillery, or their own mortars, on to that position in an effort to destroy the opposing mortar. In addition to this risk the three-inch bombs used for the Stokes Mortar, were sometimes prone to premature detonation. This meant that the bomb would explode while it was inside the mortar barrel, or as it left the muzzle of the weapon. In either event the consequences for the operators, was catastrophic. This is what occurred with one 6th ALTMB crew during the attack at Ville

---

[164] https://www.awm.gov.au/collection/C1343468

sur Ancre. As the mortar crew were serving their weapon, a mortar bomb exploded in the barrel of the weapon, instantly killing two of the crew, Private James Ashton, and Private William McGhee. Both of these men were 22 years old. Private Ashton had been a reinforcement transferred directly to the battery. Private McGhee on the other hand had been transferred to the battery from the 24th Battalion[165]. It is very likely that this incident provided Harry with the opportunity to become a mortarman.

As Private McGhee was originally from the 24th Battalion, it is reasonable to assume that the 24th Battalion would have been asked to provide his replacement. Harry may have been selected, or perhaps he volunteered for the vacant position. He might even have been engaged in carrying ammunition when the incident occurred, and then assisted the mortar section in the aftermath. In any event it appears that unofficially, as of a date in June 1918, Harry became a member of 6th ALTMB. It is not until the 14th of September 1918 that this move is officially sanctioned by the 24th Battalion. How could such a delay occur?

The logical answer to this question is that to become a mortarman, Harry would have required training. To a degree that training would have occurred on the job, but during the Brigade's time out of the line the required training would have been more intensive. Throughout the period from June to the 14th of September, he was probably on probation, and if the mortar battery commander assessed that he was not going to be an effective member of the mortar team, Harry would have found himself back with the Battalion.

During the month of June 6th Brigade units conducted a number of raids across no-man's-land and into the German trenches. These raids were part of the developing tactic of "peaceful penetration" and while the Australians suffered some casualties in pursuing this tactic, the enemy suffered far greater losses in men and equipment. During each raid the 6th ALTMB was tasked with providing vital fire support. Infantry tactics were then, and are now, based on the practise of "fire and movement". That is a group, or an individual moves, while another group or individual provides covering fire

---

[165] https://www.awm.gov.au/collection/C1343468

to keep the enemies' heads down. During the raid of the 6th of June, mortars had been employed to nullify German response to the advance of the raiding Australians. The after-action reports provided by the raid commanders, and in subsequent intelligence summaries, praised the effectiveness of the support they received from the 6th ALTMB [166]. The battery was also involved in part of Lieutenant General Monash's deception plan for an operation that was to take place early in the following month. Harry had joined a well-trained and battle-hardened organization, and it clear from his letter to his mother and the future letters and cards he pens, that he is extremely pleased to be a part of it.

---

[166] https://www.awm.gov.au/collection/C1343468?image=54

Chapter 28

July 1918

JULY 1918 WOULD PROVE TO be a particularly busy month. The new commander of the Australian Corps, Lieutenant General Monash, had chosen the 4th of July to launch a major attack at the village of Hamel. In the days preceding that date the Australian forces and supporting British and for the first time, American elements prepared and rehearsed for their part in the battle.

On the 1st of the month Harry found the time to write to his mother:

"1/7/18

Dear Mother

Just a line to let you know you are not forgotten by me also to let you know I am well hoping these few lines will find you and all in the best of health. The weather is keeping fine and very warm of a day but the nights are cool. I met Tommie Henderson yesterday he looks well. I also met a young man who used to stay at Clarkes at the Great Southern also Prte W. Canning[167] *from Springs. Dear Mother I often hear from Scotland they sent me a very nice parcel a few weeks ago. They are anxious for me to go and see them again. I have not got much time to write much this time as the mail will be collected. I must say long before you get this letter I will be in a big stunt which I hope to come through alright. Dear Mother is Mag and Jack still living in Franks house I have not heard for a long time how Will and Alice and the little ones are I should like Will if he can find time to drop a*

---

[167] Army record unavailable

line. Has Nell and Jack gone back to bards alright. Do not be disappointed if you do not hear from me regularly for we are so often on the move but I will write as often as possible. Fancy Robbie and Leslie enlisting I never thought they would leave the Valley. I will now draw to a close hoping these few lines will find you all in the best of health.

Love to all From you ever fond son Prte H.F. Withers No 6426 Australian Imperial Force 6th ALT M Bty France"

Harry is particularly reticent regarding the war, only hinting to his future involvement in "a big stunt". The "stunt" he referred to, was General Monash's planned battle for control of the village of Hamel. The two words Harry used to describe the coming battle, was as far as he could go with regard to war news, any further information would have earned the wrath of the censor. Interestingly, however, in his other news he declares he is receiving a lot of mail, including a present, from Scotland. Had a long distance relationship begun to develop, and is he softening his mother up prior to telling all?

The village of Hamel is located to the south of the River Somme and around two miles to the north-east of Villers-Bretonneux. In July 1918 the village was of strategic importance to both the Allies, and to the Germans. For the Allies, the German controlled village presented an obstacle to any future advance to the east. For the Germans the village provided a firm base from which they could continue to threaten the town of Amiens. Monash estimated the German strength in and around the village as being approximately 5600 men. He chose the Australian 4th Division as the main assault group, and he reinforced that Division by attaching the 6th Brigade from the 2nd Australian Division, and the 11th Brigade from the 3rd Australian Division. He would also deploy sixty battle tanks and four supply tanks from the British 5th Tank Brigade. Also included in his order of battle were the American 1st and 2nd Battalions of the 131st Infantry Regiment. The American infantry had yet to be committed in battle, and Monash intended that they would be embedded into battle-hardened Australian units in order to gain experience.

By including the 6th Brigade in his plans, Monash had placed Harry and his new mates in the 6th Australian Light Trench Mortar Battery (6th ALTMB), in the battle. In fact, the 6th ALTMB had been included in Monash's bombardment plan and for the two weeks prior to attack on Hamel, it had contributed to the artillery barrage Monash had ordered fired at the German positions at Hamel. Monash termed this bombardment "conditioning firing". The artillery units provided a bombardment every day at dawn for the two weeks prior to the 4th of July. The bombardment comprised of a mixture of ordnance including gas shells and smoke. The idea was to force the German soldiers to don their gas masks, restricting their field of vision and increasing their nervous tension.

Hamel was Monash's first battle as the Australian Corps Commander, and he was meticulous in his planning and preparations. A number of the tactics he employed were innovative and included parachute drops of ammunition and medical supplies, the use of tanks to carry resupply items forward (rather than work parties of soldiers), and the use of telephone and wireless by officers to send messages. Every aspect of the battle was carefully rehearsed by all those taking part, particularly infantry, tank cooperation. However, two issues arose that almost ruined Monash's plans before the battle had even commenced.

The first issue was caused by Monash's old nemesis, the war correspondent Charles Bean. Bean disliked Monash, believing he was a "thruster", one who pushed his own ambitions at the cost of others. Bean was also anti-Semitic, and he railed against the Jewish Monash's appointment to command the AIF. Along with co-conspirator journalist Keith Murdoch, Bean plotted to discredit Monash to the Australian Prime Minister Billy Hughes, in the hope that Hughes would dismiss Monash.

The conspirators almost succeeded. Hughes was misled into the belief that senior Australian officers opposed Monash. Hughes, who had been visiting England, journeyed to France with the express purpose of removing Monash from command. He arrived at the Australian Corps Headquarters two days prior to the battle. However, luckily for Monash, and the planned attack, prior to confronting Monash, Hughes chose to consult a number of senior officers and to his surprise he discovered those officers had nothing but praise for their commander. In addition, as Prime Minister Hughes was briefed on the coming battle, Monash was able to demonstrate his powers and skills, and Hughes changed his mind.

The second issue arose on the day before the battle. The commander of the American Expeditionary Force in France, General Pershing, learned of the plan to involve American troops and was not pleased. In Pershing's opinion, American troops could only be commanded by Americans, and he ordered the withdrawal of the American units planned for the battle at Hamel. A few American troops disobeyed this order and remained with the Australian units. However, most obeyed and moved to the rear. This caused a serious reduction in the size of Monash's assault force, and last-minute amendments to the overall plan had to be made to cover the gaps created by the American decision.

These distractions were soon set aside and at 3.02 am on the 4th of July the artillery and mortars began the same bombardment they had conducted for the past two weeks. Again, the German troops put on their gas masks and waited nervously in their trenches. However, on this occasion the noise of the bombardment covered the sound of the British tanks as they advanced. In the sky the Royal Flying Corps increased the noise and power of the bombardment dropping bombs to the east of the main Australian objectives. Then the artillery and mortars shortened their range to cover the infantry start line. At 3.10 am the infantry began to advance keeping just behind the barrage, and the British tanks followed in support. Ninety-three minutes later all of the Australian objectives had been achieved and the Battle of Hamel became known as a textbook victory and used as a template for later Allied battles. Hamel cost the Australians 1400 casualties (killed and wounded) and the Americans almost 200. German casualties were 2000 killed and wounded and around 1600 prisoners. [168]

The 6th ALTMB had been heavily involved. The 6th Brigade after action report stated:

---

[168] https://www.awm.gov.au/articles/blog/the-battle-of-hamel-100-years-on, also https://en.wikipedia.org/wiki/Battle_of_Hamel

> "The 6th ALTM Bty aided by two guns of the 5th ALTM Bty lent with their crews by the 5th ALTMB for the operation, barraged the enemy trench from P25.b.2.0 to P25.6.7.4 from zero to zero plus four minutes. This section of the trench was too close to the J.O.T to be effectively bombarded by artillery.
>
> Two mortars were unfortunately knocked out practically before firing but the remainder proved equal to the job.
>
> Four mortars were sent forward shortly after zero and were employed two at P.20.c.6.0. and two at P.21.c.0.5. Carry parties from the 24th Battalion put 60 rounds on each gun and then returned to their Battalion."[169]

The abbreviation J.O.T. refers to the infantry Jumping Off Tapes, tapes placed on the ground, marking the point from which the infantry was to commence the attack. Artillery and mortars worked to safety distances for the various types of ordnance used. Friendly troops who are too close to the impact zone, may well have been in just as much danger as the enemy. At Hamel, the heavier shells used by the artillery would certainly have endangered the attacking troops.

Interestingly, not all of Monash's novel resupply systems were employed. Some of Harry's former comrades of the 24th Battalion were engaged as ammunition carriers for the mortar crews. One wonders if there was any banter between Harry and his old mates as the mortar bombs were delivered. Perhaps not…

The report does not reveal how the two mortars that were destroyed met their end, and no detail regarding the two crews is recorded. However, it may be that the German artillery, or even their *minenwerfer* (mortar) batteries may have used the "conditioning bombardment" employed by the Australians over the previous fourteen days, to locate the Australian mortar position. This done, it would have been a relatively simple task to register that position as a target, and the next time the bombardment commenced, to fire a counter battery task on that position.

---

[169] https://www.awm.gov.au/collection/C1343470?image=81

Harry and the mortar team he had joined survived the battle, however, he provides no detail of his part in it. After the situation had stabilized, he penned a letter to his father:

"France 8/7/18

Dear Dad

Just a line in answer to your ever welcome letters which came to hand yesterday. I was pleased to hear Jack and all are well at time of writing as it leaves me at present. It is just the thing to know that Reg is a good ploughman for he will be *a great help to Wal. Most of the crops here look well. But a great many will not be taken off for there is hundreds of acres under shell fire*

The morning after the hop over our men were walking about looking for the Germans and when they would show up they were soon shot that was when they would appear out of the crop. It is fine to think the mine is still working as it will find employment for the men around the district. Fancy Berkley Withers returning home. I was glad to hear Mr Murry got the paddock from Reynolds for he will be a better neighbour. It was alright to know you received...."

Unfortunately, the rest of this letter has not survived, but it seems whilst Harry has become a veteran soldier, he is still a farmer at heart.

Harry makes no reference to the Battle of Hamel in his diary; perhaps the sights and sounds he had witnessed were something he had no desire to recall. It may even be that the importance of that particular battle was lost on him, after all, Hamel was not particularly large, and Harry's part in it relatively small. In any event he had little time to ponder, for on the 8th of July the Brigade received orders to form the Corps strategic reserve. The 6th ALTMB was to move with the Brigade headquarters and to stand ready to support any counterattack that may have been required.

The next week was relatively uneventful, but by the 17th of the month the Brigade was moved forward into the line again, and on the night of the 21st/22nd of July the 6th ALTMB was involved in providing fire support for a raid on a German post. During the course of providing this support the battery earned considerable praise, as outlined in the after-action report:

> "3. Telephone connected up with supporting TMs was carried by assaulting party…"
>
> 4. 2 Stokes Mortars each fired 10 rounds on to targets!.1.c.50.95 (enemy block MG position) and V.1.c.7.7. – mg position at V.1.c.50.95 was also engaged. Fire on these was controlled by Lieut Baker and shooting was accurate and most satisfactory".[170]

Then again:

> "6. Enemy resistance was slight because of the speed at which our party worked, and the extreme accuracy of mortar shooting."[171]

Harry would have been involved in this action and no doubt performed well as part of the mortar battery team.

On the following night Harry and the rest of the battery came close to disaster. The German artillery unleashed a gas attack on the Brigade area and the 6th ALTMB suffered two casualties.[172] Harry was apparently unscathed.

The next night the enemy followed up the gas attack with a raid on an Australian post, and again the mortar battery was called to action. The after-action report of this incident once again praises the efficiency of the 6th ALTMB:

> "Two Stokes Mortars at V.5.d.6.3. put down a barrage on their SOS lines (U.5.d.6.3) when the fighting commenced and maintained it till the position was re-established. If the enemy had any intention of reinforcing, this barrage effectively prevented it".[173]

Harry had joined a very professional group, and on the 31st of the month the battery was chosen to pass some of their skills on to the newly arrived American troops. The 37mm Gun Platoon, of the American 129th Regiment, was attached to the 6th ALTMB for a period of four days.[174] The American

---

[170] https://www.awm.gov.au/collection/C1343471?image=41 and 42
[171] Op. cit.
[172] https://www.awm.gov.au/collection/C1343471?image=47
[173] https://www.awm.gov.au/collection/C1343471?image=50
[174] https://www.awm.gov.au/collection/C1343471?image=70

platoon had a similar role to the light trench mortar batteries, in that they provided infantry heavy weapon fire support. There were, however, particular differences. The main armament of the American platoon was, as its title suggests, the 37mm gun. This weapon was of French design and was adopted for use by the Americans. The 37mm gun was generally employed as a direct fire weapon, but it could be used as a howitzer and in that guise could provide indirect fire similar to a mortar. The 37mm gun was transportable, but it took four to six soldiers to operate the weapon effectively. The primary ammunition fired by the weapon was a high explosive shell.[175]

One wonders what Harry thought of his new comrades and their 37mm guns. He had come across American soldiers on his leave in Scotland, and at that time he appeared to be rather dismissive of them. This meeting, however, must have been different, and it can be imagined, that even in spite of characteristic American confidence, the newcomers would have been in awe of the Aussie veterans, of which Harry was now one. There would, however, be little time for the Diggers to "strut their stuff" in front of the Yanks…August would prove to be a very busy month.

---

[175] https://www.militaryfactory.com/armor/detail.asp?armor_id=936https:// www.militaryfactory.com/armor/detail.asp?armor_id=936

Chapter 29

August 1918

ON THE 2ND OF AUGUST, the 6th Brigade returned to the line at Villers Bretonneux, the French town that had fallen to the Australians on ANZAC Day 1918. The move placed the Brigade back in the line where it assumed responsibility for the whole of the Divisional front. Harry along with the rest of the 6th ALTMB was immediately deployed to areas of strategic importance. Four mortars to a position to the south of the Villers Bretonneux railway line, six others were deployed with the forward battalions, and two more kept in reserve. There is no indication as to which of these positions Harry was sent, and he does not mention the deployment in his diary.

The only surviving piece of correspondence he sent home was an army field postcard sent to his mother on the 6th of August. The postcard is of the kind where the sender can tick, or cross out statements, printed on the card and thus affect a message. In this case Harry indicated he was well, but that he had not received any letters from home lately. These cards were ideal for the soldier on the move, or in battle, and during August 1918, Harry was both.

The lack of correspondence shrouds Harry's reaction to an event one might think was indeed newsworthy. Along with its battlefield responsibilities, the 6th ALTMB had another platoon of Americans attached to the battery to gain front line experience. This platoon was armed with Stokes Mortars, and therefore had more in common with the Australian light mortar battery than the previous American visitors. The Americans remained with the battery for two days, so they were hardly in position long enough to make a meaningful contribution to the defence. Nor were they included in the Allied offensive that was to commence a few days later.

General Rawlinson was the commander of the Fourth Army which included the British 111 Corps located north of the River Somme, the Australian Corps, situated south of the river and to the south of them the Canadian Corps. Rawlinson planned a general advance, supported by artillery, tanks and aircraft to attack German positions all along the whole of his front. This operation was scheduled to commence on the 8th of August.

The Australian part of this attack commenced from positions at Villers-Bretonneux and at Hamel. The 6th Brigade's defensive positions at Villers-Bretonneux were to provide a firm base from which the Australian attack would be launched. Those three days preceding the attack were busy for all involved. While the 6th Brigade was not going to take part in the assault, patrolling and defensive activities had to be maintained, to screen the preparations of the assaulting troops. This work was made more difficult when the weather once again took a hand in proceedings. There was heavy rain on the 5th and intermittent showers over the next two days. On the 7th the Brigade war diary recorded conditions in the trenches as "deplorable", for there was no drainage and the water simply gathered in the lowest ground and this included the Australian trenches. In spite of these conditions preparations for the attack continued.

At 4.20 am on the morning of the 8th of August, the attack began. Two hours later the Australian troops had accomplished all their objectives, and in just over three hours the whole of the enemy front line had been overrun. In total, the Allied forces captured 29,144 prisoners, 338 guns, and liberated 116 towns and villages. Ludendorff called the 8th of August "the black day of the German Army"[176]. Understandably the keeper of the 24th Battalion's war diary had a rather different opinion:

> *"Thus started what was to be a magnificent series of victories"[177]*

---

[176] https://www.awm.gov.au/articles/blog/battle-amiens
[177] https://www.awm.gov.au/collection/C1356090?image=8

The 6th Brigade maintained its position through until the 17th of the month when it began to move forward across the captured ground. During this move the mortars were distributed among the battalions and again it is not possible to trace Harry's activities. On the 18th the Brigade was once again in a forward position, and in taking up this role the mortar battery was involved in an interesting experiment. The following was recorded in the 6th Brigade's war diary:

> "An experiment was made with the carrying of the Stokes guns on Pack Mules and worked very well. The guns were taken into the line and dumped at the gun positions and the resupply of ammunition maintained the same way." [178]

Had Monash's flare for innovation been followed by the 6th ALTMB? Or perhaps the battery had been impressed by one of their recent American visitors, the 37mm Gun Platoon? The American platoon had carried its main weapons on horse drawn limbers. One can only imagine Harry, and his mates' gratitude at not having to man-pack the Stokes Mortar components and ammunition to the new location.

Whilst it may be said that the 6th Brigade was having a quieter time than most, there were still some contacts with the enemy, and they were still subject to enemy artillery bombardment. Over the period the 9th to the 19th of August the 6th ALTMB suffered two other ranks killed, and one other ranks wounded. Overall Brigade casualties during the same period, was 36 killed, 126 wounded and 35 missing.[179]

Over the period 25th to 31st of August the 6th Brigade was once again in the line, where it pursued a program of active patrolling and mopping up pockets of the enemy missed in the main assault. Then on the 31st the Brigade provided close support to the 5th Brigade for the attack on St. Quentin. "Close support" quickly resulted in the Brigade becoming embroiled in numerous assaults on well defended enemy positions. Casualties began to mount. In one assault all of the officers, and all but one of the sergeants in the leading unit became casualties. Brigade casualties

---

[178] https://www.awm.gov.au/collection/C1343475?image=81
[179] https://www.awm.gov.au/collection/C1343475?image=81

during the last two days of the month were 72 killed and 251 wounded. Enemy casualties were assessed as numerous but included 313 taken prisoner and numerous artillery and machine guns captured or destroyed.[180]

The 6th ALTMB played a very active role in these attacks. The Brigade war diary record of the battery's performance states:

> "...*Exceptionally good shooting was done in preparation for the attack by the 21st Bn on the trenches between FRISE and MEREAUCOURT WOOD. The target engaged was closely examined and 12 enemy dead were found. In addition about 50 others were forced out into the open and captured...*"[181]

During these attacks, the effectiveness of the mortar battery was placed under strain through lack of ammunition. The mules used so effectively in the battery's previous time in the line, were of no use in an open attack. The enemy artillery and machine guns would have quickly destroyed the four-legged carriers. The alternative was to revert to men carrying the vital ammunition forward, and men proved to be in short supply for such a task. Nevertheless the battery claimed to have destroyed an enemy mortar, and to have engaged targets well beyond what was considered to be the maximum range of the Stokes Mortar.[182] Aside from this issue, other aspects of the Brigade resupply system worked well, and Harry would have been most impressed when hot meals, prepared by the cooks just behind the forward areas, were delivered to the battery positions. Some meals were delivered to the forward positions by the Brigade snipers, on their way to take up positions in no-man's-land.[183]

Monash was determined to maintain the initiative this battle had established. On the 31st of August, orders were issued for the 6th Brigade to move through the positions established by the 5th Brigade and resume the advance. Zero hour for this advance was set at 6.00 am the following morning.

---

[180] Op. cit. pp 95 to 98
[181] https://www.awm.gov.au/collection/C1343475?image=100
[182] https://www.awm.gov.au/collection/C1343475?image=100
[183] https://www.awm.gov.au/collection/C1343475?image=102

Chapter 30

September 1918

AFTER HEAVY AND EXHAUSTING FIGHTING, the Australians established a stronghold in the St Quentin area and forced the complete withdrawal of the Germans from Péronne. By the night of the 3rd of September, the Australians held Péronne, and the next day they made further ground capturing Flamicourt and advancing a further two miles to the east.

The 6th Brigade had played an important role in these victories but at grievous cost. Over the period 31st of August to the 3rd of September the Brigade had suffered 72 killed in action, and 251 wounded in action. When this figure is added to the casualty figures for the earlier August battles, the brigade had suffered in total 185 killed in action and 575 wounded in action. The 6th Brigade was not alone. Australian casualties over this period numbered in excess of 3000 killed and wounded. Aside from the cost in human misery, this loss was a serious blow to the AIF's fighting capability. At that stage of the war reinforcements from Australia, and the training camps in England had slowed to a trickle, and as a result there were simply not enough available, trained men, to replace those lost. This was a situation that later in the month would place Lieutenant General Monash in a very difficult position.

In the aftermath of the St Quentin and Péronne battles, the 6th Brigade had begun training for the next operation. Key to Monash's assault on the Hindenburg Line was to be tanks, and a great deal of training time was devoted to infantry/tank co-operation. They were also afforded a little rest, and during one such moment Harry wrote one of his more revealing letters home:

"France
7/8/18

My Dear Dad and Mother

Just a line to let you see I have not forgotten you at home although it was some time since I wrote you. Nevertheless you all at home have not been absent in my thoughts. I was glad to hear all were well at time of you writing me. I was pleased to hear that the boys have got on so well with putting in of the crop. I got a letter from G Maynard today when I got yours.

Dear Dad do not be disappointed if you do not hear from me regularly for it is not always convenient especially of late for we have been in the line such a lot. We are out now for a few days spell and I tell you we can do with it for we have only had about ten days out since the 8th August the commencement of the push at Villers-Bretonneux. We have pushed the Hun a distance of 23 miles when he could not stop our advance over country like he was holding I don't like his chances anymore. We left Mt Saint Quentin[184] near Péronne a couple of days ago. It was one of the warmest times we have had the huns should never have let us take the Mt for it was full of Germans and machine guns. There was only about a hundred and fifty Aussies went over the top they soon put the Hun to flight shooting many more than the number of ours who went over capturing many guns and five hundred prisoners.

The country looks well considering after the fighting the grass it is quite green. I have not seen any of the men from the Glen or Valley for some time now. I got a letter from Barbara Anderson that is Mrs Wests niece she is the only child and is about seventeen years of age and full of life just like Violet in looks and in her actions. Mrs Anderson is about as tall as Mum and is like Mum and Aunt in her ways.

Well Dad I do not think there is any more to write just now. Today we went for a bath near the La Bassee canal and the men have been catching fish. I will ring off for this time hoping these few lines find you and Mum and

---

[184] Refers to Mont Saint Quentin

all in the best of health as it leaves me. I will conclude with love to all from your ever fond son Prte H.F. Withers xxxxxxxx

> *My address*
> *No 6426*
> *Prte H.F. Withers 6th Australia Light Trench Motor Battery*
> *AIF*
> *France*
> *Write soon"*

It would seem the possible love interest for Harry that possibly had developed during his leave in Scotland, may have become stronger:

> *"...I got a letter from Barbara Anderson that is Mrs Wests niece she is the only child and is about seventeen years of age and full of life just like Violet in looks and in her actions..."*

One wonders how his mother and father received this news. However, any response they may have sent to their son would not have reached France for some time. In the meantime, Harry and the rest of the AIF hurried forward toward their ultimate prize…the Hindenburg Line.

Harry is clearly very proud at the feat of arms the AIF had achieved in its recent battles. However, when he wrote: *"…There was only about a hundred and fifty Aussies went over the top…"* he inadvertently hints at a crisis that, unbeknown to him, was about to embroil the Australian Corps.

Under ordinary circumstances, an attack of brigade strength, or even battalion strength, would employ far greater numbers to an assault. However, the casualties suffered in the series of battles from July 1918 to September 1918, had reduced the Australian Corps to a shell of the former organization. Harry's observation as to the small numbers of Diggers who "went over the top" at St Quentin, was in fact an indication of a crisis in manpower, for quite simply there were not enough men left, to commit a greater number to the assault. This fact of life, and death, would prove to be a particularly difficult issue for Lieutenant General Monash.

Perhaps in the euphoria of success, Monash had overlooked the condition of his men. Battalions that should have consisted of around 1000 men, were hardly able to call a few hundred together, and those who could still fight were exhausted. It would seem Monash could only see that a final, decisive victory was within his grasp. Surely, all he had to do was continue the advance, and the Germans would be finished? So he continued to push his command hard. Too hard as it transpired, for on the 14th of September, some overworked AIF battalions refused to re-join the fight.

Monash's troubles did not end there. Unable to replace the casualties, one solution offered, was to disband some of the most decimated units, and to redistribute the men to those battalions that were to be retained. This initiative would also enable the AIF to reorganize and follow the British Army structure, with three battalions to a brigade, rather than four. Monash decided to run with the idea and the brigade commanders were directed to identify a battalion, within their commands, for disbandment.

Seven of the AIF's battalions were earmarked for this fate. In the 6th Brigade the 21st Battalion was chosen. However, there was to be an unexpected twist in this saga, for on the 20th of September, after the Australian Corps Headquarters issued the order for the disbandment, one of the identified battalions, the 21st Battalion, refused to obey the order.

When the Commanding Officer of the 21st Battalion informed his unit they were to be disbanded, it is safe to say the men did not receive the news well. Three days later the CO informed the Brigade Commander that whilst his officers would obey the disbandment order, his men would obey every order given them, but not the order to disband. This was a very serious situation, and whilst the 6th Brigade war diary entry for the 25th of September began:

"Fine sunny morning" [185] that singular statement was the only good news for the day. The majority of the war diary entries for that day detailed the situation at the rebellious battalion.

General Monash was informed of the situation, and he instructed the brigadier commanding the 6th Brigade that the Brigade was to continue its work as if nothing unusual had occurred, and to use tact in dealing with the men of the 21st Battalion.[186]

---

[185] https://www.awm.gov.au/collection/C1343479?image=26
[186] https://www.awm.gov.au/collection/C1343479?image=70

The 21st Battalion was not the only Australian unit to mutiny over the disbandment issue. Similar circumstances were facing other brigade commanders across the Australian Corps. In an effort to curtail the spread of the unrest, senior AIF commanders made every effort to distract their men from news of the mutiny and unrest. Sports days, and training of various kinds were organized no doubt in an effort to occupy the men on matters other than rumours of unit disbandment. Over the period of the 12th through to the 16th of September the brigades of the 2nd Division, including the 6th Brigade, conducted a series of sports days. On the 13th Harry appears to have taken an active part in the 6th Brigade's sports day. During these activities the best performers were selected to represent the Brigade at the Divisional Sports Meeting which was held on the 16th of the month. Harry must have made a good showing for his diary records his participation at the Divisional meet, where he competed in the high jump, and the tug of war.

> "Thursday 16th went on parade in morning. In afternoon went to sport I pulled in tug-a-war with eight other men. The sixth beat the seventh brigade.
>
> 17th The seventh came down to give the sixth a few pulls to represent division. There was eight men from the seventh came down to our camp four of the seventh pulled, four of the sixth and the sixth best in both pulls. I was pulling with sixth brigade team. The final pull came off on the 18th at the divisional sports which were held near Cappy. We have three pulls one against details and one against a team of Tommies we beat both of these teams and the 5th Division beat us in the high jump and I was third. The winner jumped 4 foot 10 in beating me by two inches."

Organized sport was followed by some recreation and more training, as Harry's final diary entries indicated:

> "19 Sunday I went for a walk out to St Ledges.
> 20 Monday went out and done musketry.
> 21 Tuesday Did not leave the camp formed up in squads and

> were instructed on the Lewis Gun. Last evening Fritz dropped bombs about five hundred yards from our camp also two down in Berteaucourt and killed two French people.
>
> 22 Wednesday Nothing of importance to mention. Parades during the day I am tired.
>
> 23rd and 24th on Gun drill. 25th went to Church of England in the morning at church parade on bank of river. After dinner I went for a walk out on the hills and came back by four o'clock and went to the pictures at night.
>
> 26th Went on fatigue at quartermaster store and got paint for the tents. In afternoon went on guard from 2 o'clock till six. Vince McDonald called to see me. I had to meet him on evening after the pictures but he was too late as I had to be in camp by 9 o'clock."

Throughout this period, Harry's diary entries make no mention of the developing disbandment situation, so perhaps the senior commanders' strategy to distract their men, had worked. However, it is inconceivable that he was unaware of the situation, almost certainly the disbandment order would have been a topic of conversation from the lowest to the highest, ranking members of the AIF.

To return to developments on the 25th of September. At 11.00 am the officers of the 21st Battalion departed the Battalion for their new postings. However, the men refused to leave for their new units, and began to manage the Battalion themselves. At a representative meeting the men decided that any man who might take advantage of the situation and absent himself without leave, would be dealt with harshly, by the men of the Battalion.[187] In an effort to validate these proceedings a letter[188] was sent from the representative committee to the Commander 6 Brigade:

> "During the withdrawal of the officers from this unit, on their reporting to the respective Battalions it was considered necessary, by a representative meeting of Other Ranks of the

---

[187] https://www.awm.gov.au/collection/C1342439?image=10
[188] https://www.awm.gov.au/collection/C1343479?image=27

> 21st Battalion, that certain NCOs should, for the time being, be given certain powers for the maintenance of order.
>
> Acting in the capacity of CO – 310 CSM Trevascus W.C.
>
> Acting in the capacity of Adjutant – 929 Sgt Montgomery W.
>
> Signed W Montgomery Sergeant
>
> 21st Battalion A.I.F."[189]

The signatories to this letter had placed themselves in a difficult position. They had clearly identified themselves to the authorities, as "ring leaders" in the mutiny, a brave, some might say foolhardy, thing to do. However, Monash must have been aware that every man in the AIF was watching and waiting for his decision regarding these two men, and he knew he had to act carefully if he was to retain the trust of his soldiers. The refusal to obey his disbandment order must have greatly annoyed Monash, and yet he understood the sentiment that drove that disobedience. He knew the men were fiercely proud of the battalion to which they belonged, and that they bitterly resented the decision, to disband their particular battalion. On the other hand, he had a battle to plan… the attack on the much-vaunted Hindenburg Line. If this attack was to succeed, he needed his units to be ready and willing to participate in the coming fight. By 5.30 pm of the 25th, Monash had proposed a compromise. The 21st Battalion and other battalions earmarked for disbandment would receive a temporary reprieve. However, every battalion would be required to undergo an immediate internal restructure, reducing the companies in each unit from four to three. The battalions would still be understrength, but the restructure would enable the best use of the existing manpower.

The 6th Brigade war diary for that day provides brief and explicit details as to how the compromise was to be implemented:

> "Instructions contained in Bde Special Order of 24th Inst re disbandment of 21st Bn to remain in abeyance. Officers of 21st Bn to re-join their Bn at once. All Bns to reorganise on a 3 Coy basis at once…" [190]

---

[189] https://www.awm.gov.au/collection/C1343479?image=71
[190] https://www.awm.gov.au/collection/C1343479?image=28

Further drama had been avoided and Monash and his men, including Harry, began to make their final preparations to attack the Hindenburg Line.

During the 21st Battalion's preparations, Company Sergeant Major Trevascus and Sergeant Montgomery were retained in their current positions, but both men must have realised that after the battle, their part in the mutiny was likely to catch up with them. It seems they both determined to make such a good showing in the coming battle, that they would perhaps be forgiven. So it was that during the Battle of Montbrehain, the AIF's attack on the Hindenburg Line, both men placed themselves in the very thick of the fighting.

Montgomery was leading his men when he was critically wounded, and he later died of his wounds[191]. Trevascus also fought with great courage and was awarded a Bar to his previously awarded Distinguished Conduct Medal. However, after the battle, as he possibly feared, he did not long remain with the 21st Battalion. He was first transferred to the 24th Battalion, but soon after that, in what must have seemed like a backhanded compliment, he was sent to an Officer Cadet Training Unit in England, from where he was commissioned as a second lieutenant. He survived the war and returned to Australia. He died in 1956.[192]

---

[191] https://vwma.org.au/explore/people/328731
[192] http://adb.anu.edu.au/biography/trevascus-william-charles-8850

Chapter 31

October 1918

ON THE 29TH OF SEPTEMBER the Fourth Army, which included the Australian Corps attacked the Hindenburg Line and the Hindenburg Support Lines. By the 1st of October both of these lines had been breached and preparations were being made to attack the Beaurevoir Line. That attack commenced on the 3rd of October. However, Allied successes were limited. The British 46th Division had captured the village of Montbrehain but were driven out of it again by a strong German counterattack. The 2nd Australian Division had attacked the Beaurevoir Line and made some gains. Then on the 4th of October the 6th Brigade, which had spent much of the previous day in reserve, took over the divisional area of responsibility and conducted a series of battalion strength attacks between Beaurevoir and Montbrehain.

At this stage of the operation the mortars of the 6th ALTMB were allocated out to each of the battalions, there to be employed at the relevant CO's discretion. This would seem to be counter to the best way to employ mortars, given the weapon's characteristics, however the attacks were supported by a massive artillery commitment, and a large number of tanks. To employ the mortars as a battery must have seemed to the 6th Brigade planners as an overkill.

It has proved impossible to establish which battalion the mortar team to which Harry belonged, was allocated to. All that is certain is that he was a member of a mortar team, and that he was committed to the battle. It may also be assumed that at certain times during the battle, his team would have established a firing point from a position of cover, and at others they would have been required to advance with the infantry. Carrying one or more tubes from the battery, during an attack was not unheard of, although rarely were all of the mortars from a battery man-packed forward. To man-pack a mortar in an attack was hard work for a mortar team of three men. To do so, each weapon would be broken down into its three separate components, the barrel, or tube weighing forty pounds, the base plate weighing twenty-eight pounds and the bipod thirty-seven pounds. Add to this the weapon's first line ammunition, each shell weighing ten pounds. There was also additional paraphernalia such as sights and aiming sticks to be carried. In addition to this load the mortarman also carried his rifle and ammunition and his basic equipment and pack. As a result, the mortar crew were generally slower to move across the battlefield than other infantrymen. Harry and his mates were in for a rough day, but they would have been buoyed by the news that the Americans were coming to relieve them, and that after the assault on the 4th they would enjoy a period of rest. Their main thought as they approached the coming battle, must have been…all we have to do is survive.

Survival, however, was not a general expectation. By this late stage of the war, many soldiers on both sides believed the war would grind on until they were all dead. This fatalism, some might say desperation, is well illustrated by the famous World War One poet and soldier Siegfried Sassoon in his poem "I Stood With the Dead":

> *"I stood with the Dead, so forsaken and still:*
> *When dawn was grey I stood with the Dead.*
> *And my slow heart said, 'You must kill, you must kill':*
> *Soldier, soldier, morning is red.*
>
> *On the shapes of the slain in their crumpled disgrace*
> *I stared for a while through the thin rain…*
> *'O lad that I loved, there is rain on your face,*
> *And your eyes are blurred and sick like the plain.'*

> *I stood with the Dead...They were dead; they were dead;*
> *My heart and my head beat a march of dismay:*
> *And gusts of the wind came dulled by the guns.*
> *'Fall in!' I shouted; 'Fall in for your pay!'"*[193]

There was of course little hope of reprieve, save for the luck of receiving a wound severe enough to be evacuated to England, or for this particular battle, the arrival of the promised American relief. As fate would decree, while the former hope remained as a painful alternative, the latter would arrive late...too late for many Australians.

The initial plan of the battle scheduled the 2nd Division to be relieved by the 11th American Corps on the 5th of October. However, the Americans advised they would not be ready to make this relief by that date. As a result, the Fourth Army Commander, General Rawlinson retained the Australians in the line for an additional day and ordered them to join in the attacks of the 5th of October. The Australian attack was to be part of a wider coordinated assault by the Fourth Army. To the north of the Australians, the British IX Corps was to advance to the north-east of Sequehart and recapture Mannequin Hill, which overlooked the village of Montbrehain. The British attack was timed to commence at 6.00 am, the Australian at 6.05 am.

For the Diggers, the hoped-for rest had evaporated as they once again took a forward place in an attack. The 6th Brigade objective was to push the Germans out of the village and to secure an area to the north of the village. If this could be achieved the Allies would have secured the newly won line at Beaurevoir, and they would have provided themselves a firm base for future attacks.

For this particular attack, the 6th Brigade had been reinforced by the 2nd Pioneer Battalion. This battalion was a divisional asset whose soldiers were trained as infantry, but whose main role was light engineering tasks and road building. This attack was the first time they would fight as infantry. As for the previous seven days the 6th ALTMB mortar tubes were allocated out to the battalions to be controlled by the battalion commanders. The battalions attacked with three companies in extended line formation, with two platoons

---

[193] https://warpoets.org.uk/worldwar1/blog/poem/i-stood-with-the-dead/

forward and one providing depth. During the advance the two mortars attached to the battalion were generally located with the centre company of the formation. At the start of the battle the 6th ALTMB numbered, two officers and forty-three other ranks. The number of mortar tubes carried into battle that day is a little vague, it might be assumed there were eight in total. This figure allows for three men on each mortar, while the remainder would probably have been employed in the carriage of ammunition for the weapons, and as replacement crew members when casualties occurred in the mortar teams. However, it is also possible that the Australian light mortar batteries found that they had to adopt different tactics to meet the requirements of being part of the assaulting force. Two days previous to the attack on Montbrehain, the 7th ALTMB were committed to an attack in support of the 26th, 27th and 28th Battalions on the Beaurevoir Line. In that attack the mortars were deployed quite differently to the more usual method of employment as the officer commanding the 7th ALTMB recorded:

> *"On the 3rd of October 1918 I have to report as follows:*
> *Mortars as under were attached to Battalions carrying out the assault.*
> *Two under Lieut G.J. Rodger to the 26th Bn*
> *Two under Lieut A.H. Stewart to the 27th Bn*
> *Two under Sgt M. McEvoy to the 28th Bn.*
> *The remaining two mortars were held in reserve at Battery H.Q.*
> *In all cases mortars and ammunition were taken up as far as possible by limber prior to zero hour, but as the Battalions were unable to provide carrying parties, it was found necessary to accompany each of the assaulting Battalions with one mortar only, the crews from the second mortar in each case being used as ammunition carriers..."* [194]

The key to this situation is the inability of the infantry battalions to provide ammunition carriers, for as has been previously outlined, they barely had enough men to carry out the assault. It is reasonable to assume that for the assault on Montbrehain the supporting light trench mortar batteries

---

[194] https://s3-ap-southeast-2.amazonaws.com/awm-media/collection/RCDIG1009446/large/5089543.JPG

adopted the same tactics. Indeed, in his after-action report, the Commanding Officer of the 21st Battalion in referring to his employment of the mortar section attached to his battalion, refers to only one mortar tube.[195] So where was Harry positioned during the attack?

In a letter sent after the battle, from Mrs West to Mrs Withers, it is apparent that Harry was part of a mortar team working one of the tubes. This would indicate that by the time of the attack at Montbrehain, he was a skilled and trusted mortarman. However, the battalion to which his team was assigned is not recorded.

The 5th of October was to be a day of high drama, and the drama began even before the attack commenced. During the early hours of the morning, while the men of the 6th Brigade were being guided toward their start lines, screening patrols from the 5th Brigade were sent forward to ensure the enemy were kept away from the 6th Brigade assembly areas. Assembly areas are places where a force can be gathered together and sorted out into formations suitable for the task at hand, in this case the assault on the village of Montbrehain. Should the enemy have discovered the 6th Brigade assembly area they would have trained their artillery assets on it with the certain knowledge they would have inflicted heavy casualties on the Brigade as it assembled. Thus, the 5th Brigade screening patrols were vital for the success of the 6th Brigade preparations. The drama of the occasion was heightened when one of the 5th Brigade patrols, as it moved across the section of no-man's-land to be crossed by the 23rd Battalion, made an unpleasant discovery. A German machine gun post had been established in a railway cutting. The location was noted, and when the patrol returned it was arranged that the Stokes Mortars (possibly from the 5th Brigade) would deal with the enemy post, and a platoon was readied to immediately move into the German position after the mortar shoot ended. This plan was about to be enacted when a second patrol returned with news of another German post at a nearby level crossing. This news was passed on to the 6th Brigade headquarters, where, after some consideration, it was decided to leave the two German posts alone until after zero hour. The rationale behind this

---

[195] https://www.awm.gov.au/collection/C1343874?image=100

decision would seem to be that any attack on these two enemy posts would jeopardise the element of surprise for the main attack.

6.00 am, and off to the north the British attack to secure a feature to the Australians' flank known as Mannequin Hill, commenced in a cacophony of noise, light, and death. Every German eye would have swung toward it. Then at 6.05 am the men of the 6th Brigade climbed out of their trenches. They began to advance behind the cover of a massive Allied artillery barrage, and tanks clanked and rattled along behind the advancing infantry. The noise of this advance would have been horrendous and for a few minutes the Germans had been taken by surprise. However, they then responded fiercely with artillery and machine gun fire. The total sounds of battle would now have assumed a physical form, in that it could be felt as well as heard, adding to the terror of the moment.

The attacking Australians began to take heavy casualties. In an effort to counter the German fire, the 6th Brigade companies began to advance in short sharp rushes, perhaps 50 yards at a time, across open farmland toward the village. This tactic must have been extremely difficult for the mortar crews with their cumbersome loads, to manage.

As the Australians fought their way into the village, the fighting became a confused and bloody brawl. On several occasions the Allied artillery fire dropped short, killing and wounding Australian troops. Then when the lumbering tanks caught up with the infantry, they turned their machine guns and cannon onto the attacking force, adding to the Australian casualties. In some areas the Germans used gas in an effort to repel the attacking force, in others the German artillery fired point blank, over open sights into the Australian infantry.

As the 21st Battalion fought its way through the village it suffered heavy casualties. The CO had endeavoured to employ the mortar assigned to him, but that effort proved counterproductive. The mortar had fired no more than two rounds at a target indicated to them, but that action immediately provoked heavy German artillery counter-battery fire. It also attracted the unwelcome attention of German snipers. This response by the Germans endangered not only the Australian mortar crews, but also those other

Australians in the vicinity of the mortar. The officer accompanying the mortar was wounded, and the CO, judging that a single mortar was unlikely to be effective in supressing German counterattacks, ordered the mortar crew back to the relative shelter of a quarry to await further orders. Other battalions were making similar decisions regarding the mortars, and most of the 6th ALTMB mortars were out of action by midmorning.

In spite of their losses, by 9.00 am the 21st, and 24th Battalions along with the 2nd Pioneer Battalion had reached their initial objectives. However, the British attack to secure Mannequin Hill had failed. This was to have serious consequences for the Australians, for as they endeavoured to consolidate their positions in the village, they were subjected to flanking machine gun and sniper fire from the German positions on the hill, a situation that extended throughout the day. In addition to this, a murderous German artillery bombardment was unleashed on them, followed by several furious counterattacks by German infantry. Hand to hand fighting ensued, and for a time, the Australian position was desperate, and they were pushed back through the village of Montbrehain. However in a counterattack they regained some of the lost ground and established a line on the forward outskirts of the village.

It was in this maelstrom of death and destruction that the mortar crew of which Harry was a member, tried their best to operate and to survive. It is difficult to assess what posed the greater danger to them. Artillery and machine gun fire tended to be impersonal. The artillery gunners generally fired at an area, although as has been noted earlier some German artillery pieces were fired over open sights at the attacking Australians. Likewise, machine gun crews tended to fire their weapons on a fixed line, not swivelling back and forth as is often displayed in Hollywood pictures. However, if a priority target was identified, such as an enemy mortar, machine guns were often ordered to engage such a target directly. There was also a more stealthy foe for a mortar crew to contend with…that of enemy snipers.

Snipers on either side were expert marksmen, and German snipers had a particularly lethal reputation. The sniper would establish a relatively secure position, perhaps in the cover of a trench, or a building. From his position he would watch and select his targets. He would take his time, aiming carefully, perhaps only firing one shot from his position before moving to another. His targets were officers and NCOs, or any enemy soldier showing leadership, or particular courage. In addition to these targets, if a sniper identified a machine gun or mortar crew he would endeavour to kill key members of the crew in an effort to render the crew-served weapon inoperable. There was little those who found themselves under the attention of a sniper could do but move as quickly as possible from cover to cover, and hope.

There were two problems for a mortar crew faced with an enemy sniper. The first, if the mortar crew was on the move, the weapon parts they carried identified them as mortar crew, and therefore a priority target. The second problem was the signature flash and sound of a mortar when it was fired. This identified the mortar position to a sniper, and also to any enemy soldier who had the capability to direct artillery or machine gun fire against the mortar position. This second problem tended to make any supporting infantry close to the mortar, rather nervous, for they feared the enemy reaction once the tube was fired. By this stage of Harry's war, he knew what was required of him and his reactions to the battle going on around him would have been almost automatic. This is not to say he would not have been frightened. Indeed, he must have been terrified. However, overriding that fear would have been a grim determination to do his job, look after his mates, and to take care, as far as possible of his own safety. As they moved across the battlefield, he and his fellow mortar men would have employed a tactic known as fire and movement. The tactic requiring one man, or a group of men to provide covering fire, whilst another man or group moved. The idea being that the covering fire would force the enemy to keep under cover, enabling the man or group that was to move, to do so with slightly more safety. It is likely that the mortar crew would move together, under the covering fire of the supporting machine guns, artillery and the infantry. Fire and movement did not guarantee safety, and at best under World War One conditions, it reduced the casualty rate. For Harry and the other advancing Australians, it was all a matter of trust, and luck.

Trust that your mates would do their job, and that good luck would not desert you.

Many soldiers believed in luck. Harry may have interpreted "luck" as "God's will", but at some point during the morning, on the outskirts of Montbrehain, Harry's luck ran out, or God was momentarily distracted, for as Harry's mortar crew was moving from cover to cover, Harry was killed.

The immediate reaction of those who were with him can only be imagined...shock, certainly...fear, they would be terrified...bewilderment. They would be desperately trying to establish where the enemy was who killed Harry. Practically though, there was in all likelihood, little time for them to do anything but the essentials...check that Harry was indeed dead, remove one of his identity tags from the leather strip warn around the neck of every soldier, make a brief note of the location where the body lay, retrieve any essential items Harry had been carrying, and then they got on with the battle. Death had probably become so familiar to the survivors, that any sorrow they felt at the demise of a comrade came later. They may even have felt a degree of relief that it was Harry who had died and not them. The death of one man hardly mattered, the battle continued, and Harry's body was left where it fell.

For those living Australians, the period between 10.15 am and 12.30 pm was particularly desperate. Ammunition supplies ran low, and until resupply could be implemented, captured weapons and ammunition were freely used. The German forces mounted several counterattacks which were driven off by artillery and machine gun fire. Finally though the Australians consolidated their positions, and the Germans did not press them again.

Relief was finally at hand for the Australians. American troops had been arriving throughout the late morning of the 5th, gradually taking over the Australian positions. By 2.45 pm the relief was complete, and the 6th Brigade AIF was out of the battle.

Montbrehain was the last Australian action of the First World War. It cost the 6th Brigade 127 killed in action, 408 wounded in action and 25 missing in action. Many military historians have questioned why the Australians had been committed to that battle, arguing that the battle was in fact unnecessary.

Others, however, hold to the view that the Montbrehain battle maintained pressure on the Germans, ultimately helping to bring the war to a swifter end.

As for Harry, he was the only member of the 6th ALTMB to be killed that day. He and the other Diggers who died at Montbrehain had so nearly survived the war. It seemed so unfair to fall in the AIF's very last battle.

Chapter 32

How did Harry die?

THE WORDS SPOKEN BY THE Duke of Wellington after the British victory at the Battle of Waterloo might just as easily have been applied to the Australians after the Battle of Montbrehain:

> *"My heart is broken by the terrible loss I have sustained in my old friends and companions and my poor soldiers. Believe me, nothing except a battle lost can be half so melancholy as a battle won".*[196]

This was certainly the feeling at the 24th Battalion, where immediately after the battle the keeper of the war diary recorded the following observation:

> *"The price of victory was paid with the loss of many very gallant officers, NCOs and men whose loss in the closing stages of the war, perhaps in our last battle, all regret".*[197]

Indeed, it seemed so unfair to fall at the very end. However, for the living there was one last task to perform before they could rest... battlefield clearance.

In other World War One battles the task of battlefield clearance was hardly an issue. It was rarely possible to retrieve the wounded and the dead from no-man's-land, for those who fell simply disappeared into a sea of mud, or were buried, or blown to atoms by artillery fire. Thousands of the dead had no known grave. Montbrehain was a little different, there was no

---

[196] https://en.wikiquote.org/wiki/Arthur_Wellesley,_1st_Duke_of_Wellington
[197] https://www.awm.gov.au/collection/C1342829?image=11

mud to swallow the casualties of either side, and once the fighting died away, the wounded and the dead remained visible. As soon as it was reasonably safe to do so, the surviving Australians began the awful task of accounting for those who failed to answer "present" at a unit roll call. Some of those missing would have been confirmed by the survivors as being wounded. Most of the wounded would have been moved to casualty clearing stations for initial treatment prior to evacuation to field hospitals. In a similar vein, others, like Harry, would have been confirmed as having been killed and the approximate location of the body provided. Work parties from various units would have then commenced the task of finding and providing the dead with a rudimentary burial. It must have been a gruesome task, for unlike the movies, real bullets and high explosives tear and mangle the victims, and the warmth of that October day would have hastened decomposition. According to Mrs West's correspondence, a burial party from the 24th Battalion, Harry's former unit, were directed to where his body lay, and buried it in situ. The location of this temporary grave was registered on a map, to be used at a later date by the War Graves Commission whose task it was to disinter the dead from their temporary graves, from where they were taken for formal reburial in a military cemetery.

Unlike the process that followed Jack Mitchell's death, there was no need for either the 6th ALTMB, or the 24th Battalion to hold a court of inquiry into Harry's death. He was not missing, and the surviving members of the mortar crew, and the 24th Battalion burial party, could confirm that he was dead. As a result, on the 14th of October a cable was dispatched to AIF Headquarters in Australia listing those killed in action, a list that included 6426 Harry Francis Withers. On receipt of the cable in Australia, a headquarters clerk would have composed a telegram for each of the dead listed on the cable. These telegrams were then forwarded to the unsuspecting families. The details of the telegram would have been brief and to the point. In Harry's case words to the effect:

We regret to inform you that your son 6426 Private Henry Francis Withers has been killed in action on the 5th of October 1918.

These telegrams were hand delivered, generally by young men mounted on bicycles. There was no accompanying padre, or military officer, to gently break the news and offer comfort. The delivery person would knock at the door, ensure the person to receive the telegram lived there, then the telegram was handed over and the delivery person rode away. For those with people serving overseas, the telegraph delivery persons became objects of fear. For all knew the news they carried was generally bad. One can only imagine the gut-wrenching grief the telegram concerning Harry's death caused the Withers family.

Often the news of a loved one's death was made even more poignant, as the telegram often arrived well before the last letter sent from the front, which when it arrived, stated the soldier was fit and well and looking forward to finally coming home. Or perhaps the family had only recently written a letter to their soldier, giving all the news from home, and begging him for news. Now that letter would never be opened.

Some of the bereaved were unable to accept the news the telegrams brought, and for many months they clung to the hope that it was all some kind of dreadful mistake, and they would hear from their loved one once again. Mistakes did happen, but rarely were the dead resurrected.

More often the mistakes that occurred compounded the grief of those left behind. For example, on the 8th of October 1917, a soldier with the name of J.J. Mitchell, formerly of Wollongong, was killed in action. His mother was officially advised of his death, but then things went badly wrong.

In an almost inexplicable administrative muddle, another soldier, J.J. Mitchell's personal effects were sent in error to Harry's sister, Margaret Stewart (nee Withers), the guardian of Ruth Mitchell, and the nominated next of kin of her brother-in-law Jack Mitchell. It will be recalled Jack had been killed in action in April 1917, and when Margaret received the erroneously sent package, her initial thoughts must have been that some more of Jack's effects had been found and sent home. Some people, on the erroneous receipt of such a package might have discarded the contents or returned it to the sender. However, Margaret had the strength of character to forward the package to its rightful owner, and to write to the officer in charge of the army's Office of Base Records explaining what she had done:

> "Chiltern Valley P.O.
> June 5th 1918
> To
> The Officer in Charge Base Records
>
> Dear Sir,
>
> Some weeks back, I received from you, a wallet containing, letters, post cards, & photos. On opening it I found it was not for my ward whose name is Ruth Annie Mitchell, her father, John James Mitchell (whose number was 3833 the same as those of the late J.R. Mitchell (whom this wallet belonged) was killed 11th April 1917. I wrote to the address I found on the letters in the wallet. I received an answer, so today I have forwarded on, under registration, the wallet just as it came to me. Trusting I have done the right thing.
>
> I am yours sincerely
> (Mrs) M. Stewart
> P.S. This is the address of the lady: Mrs A Mitchell
> Hercules St
> Garden Hill
> Wollongong N.S.W." [198]

Margaret's action was greatly appreciated by Mrs Mitchell as is shown in the following response she received to her initial letter explaining the mix up:

> "Wollongong
> Hercules St
> Garden Hill
> May 31/18
>
> Dear Mrs Stewart
>
> It came as a great surprise today to receive a letter from you stating that you had received a wallet and letters from my Son. I had a small parcel returned last week but I was wishing for his pocket book and think that it

---

[198] https://recordsearch.naa.gov.au/SearchNRetrieve/Interface/ViewImage.aspx?B=7980590

should have gone to Victoria, I will forward you a letter I had from your brother JJ Mitchell 3833. I had a letter returned to me from a Cyclist Mitchell the same No (3833) that made three at the same No & Name. I wrote several times to your brother in law and had two letters from him, do you by chance come from Warracknabeal there is Mitchells there our relations and my husband's name is James John Thanking you very much for your kindness in writing to me

I remain yours sincerely

A Mitchell

Please forward me your brother's letter back as I would like to keep it. My poor boy was killed Oct 8/17"

There is no record of any response from the Office of Base Records being sent to Margaret. However, one wonders why someone within that office had not made the same rudimentary check Margaret made regarding addresses. In fairness, the Western Front was producing so many fatal casualties, it is a wonder such errors were not more frequent than they were.

The issue of the same army number, 3833, being issued to at least three men would seem to be a major administrative blunder. However, during the early part of World War One, the duplication of numbers was not an unusual occurrence. On enlistment a soldier was issued with a number, however, on transferring from one unit to another, that number was often changed, a practise that inevitably led to confusion and administrative errors. So much so that during the Gallipoli campaign a special administrative order was issued in an attempt to control the situation that had developed:

> "Units at Anzac are still in many cases changing the numbers of reinforcements joining their Units. Please issue strict orders that the number allotted to any man in Australia must be retained in every case otherwise the work in Records Section impossible. Where such changes have been made the change should be cancelled and the original number reallotted. Duplication of numbers in Units cause less confusion than is caused by alteration. General Carruthers."[199]

---

[199] https://www.awm.gov.au/articles/encyclopedia/numbers/regimental

However, the damage was already done. As the war progressed, other orders were issued in an attempt to further rectify the situation. Letters were used as a prefix to a number such as an "A" or a "B" to differentiate between two soldiers with the same number. However, this was of limited success, and it was not until 1917 that AIF recruits began to be issued with numbers from 50,000 to 80,000, and from that point onward regimental numbers were not duplicated.[200]

In the meantime, of course, errors such as the one the Withers family faced, continued to plague the AIF records system, and the unfortunate families who were impacted by the issue. This sometimes made obtaining information regarding the death or injury of a loved one, very difficult. Understandably many bereaved families were desperate for details as to how their loved ones had died. Had they suffered? Did they leave any last message? Official accounts were generally lacking in detail. "Killed instantly" or "Died of wounds" were descriptions most commonly used, and even then, such official detail was not provided until months after the death had occurred. Unofficial or semi-official letters often provided more timely answers to these questions. On the 16th of October a chaplain attached to the 6th Brigade wrote on behalf of the officer commanding the 6th ALTMB, to Harry's father:

"France
Oct 16th 18

My Dear Mr Withers,
The Commanding Officer of the 6th ALTMB, to which your son was attached from the 24th Battalion, tells me he is sending you the particulars of his death on Oct 5th. It will be a morsel of comfort to you to know that it was caused by a bullet on the head and that he died instantly, suffering no pain.

These have been heavy and anxious days to us all & our sympathy is with you in your heavy sorrow. Our men have bravely borne their part in joining a great victory and I am sure that God will bless them for their heroic spirit & sacrifice, both those who have survived & those who fell. May He give

---

[200] Op. cit.

you strength & peace as the great Comforter in these heavy days of mourning.

With deepest sympathy
Yours sincerely
Sydney Buckley
Chaplin"

This letter obviously sought to comfort the Withers family. However, *"a bullet on the head and that he died instantly"*, is almost a clichéd explanation. In Harry's case, it is highly unlikely that the chaplain, or the officer commanding the battery, had been with Harry when he died, and even if they had, they would hardly have provided graphic details of the incident. The chaplain's main focus in writing was to confirm the terrible news and to shield Harry's family from any thoughts of his having suffered. This theme is continued in the following letter from an officer in the 6th ALTMB to Harry's mother:

"France
2/12/18

Dear Madam

It is with deepest sympathy & regret that I write you re the decease of your son H.F. Withers.

He was killed on Oct 5th on the outskirts of the village of Montbrehain by a machine gun bullet which passed through his head. Death was instantaneous.

I regret delay in writing you, but as we were advancing at the time of his death we were not able to bury him on the spot. However a burial party from his old Bn (24th) buried him the next day. And since then his remains were removed from the battlefield & laid at rest in the military cemetery at Montbrehain and a cross erected. He had not been with us for any length of time, but during his stay with us he became a favourite amongst the men and had the respect and confidence of the officers and men. I tender you our deepest sympathy

Yours faithfully
Lieut (signature illegible*)*
6 ALTMB"

It must have been very difficult to write letters such as this, to the loved ones of the dead. However, this letter is almost off hand in tone, and smacks of being written by one who hardly knew Harry. The statement *"he had not been with us any length of time"* is inaccurate, Harry had first been detached for duty from the 24th Battalion to the 6th ALTMB on the 13th of June. However, his transfer had not been ratified until the 14th of September. It would seem that J.A. Reid had used the September transfer date as the basis for his statement. It might also suggest that Reid himself may have been new to the battery, and as a result may have been unaware of the length of time Harry had spent with the mortars.

It is unusual for a letter of condolence to be written by an officer with scant knowledge of the deceased. For example, in an infantry platoon, the platoon commander would generally write such a letter, or at the very least the relevant company commander. To be sure, having to write such a letter was an unpleasant task, particularly if there had been heavy casualties. However, Harry was the only fatal casualty the battery suffered on the day, so why had the task been performed by a junior officer? Does the apparent farming out of this responsibility point to a flaw in leadership?

The war diary of the 6th ALTMB for 1918 is not available, or has not survived, and as a result no unit explanation can be gleaned. However, a 6th Brigade strength state for the 12th of October, recorded in the Brigade war diary, provides a possible explanation. The strength state details how many officers and men from each unit in the Brigade, were committed to the Battle of Montbrehain, and the actual fighting strength that remained after the battle. In the case of the 6th ALTMB, the strength state indicates that on the 5th of October, the battery had two officers and 43 other ranks. On the 12th of October the battery strength is given as one officer and 42 other ranks. The reduction in officers was as a result of one officer being wounded and evacuated to hospital for treatment. The reduction in the other ranks figure was the result of Harry's death.[201] It seems therefore likely that Lieutenant J.A. Reid had been left alone to carry out the battery's after battle administration. That administration included writing to Harry's mother.

---

[201] https://www.awm.gov.au/collection/C1343480?image=101

On receipt of advice that a loved one had died in action, and the various letters that followed, all sent from no doubt well intending officers, many families were still not prepared to accept the official version of events. These folks sought information from other sources regarding the demise of their loved one. It would appear that soon after news was received of Harry's death, the Withers family in Australia, and the West family of Ross-shire, Scotland, were in communication. Ships carrying the mail no longer ran the risk of U-boat attack, and as a result, letters were being delivered safely and swiftly. By December 1918 letters between the Wests and the Withers must have been passing freely, as both families tried to establish the circumstances of Harry's death. The first part of the following communication between the two families is an extract of a letter from Mrs West. The second part is a letter obtained by a friend of the Wests, Lance Corporal J Millar, regarding Harry's fate:

"This is a letter we got from a friend that is staying near us he was in the same Coy as Harry and knew him well.

We asked this soldier about Harry when he was so long in writing so he wrote to France and got this reply back so he sent it to us. We inquired about Oct but got your note first letting us know.

Mrs West
Belgium
24/12/18

Dear L/CPL J Millar

Your letter of 9th instant to hand re 6426 Pte H.F. Withers I greatly regret that I have to inform you that this soldier was killed in action on 5th October at Montbrehain a small village north east of Estrées. He was one of the gun crew that went over the top that morning they had just gained their objective when a sniper picked them up he fired once and a bullet penetrated the rim of his tin hat without injuring him. About 10 minutes later he got on to the party again striking Pte Withers in the head killing him instantly.

I wrote to his next of kin telling them full particulars

I remain yours sincerely

J A Reid for OC 6th ALTM Bty"

The letter to Mrs Withers and the letter to Lance Corporal Millar pose a number of issues. The first being, the signatures on the original of both of these letters, are very difficult to read. Indeed, it appears that it was the custom during the war, for the drafter simply to sign the letter (no matter how illegibly) and that there was no requirement to clearly identify him, or herself, in type or clear print, as the drafter. However, in the case of these two letters, there are sufficient similarities in the writing style, to assume it is the same person that signed both. The writing for the first letter is somewhat clearer, and it would appear to have been drafted by J.A. Reid on behalf of the officer commanding the 6th ALTMB. Further evidence supporting this assumption is the claim in the first letter, that the writer had already written to Harry's next of kin. Therefore, it seems reasonable to assume the second letter is the one J.A. Reid states he sent to Mrs Withers.

The second issue, again assuming the author of this letter is J.A. Reid, is that in his letter to Millar, he has changed his version regarding the nature of Harry's death. In his letter to Mrs Withers, he had stated Harry was struck by machine gun fire, and that version of the death, is the one recorded in Harry's official army record. However, in the letter Reid sent to Lance Corporal Millar, a more graphic description of the situation surrounding Harry's death is provided. This letter has the tenor of one soldier talking to another and he provides the kind of detail that was probably more accurate, one hesitates to say truthful, than the official version. Mrs West stated in her note that Lance Corporal Millar was a member of the same company as Harry. However, did she mean that Millar was a member of the 24th Battalion, or of the 6th ALTMB?

On reflection, Millar was probably in the 24th Battalion. If he had been a battery member, he would have known Harry was dead, and he would have been aware of the nature of that death. However, would Millar as a lance corporal, have been so bold as to write directly to Reid, an officer?

The AIF Diggers were notoriously unimpressed by rank, so Millar would have been unlikely to give the matter a second thought, and he would have written as soon as Mrs West made inquiries about Harry. Besides, by the time Millar and Reid corresponded, the war was over. Any misgivings regarding interaction between the ranks that either man might have had during the fighting, would almost certainly have ceased to exist.

So where does the truth lie? How did Harry die?

Of the many ways a soldier might die on the 5th of October 1918, machine gun and artillery fire were two of the most likely causes. However, on that day, German snipers had also been particularly active. Reid's explanation to Lance Corporal Millar was written almost two months after Montbrehain. In the interim period Reid would have had time to talk to the men of 6th ALTMB about the battle, particularly the men who had been with Harry when he had been killed. They would most likely have wanted to talk about the unfairness of being killed in the very last battle. Reid, as their leader, was obliged to listen, and perhaps to his surprise he gained what is probably a more accurate account, than the one that was available to him immediately after the battle. That was that a sniper, not a machine gun, had killed Harry.

Further to this argument the following scenario is presented. Snipers were selective killers. They looked at the battle unfolding before them and carefully chose their targets. Generally, they selected officers and NCOs, those leading the enemy soldiers. However, snipers would also target the enemy crews of machine gun crews…or mortars. On that 5th of October morning, at Montbrehain, that particular German sniper saw Harry's mortar crew, and decided to engage it. However, of the three members of the mortar crew, the sniper seems to have selected Harry as his victim, and he does this twice. Perhaps, as the mortar crew had been striving toward their objective, Harry had been encouraging the others. This would have marked him, so far as the sniper was concerned, as a leader. Or, perhaps, Harry was carrying a piece of the mortar the sniper judged to be essential for the mortar to operate. The sniper does not seem to have considered any of the other mortarmen for his target, only Harry. In addition to this, the sniper was not aiming at the body bulk of his target, as perhaps a less expert marksman might have done. He was aiming for head shots.

To follow the machine gun bullet as the cause of Harry's death the following should be considered. The machine gun tended to be an impersonal killer, in that machine gunners looked to kill numbers of men with each burst of fire, rarely would they engage a single man as a target. In addition, if a machine gun had been fired directly at Harry it is likely he would have been hit by more than one bullet, and in other parts of his anatomy. There was of course a great deal of machine gun fire being aimed at the attacking Australians, so it is possible that Harry was killed by a single bullet from that volume of fire. However, to be hit twice in the head, several minutes apart? That would seem less likely.

On the other hand, the sniper supposition is strongly supported by Reid's statement that the sniper fired at Harry twice. The first shot hitting the rim of Harry's helmet without causing injury. In the moments immediately following that first hit, the fear each man in the mortar crew would have felt, must have been palpable. They would have been checking and calming Harry and trying to work out if the shot that hit Harry's helmet had been deliberately aimed, or a random round. The noise of the battle taking place around them must have been horrendous but being experienced soldiers, they would have been able to distinguish the signature sounds of individual weapons being fired around them… those fired by friendly forces, and those of the enemy. Even so, as they huddled in the nearest available cover, there was probably some hasty debate as to where that single bullet that had hit Harry's helmet, had originated. A machine gun bullet was bad enough, but a sniper… that would have been a particularly terrifying alternative. A sniper would know where they had taken cover, and unless his attention had been taken by another target, he was almost certainly waiting for the mortar crew to reappear. To add to the stress of the situation, the mortarmen would have known that they could not simply remain where they were. It was possible that at any moment they might be called on to engage a target, they had to move forward to be ready to support their mates. It would have taken tremendous courage for them, and particularly for Harry, to break cover and resume the advance.

The sniper on the other hand could afford to wait until his quarry reappeared. When the Australians finally broke cover, he may even have been surprised to see that the fellow he thought he had already killed, was apparently unharmed. Having already identified Harry as a key target, he fired again and his second shot struck home.

Chapter 33

The aftermath

IF REID'S EXPLANATION OF THE sniper is accepted as the real cause of Harry's death, why didn't the official version of the cause of his death change? The answer is probably as brutal as it sounds…it was hardly worth the effort. Indeed, any attempt to change the official record may have resulted in untold confusion in the administrative system. It would make no difference to Harry, and probably not to his family, for sniper, or machine gun, Harry was still dead. Thus, the official cause of Harry's death remains as *"machinegun bullet wound in head"*.[202]

Whoever fired the bullet that killed Harry, destroyed much more than Harry's life and his dreams of returning home to the valley. There was Margaret and William Withers who lost a much-loved son. Then there were Harry's siblings, bereft of a brother, and his nephews and nieces, that of an uncle. The West family would never see their newly found cousin again. His friends back in the valley would never see his familiar face on the sporting field, or at the church. The men of 6th ALTMB, and many in the 24th Battalion, had lost a comrade and mate. Then there was that Scottish lass, Miss Anderson… what had she lost? If only that bullet had missed.

Harry's family's war did not end with his death. Indeed, it did not even end with the Armistice. For now, the army's bureaucratic system took control of Harry and his effects, and the family received numerous

---

[202] https://recordsearch.naa.gov.au/SearchNRetrieve/Interface/ViewImage.aspx?B=8855783

communications, requesting this, and questioning that. The first of these was a package containing Harry's personal effects, sent on the 21st of May 1919. An accompanying letter demanded a strict protocol be followed prior to opening the package, and that once the protocol was completed, a receipt be sent to the Base Records Office at Victoria Barracks in Melbourne.

For a man who had been away from home for almost two years, Harry's effects were few. However, a soldier on deployment must of necessity, travel light. Inside the package another accompanying letter listed the following items under the heading of:

> *"Effects received from the field (3/9674) 5.11.18. 1 parcel (sealed) containing:-*
>> *2 wallets,*
>> *Religious book,*
>> *Photos,*
>> *Cards,*
>> *2 note books,*
>> *Watch and chain,*
>> *Belt with souvenirs attached."*[203]

It was all so cold and impersonal. No expressions of regret, or of support, merely a statement of all that was left.

On the 26th of May 1919, William Withers signed the Receipt of Consignment from the Defence Department and returned the same to the Officer in Charge of the Base Records Office as directed. It was a sad duty for a father, who had hoped for the return of his son, not a package with a few trinkets. On the 3rd of October 1919 the bureaucrats in the Base Records Office, contacted the Withers again:

> *"Dear Sir,*
>
> *With reference to the report of the regrettable loss of your son, the late No 6426, Private H.F. Withers, 24th Battalion. I am now in receipt of advice that he was Killed In Action (machine gun bullet wound in the head) on 5th October, 1918, at*

---

[203] Ibid

> Montbrehain, death being instantaneous. He was buried in the Montbrehain cemetery.
>
> The utmost care and attention is being devoted to the graves of our fallen soldiers, and photographs are being taken as soon as possible for transmission to next of kin.
>
> These additional details are furnished by direction, it being the policy of the Department to forward all information received in connection with the deaths of members of the Australian Imperial Force.
>
> Yours faithfully
>
> Major
>
> o/ic Base Records." [204]

The only piece of news in this missive concerned the intention to photograph Harry's final resting place. As for the rest…another painful reminder of loss, delivered in cold impersonal tones.

There were other administrative matters to attend to, such as Harry's will, and state probate. Harry's brother Walter was the main beneficiary. In July 1919 Harry's mother wrote to the Base Records Office to obtain a death certificate for Harry. A proud lady, she had no intention of receiving any kind of charity and enclosed a postal order for seven shillings and six pence to cover the cost of the certificate and postage. This money was promptly returned with an explanatory note:

> "Dear Madam
>
> No. 6426, Private H.F. Withers, 24th Battalion.
>
> Postal note for 7/6 enclosed by you is returned herewith, as there is no charge made for Certificates in connection with any member of the A.I.F."

Interestingly, the system studiously ignores the fact that Harry had been transferred to the 6th Australian Light Mortar Battery, and the 24th Battalion appears to have reclaimed him. This is possibly due to the comparative size of the two units. The Battalion being a far larger organization had a far greater capacity to deal with administrative issues,

---

[204] Ibid

so it is likely it was directed to assume control of Harry's effects and related administration.

In October 1920, the family was again contacted by the Base Records Office regarding an inscription and symbol to be inscribed on Harry's tombstone. It would appear that initially Margaret Withers responded to the request, indicating that the symbol she desired to appear on the tombstone was a star. This drew the following response:

> *"Dear Madam,*
>
> *With reference to the Circular Form "A" completed by you, in respect of your son, the late No. 6426, Private H.F. Withers, 24th Battalion, it is noted you have expressed the desire to have the Star of David inscribed on the headstone to erected over the late soldiers grave.*
>
> *For your information I would point out that the Star of Davin is the emblem of the Jewish Faith, whereas the cross is symbolic of Christianity and not of any particular religious denomination.*
>
> *I should therefore be glad to learn if you are agreeable to having the Cross inscribed in lieu of the Star of David. Neither will be inscribed if you so desire.*
>
> *The favour of an early reply will oblige ..."* [205]

This letter elicited the following response:

> *"To the Major of Base Records*
>
> *Melbourne*
>
> *Dear Sir,*
>
> *We would just like the two words "Peacefully Sleeping" put on the cross to be placed to the memory of the late Harry F. Withers, No. 6426, 24th Batt.*
>
> *I am yours faithfully*
>
> *(Mrs) M. Withers."* [206]

It took some time for the photographs of Harry's grave to become

---

[205] Ibid
[206] Ibid

available, and it would appear that when it was finally ready, the family was required to request it. In December 1921 William wrote:

> "To
>
> Base Records
>
> Victoria Barracks
>
> Will you please forward me three photograph copies of the grave of the late No6426 Pte H.F, Withers 24th Battal. Enclosed find stamps for same. Trusting you will forward same as soon as possible.
>
> Yours truly
>
> William Withers" [207]

The three photographs of the grave were dispatched to the family on the 15th of May 1922.

Harry's campaign medals were also issued. He had earned the 1914/15 Star, the British War Medal, and the Victory Medal. These decorations were issued on the 20th of May 1921 but were not received by the family until the 28th of April 1923.

Along with the medals, a Memorial Scroll was issued and a Memorial Plaque plus a message from the King. The plaque was commonly referred to as the "Dead Man's Penny" because of its similarity to the smaller coin of the realm, the single penny. The plaque featured an image of Britannia holding a trident and standing with a lion. In Britannia's outstretched left hand, she holds an olive wreath above a rectangular tablet that bore the deceased's name cast in raised letters. Across the British Empire 1,355,000 plaques were issued, made from a total of 450 tons of bronze. The numbers of war dead were so great, plus the requirement to include the name of the individual deceased on the relevant plaque, meant that the issuing of the plaques continued into the 1930s. The Withers received Harry's plaque and regal message on the 2nd of December 1922.[208] No doubt this gesture made on behalf of a grateful Empire, was received by Harry's parents with pride. However, it must have also re-opened the anguish of having lost a son. In

---

[207] Ibid
[208] https://www.awm.gov.au/articles/encyclopedia/memorial_scroll also https://www.forces.net/services/tri-service/story-dead-mans-penny

fact, it is doubtful that they ever truly recovered from Harry's death. We may be sure he was never far from their thoughts… ANZAC Day's must have been particularly poignant.

The surviving Withers siblings went on to live reasonably happy and productive lives, however the spectre of their lost brother remained with them for the rest of their lives. They were not alone in their grief and pride. Harry was one of 60,000 Australians soldiers, sailors, airmen, and women of the Australian Army Nursing Service, who died in World War One. Like most of these men and women, Harry had loved his parents and his siblings dearly, and had longed to return to Australia and the life he had left behind. In Chiltern Valley the only local reference to his sacrifice may be found on the Shire of Chiltern World War One Honour Roll, where his name is proudly displayed. However, an asterisk appears alongside Harry's name and that of thirty-nine other Chiltern men, showing that that person paid the supreme sacrifice. Forty men who did not come home, a high price to pay for a relatively small community.

All of the soldiers, sailors, airmen and nurses, who served during that war showed great courage in continuing to face their daily duties, often at great peril. However, in Harry's case it would have been so easy for him to opt out of army service…all he had to do was tell the truth regarding his brain injury and he would have been sent home. However, loyalty to his King and Country, pride in his unit, and a determination to stick with his mates, gave him the strength to honour his oath of duty. He was quite a man.

Harry now lies at the British military cemetery at Calvaire, Montbrehain, in Plot 1 Row B 4.

Lest We Forget.

Bibliography

1. Benalla Standard 17 October 1913
2. Ed Margaret Young **We Are Here Too,** Published by Margaret Young 2014
3. Ed. Sir John Hammerton, **The Great War I Was There**, Volume One London Amalgamated Press Ltd, Volume 1
4. Ed. Sir John Hammerton, **The Great War, I Was There, Volume Two,** London Amalgamated Press Limited
5. acms.sl.nsw.gov.au/_transcript/2012/D14087/a3370.htm
6. adb.anu.edu.au/biography/james-william-edward-6825
7. alh-research.tripod.com/Light_Horse/index.blog/1846485/australian-militia-activity-location-list-1910/
8. allpoetry.com/Base-Details
9. www.amazon.com/Captured-Germans-British-Camps-First/dp/1783463481
10. www.ancienthistorylists.com/world-war-1/top-10-diseases-that-were-spread-in-world-war-1/
11. anzaccentenary.vic.gov.au/history/australias-contribution-wwi/index.html
12. anzacportal.dva.gov.au/wars-and-missions/ww1/military-organisation/training
13. anzac-22nd-battalion.com/training-camps-england/
14. anzac-22nd-battalion.com/training-camps-france/
15. anzacportal.dva.gov.au/wars-and-missions/ww1/military-organisation/transport#4
16. artilleryhistory.org/documents/artillery_abbreviations.pdf
17. australianfoodtimeline.com.au/1890s-depression/

18. books.publishing.monash.edu/apps/bookworm/view/Australians+in+Britain%3A+The+Twentieth-Century+Experience/137/xhtml/chapter06.html John Oxley Library, State Library of Queensland, OM64-31/7.
19. bulletin.accurateshooter.com/2017/10/mad-minute-marksmanship-the-one-minute-lee-enfield-drill/
20. dictionaryofsydney.org/entry/great_strike_of_1917
21. en.wikipedia.org/wiki/First_Australian_Imperial_Force
22. en.wikiquote.org/wiki/Arthur_Wellesley,_1st_Duke_of_Wellington
23. journals.lww.com/ajpmr/Fulltext/2010/08000/The_History_and_Evolution_of_Traumatic_Brain.13.aspx
24. lachlan.bluehaze.com.au/aaf/awake.html
25. researchdata.ands.org.au/registers-purchases-section-act-1869/156027
26. sydneylivingmuseums.com.au/ww1/arthur-mcphail-kilgour-1896%E2%80%931941
27. trove.nla.gov.au/newspaper/article/28588259
28. trove.nla.gov.au/newspaper/article/198637717
29. unsworks.unsw.edu.au/fapi/datastream/unsworks:36626/SOURCE02?view=true
30. Letter from Chaplin S Buckley to Mr Withers dated 16 October 1918
31. Letter from Lieutenant in 6ALTMB to Mrs Withers dated 2nd of December 1918
32. Letter from Lance Corporal Millar to Mrs West dated 24th of December 1918
33. London and the First World War 20-21 March 2015 Institute of Historical Research, University of London Imperial War Museums
34. Please Give Me A Penny Sir, nla.gov.au/nla.obj-190803035/view?partId=nla.obj-211068211
35. National Archives of Australia: B2455 E BOTTERAL Service Record recordsearch.naa.gov.au/SearchNRetrieve/Interface/ViewImage.aspx?B=3100413
36. National Archives of Australia: B2455, GRAIL W Service Record recordsearch.naa.gov.au/SearchNRetrieve/Interface/ViewImage.aspx?B=4669655
37. National Archives of Australia: B2455, HARVEY D F Service Record recordsearch.naa.gov.au/SearchNRetrieve/Interface/ViewImage.aspx?B=4735906
38. National Archives of Australia: B2455, HENDERSON T Service Record

recordsearch.naa.gov.au/SearchNRetrieve/Interface/ViewImage.aspx?B=5338713

39. National Archives of Australia: B2455, WITHERS HARRY FRANCIS Service Record www.awm.gov.au/collection/C1342343?image=11
40. National Archives of Australia: NAA: B2455, MITCHELL JOHN JAMES Service Record recordsearch.naa.gov.au/SearchNRetrieve/Interface/ViewImage.aspx?B=7980590
41. National Archives of Australia: B2455, VANCE CHARLES Service Record recordsearch.naa.gov.au/SearchNRetrieve/Interface/ViewImage.aspx?B=839733
42. War Diary 24th Infantry Battalion www.awm.gov.au/collection/C1342340?image=4
43. War Diary 6th Infantry Brigade www.awm.gov.au/collection/C1343468
44. War Diary 21st Battalion www.awm.gov.au/collection/C1342439?image=10
45. encyclopedia.1914-1918-online.net/article/religion_australia
46. medium.com/war-is-boring/the-303-lee-enfield-was-a-british-tommy-s-best-mate-d7f18ece0e88
47. spartacus-educational.com/FWWtrenchfood.htm
48. trove.nla.gov.au/newspaper/article/69594366?searchTerm=&searchLimits=l-publictag=WWI+letter+in+a+bottle quoting the Wodonga and Towong Sentinel (Vic: 1885 – 1954) Friday 6 June 1947
49. www.awm.gov.au/articles/blog/battle-of-passchendaele-third-ypres
50. www5.austlii.edu.au/au/legis/cth/consol_act/ca191482/s21d.html
51. www.awm.gov.au/collection/E84708
52. www.awm.gov.au/collection/event/ww1/1916/essay
53. www.awm.gov.au/collection/C175198
54. www.awm.gov.au/articles/blog/so-far-home-sending-and-recieving-mail-trenches
55. www.bl.uk/world-war-one/articles/prisoners-of-war
56. www.diggerhistory.info/pages-asstd/schwinghammer.htm
57. www.bbc.co.uk/religion/religions/christianity/subdivisions/methodist_1
58. www.britannica.com/topic/Balkan-Wars
59. www.britannica.com/topic/drill-military
60. www.google.com/search?client=firefox-b-d&q=bromide
61. www.google.com/search?client=firefox-b-d&q=mouse+plague+in+australia+1918

62. www.iwm.org.uk/history/voices-of-the-first-world-war-home-on-leave
63. www.nfsa.gov.au/collection/curated/australia-will-be-there
64. www.nma.gov.au/defining-moments/resources/conscription-referendu
65. www.nma.gov.au/defining-moments/resources/free-education-introduced
66. www.parliament.vic.gov.au/papers/govpub/VPARL1894-95No3.pdf
67. www.poheritage.com/Upload/Mimsy/Media/factsheet/93338HORORATA-1914pdf.pdf
68. www.salcombemuseum.org.uk/rw_common/plugins/stacks/armadillo/media/SalcombeMuseumDisplay2017.pdf
69. www.sl.nsw.gov.au/sites/default/files/3._elise_edmonds_-_london_and_the_first_world_war.pdf
70. www.thoughtco.com/history-of-the-hand-grenade-1991668
71. www.victorianplaces.com.au/chiltern-valley
72. www.westminster-abbey.org/abbey-commemorations/commemorations/henry-withers-henry-disney
73. www.worldwar1postcards.com/5-the-leaning-virgin-of-albert.php
74. www.ymca.org.uk/about/history-heritage/ymca-and-ww1
75. Harry Withers' cards and letters
76. Jack Mitchell's letters
77. Lance Corporal E Bottrell letter to Mrs Withers 19 June 1917
78. Mrs Withers' Letters
79. Please Give Me A Penny Sir, nla.gov.au/nla.obj-190803035/view?partId=nla.obj-211068211
80. www.gov.uk/government/case-studies/ww1-australian-vc-recipient-william-ruthven
81. www.militaryfactory.com/smallarms/detail.asp?smallarms_id=651
82. www.awm.gov.au/articles/blog/trench-mortar
83. www.awm.gov.au/articles/blog/the-battle-of-hamel-100-years-on
84. en.wikipedia.org/wiki/Battle_of_Hamel
85. www.militaryfactory.com/armor/detail.asp?armor_id=936www.militaryfactory.com/armor/detail.asp?armor_id=936
86. www.awm.gov.au/articles/blog/battle-amiens
87. vwma.org.au/explore/people/328731
88. warpoets.org.uk/worldwar1/blog/poem/i-stood-with-the-dead/
89. www.awm.gov.au/collection/C1342829?image=11
90. Letter from Mrs A Mitchell to Margret Stewart dated 31 May 1918

91. www.awm.gov.au/articles/encyclopedia/numbers/regimental
92. recordsearch.naa.gov.au/SearchNRetrieve/Interface/ViewImage.aspx?B=8855783
93. www.awm.gov.au/articles/encyclopedia/memorial_scroll
94. www.forces.net/services/tri-service/story-dead-mans-penny

Other titles by Max Carmichael

In Kilted Company, a story of Part Time Soldiering

With Skill and Fighting, Craftsmen of the Australian Army 1942 – 2014

Attack on the Black Cat Track

The Map of Honour

The Cost of Duty – A family's reflection on the 9th Battalion Royal Australian Regiment's service in Vietnam 1968 – 1969 and of the impact that tour had on their lives.

About the Author

MAX CARMICHAEL WAS BORN IN country Victoria, and spent most of his formative years in boarding school. On leaving school he has worked in a variety of fields including agriculture, education, the Australian Army (including three operational deployments), and the Australian Public Service.

Max is now retired and lives with his wife in Ballarat. His interests include writing, reading, gardening and Australian Cattle Dogs.

www.ingramcontent.com/pod-product-compliance
Lightning Source LLC
Chambersburg PA
CBHW070248230426
43664CB00014B/2449